Stephanie Rohlfing-Dijoux | Uwe Hellmann (eds.)

Culture and Law

Multidisciplinary Cross-fertilization of Views on the End of Life

Nomos

The Deutsche Nationalbibliothek lists this publication in the Deutsche Nationalbibliografie; detailed bibliographic data are available on the Internet at http://dnb.d-nb.de

ISBN 978-3-8487-7731-0 (Print)
978-3-7489-2127-1 (ePDF)

British Library Cataloguing-in-Publication Data
A catalogue record for this book is available from the British Library.

ISBN 978-3-8487-7731-0 (Print)
978-3-7489-2127-1 (ePDF)

Library of Congress Cataloging-in-Publication Data
Rohlfing-Dijoux, Stephanie | Hellmann, Uwe
Culture and Law
Multidisciplinary Cross-fertilization of Views on the End of Life
Stephanie Rohlfing-Dijoux | Uwe Hellmann (eds.)
206 pp.
Includes bibliographic references.

ISBN 978-3-8487-7731-0 (Print)
978-3-7489-2127-1 (ePDF)

Onlineversion
Nomos eLibrary

1st Edition 2022

Preface

The articles collected in this book have been presented at an international symposium held on 10 and 11 March 2020 in Paris. The symposium topic was a multi-disciplinary approach of "end-of-life" by aspects of culture and law.

The subject of the symposium, " end-of-life " concerns each one of us. Every person is moving to death. Death is a truth and linked to life. It is subject to strong cultural and religious influences. Nor can the subject be dealt with in legal terms alone, but must include other disciplines, such as medicine, philosophy, history. Different religions also have different philosophies on end-of-life.

Chapter I deals with the place of death in our societies, the religious influence and the dignified death. The first article from *Jeanne Mesmin d'Estienne*, dedicated to a general approach to end-of-life, introduces the topic before focussing on philosophical and historical concepts of end-of-life. The second article from *Florence Bellivier* examines the influence of bioethics on end of life legislation.

Birgit Daiber gives a general overview of the dignity topic that also includes the well-being of the person. The whole environment of the person, such as psychological, religious, family situation, must be taken into account. Therefore, death should be considered holistically as a whole. All religions have the concept of dignity in death. In the Hindu religion and Buddhism, the end of life is seen more as liberation. Assumes that death is not an end but that the soul survives. Death can be celebrated as a festival. But due to the influence of the Western view, the medical approach to death is being applied more and more there today, and the philosophy is moving more to a concept of western individuality so that differences tend to diminish.

Dying with dignity is considered the central concept for end-of-life questions and is also a major issue in jurisprudence. This field of law is still subject to constant transformation because it is linked to the sociological transformation of our societies. This can be illustrated by the latest German case-law around the constitutionally guaranteed right to self-determination enclosing a right to self-ending one's life. The latest case of the German Constitutional Court, in this field, of February 2020 is explored in the article of *Michael Eichberger*. However, the legislature is expected to intervene in the next few years to regulate this.

An essential aspect of dying with dignity, especially in the western system, is that death should not be associated with pain but that the pain should be lifted or alleviated by medical interventions. That is why palliative care has developed to a large extent in Western countries, probably not yet enough. That is why several articles will be devoted to the issue of palliative care in different countries in Chapter II of this book. The contributions of *Tobias Lettl* and *Kerstin Peglow* for Germany, *Sophie Garcelon* and *Louis-Charles Viossat* for France are dedicated to palliative care and sedation. Even in other cultures, where suffering is more a part of the concept of dying because suffering is considered necessary in order to be freed from bad karma, such palliative care initiatives have been founded in recent years. For example, in the state of Kerala, which is considered to be the most socially progressive in India, there is now a state palliative care plan, which should lead to all citizens being able to benefit from palliative care.

The question of the right to self-determination of one's own life arises in this context, especially for minors and persons who are under care or who cannot decide for themselves because of their condition. The protection provided for these persons in the various countries is dealt with in chapter III's contributions for Germany by *Angie Schneider*, for French law by *Stephanie Rohlfing-Dijoux*, and England and Wales by *Kartina A. Choong*.

Another essential issue is the voluntary termination of life. The legal impunity of suicide is now undisputed in most countries. Even in India, where suicide is still punishable under the Penal Code, the provision is generally no longer applied by the courts. But the question is rather to what extent assisting suicide is exempt from punishment, especially medical assistance by doctors or medical staff, which goes close to the question of active euthanasia. Here are also many differences in the various European countries, from countries that go so far as to allow active euthanasia to Catholic tradition countries that also prohibit passive euthanasia. Germany, France and England, which are examined here as representatives of the European countries, take a middle position, in which passive euthanasia is permitted, but active euthanasia remains prohibited. Germany has gone the furthest in this respect since the most recent case law, the state can even be obliged to provide a lethal dose of drugs to a person who has no other issue than a self-determined death. There have been significant decisions on this very issue in Germany, which have been analysed in Chapter IV by *Uwe Hellman* and in a comparative way by *Volker Lipp*. *Geraldine Demme* dealt with the same issue for Swiss law. But in Germany, the question has not been finally clarified; instead, we are waiting for a legal clarification here in the next few years. Physicians need clarification and a clear legal concept regarding their options for reasons of legal certainty. And ultimately, only the legislator can create this. Palliative medicine is also extremely important because alleviating pain can help mitigate the urgent wish to die. There have already been two initial draft laws on this in Germany in recent weeks and an extensive debate in the Bundestag. It is interesting that these draft laws are cross-party or even come from academia. This shows that political boundaries are being crossed in this area. The draft legislation deals with ethical questions of euthanasia and, above all, the question of the authorisation of euthanasia associations and the specifications of procedures and behavioural requirements that are to be imposed on them in the future (such as mandatory counselling, time limits, access requirements). This also raises the question of whether euthanasia as a whole should be regulated in a uniform set of laws (as in France, for example) or whether it should continue to be regulated in various special laws. Furthermore, it will also be necessary to change the professional regulation of physicians.

The book will also explore how other legislation in European countries, but also other cultures, such as India and Japan, deal with end-of-life issues in Chapter V, where a comparative table of the laws in England, India and Japan is drawn up by *Tetsu Isobe* and *Haluna Kawashima* for Japan, *Anand Raut* for India.

Unfortunately, the Covid pandemic has brought the question of the end of life back into the spotlight, because in many countries, there were or are questions about the extent to which medically available resources, such as beds in intensive care, are distributed when there are not enough resources for all those in need. This too was already explored to some extent in the colloquium by the contribution of *Richard Law* for England and Wales. However, at the time it took place, on 10 and 11 March 2020, it was still before the actual covid pandemic and the strict lockdown in almost all countries in the world.

Our warm thanks to all authors of the book for their valuable contributions and the German-French University in Saarbrücken that sponsored this scientific event. We hope that the book may contribute and give some inputs to the ongoing discussion on end-of-life issues.

Nanterre, Potsdam, July 2021
Co-editors: Stephanie Rohlfing-Dijoux, Uwe Hellmann

Table of contents

CHAPTER I: The place of death in our societies: the constitutional right to life or die/ Medicalisation of death/ Religious Influence

Jeanne Mesmin d'Estienne, Lecturer at the University of Lyon II – Lumières, Avocat à la Cour, *Discourses on the end of life, from politics to law: historical dynamics and contemporary perspectives.*

The notion of the end of life is rooted in the concept of palliative care, the hidden face of curative medicine, that can be defined as all treatments which cater to the specific needs of those who are terminally ill. The semantic variations surrounding the term "palliative care" have revealed interesting differences. On the one hand, it has the virtue of providing temporary relief, but it is also, more bluntly, a treatment that alleviates the symptoms of an illness without addressing the cause. Linguistic variations of the notion of palliative care were highlighted by the Anglo-Saxon distinction between the verb "*to cure*" and the verb "*to care*", meaning, to take care. Given its usage in the term "palliative care", this term can thus be considered an all-encompassing form of treatment. Its objective is to relieve physical pain and other symptoms and take into account the psychological, social and spiritual suffering of an individual at the end of their life. With that said, however, the end of one's life is not limited to palliative care. Being conscious of one's immortality has often given rise to existential questions. To understand the enigmatic concept that is the human condition, many have resorted to creating myths[1] and rituals as a coping mechanism to ease one's nerves as death approaches.

Going beyond mystical and mythological approaches, the social sciences have sought to understand man's relationship and his own death. As we see in Plato's questioning of suicide, the idea of "being-towards-death" from Heidegger and the concepts of Stoicism and Existentialism, the confrontation of the individual with his own demise underlies the whole

1 From the epic of Gilgamesh, the man "who did not want to die" in Assyrian mythology, to the torment of Prometheus, the man is condemned to suffer eternally in Greek mythology, to the sacrifice of Antigone who braves Creon's prohibition to offer a burial to his brother Polynices.

history of philosophy. Philosophers such as Vladimir Jankélévitch[2] (1903–1985) have devoted a large part of their thinking to this subject. The end of life is also a prism of knowledge of the human psyche, as shown by the work of Sigmund Freud[3] (1856–1939)[4].

Nevertheless, the end of life cannot be reduced to individual philosophical and spiritual approaches, as it also, in turn, enlightens our modern

---

2 JANKELEVITCH V., *La mort,* Paris, Ed. Flammarion, coll; " Champ Essais ", reed. 2008.

3 FREUD S., *Our Relationship to Death. La désillusionée causée par la guerre,* Paris, Ed. Payot, reed. 2012; *Deuil et mélancolie,* Paris, Ed. Payot, reed. 2011.

4 For studies on the conceptions of death and the funerary rites of prehistoric men see: MOHEN J.-P. and TABORIN Y., *Les sociétés de la Préhistoire,* Paris, Ed. Hachette, 1998; LEVY-BRUHL I., *Le surnaturel et la nature dans la mentalité primitive,* Paris, Ed. PUF, reed. 1963; PICQ P., *Au commencement était l'homme. De Toumaï à Cro-Magnon,* Paris, Ed. O. Jacob, 2003; TATTERSALL I., L'*émergence de l'homme, Paris, Ed.* Gallimard, 1998; TILLIER A.-M., *L'homme et la mort : l'émergence du geste funéraire pendant la Préhistoire,* Paris, Ed. C.N.R.S., 2013.
For studies in philosophy and psychoanalysis on death v° : ANDRIEU G., *Etre, paraître, disparaître : Au-delà de la vie et de la mort,* Paris, Ed. L'Harmattan, 2014; BAUDOIN B., *La mort dévoilée : un autre sens donné à la vie, Paris, Ed. De* Vecchi, 2004; COMTE-SPONVILLE A., *Pensées sur la mort, Paris, Ed.* Vuibert, coll " Petits carnets de philosophie ", 2012; CONCHE M., *La mort et la pensée,* Paris, Ed. C. Defaut, 2007; CORDONNIER V., *La Mort,* Paris, Ed. Quintette, "Philosopher" collection, 1995; DASTUR F., *Comment affronter la mort,* Paris, Ed. Bayard, "Le temps d'une question" collection, 2005; DASTUR F., La *mort : essai sur la finitude, Paris,* Ed. PUF, 2007; DUPOUEY P., La *mort, Paris, Ed.* Flammarion, "Corpus" collection, 2012; DUCLUZEAU F., La mort *dans tous ses états. Essai sur la quête du vrai sens de la vie,* Paris, Ed. Dervy, coll. " Essence du sacré ", 1998; FEUERBACH L., *Pensée sur la mort et l'immortalité, Paris,* Ed. Cerf, coll. " Nouveau horizons ", reed. 1991; FOUCAULT M., *La volonté de savoir : droit de mort et pouvoir sur la vie,* Paris, Ed. Folio, 2006; FREUD S., *Notre relation à la mort. La désillusion causée par la guerre,* Paris, Ed. Payot, reed. 2012; FREUD S., *Deuil et mélancolie, Paris, Ed.* Payot, reed. 2011; GEORGES E., *Voyages de la mort, Paris, Ed.* Berger-Levrault, 1982; GUIOMAR M., *Principes d'une esthétique de la mort, Paris,* Ed. J. Corti, 1989; HARRISON R.., *Les morts,* Paris, Ed. Le Pommier, coll " Essai ", 2003; HEUSER G., *Guide de la mort, Paris, Ed.* Masson, 1975; JANKELEVITCH V., *La mort, Paris,* Ed. Flammarion, coll; " Champ Essais ", réed. 2008; LAPLANCHE J., *Vie et mort en psychanalyse,* Paris, Ed. PUF, 2013; SAUJOT C., *La mort : notre destin,* Paris, Ed. L'Harmattan, 2012; MAETERLINCK M., *La mort, Paris, Ed. La* République des lettres, 2013; MALEBRANCHE, *Entretiens sur la mort, Paris,* Ed. Actes Sud, reed. 2001; SCHOPENHAEUR, *Métaphysique de l'amour, Métaphysique de la mort,* Paris, Ed. 10–18, coll. " Bibliothèque ", reed. 2001; SCHUMACHER B., *Confrontations avec la mort : la philosophie contemporaine et la question de la mort,* Paris, Ed. Cerf, 2005; VANIN-VERNA L., *La sagesse de vivre : les philosophes et la mort,* Paris, Ed. De la Mémoire, coll. " Les carnets de l'Olympe ", 2009.

societies. Sociological and anthropological doctrines convey the end of life as a central component to understanding communities. Studies in Social Sciences have multiplied over the last fifty years, attesting to researchers' interest in this crucial stage of life. Patrick Baudry[5], Jean Baudrillard[6], Louis Vincent Thomas[7], Philippe Aries[8] and Michel Vovelle[9] specifically chose the subject of death as their topic of research. These studies have been undertaken to better understand societies' relationship with death, from antiquity to the contemporary era[10].

---

5 BAUDRY P., *La place des morts, enjeux et rites,* Paris, Ed. Armand Colin, 1999.

6 BAUDRILLARD J., *L'échange symbolique et la mort,* Paris, Ed. Gallimard, coll " bibliothèque des Sciences humaines ", 1976.

7 THOMAS L.-V., *Anthropologie de la mort,* Paris, Ed. Payot, 1975; *Rites of Death,* Paris, Ed. Fayard, 1985.

8 ARIES P., *Essai sur l'Histoire de la mort en Occident* du *Moyen Age à nos jours,* Paris, Ed. du Seuil, coll " Points/Histoire ", 1975; *Histoire des populations françaises et de leurs attitudes devant la vie depuis le XVIIIe siècle, Paris,* Ed. Self, 1948; *Images de l'homme devant la mort,* Paris, Ed. du Seuil, 1983.

9 VOVELLE M., *L'heure du grand passage, chronique de la mort,* Paris, Ed. Gallimard, 1993; *La mort et l'Occident de 1300 à nos jours,* Paris, Ed. Gallimard, 1983.

10 For sociological and anthropological studies see: ABIVEN M., *Une éthique pour la mort,* Paris, Ed. Desclée de Brouwer, coll. "Ethique sociale", 1995; BARRAU A., *Socio-économie de la mort : de la prévoyance aux fleurs de cimetière,* Paris, Ed. L'Harmattan, coll. "Logiques sociales", 1992; BAUDRILLARD J., "Logiques sociales", 1992, *L'échange symbolique et la mort,* Paris, Ed. Gallimard, coll " bibliothèque des Sciences humaines ", 1976; BAUDRY P., *La place des morts, enjeux et rites,* Paris, Ed. Armand Colin, 1999; DECHAUX J.-H., HANUS M. et JESU F., *Les familles face à la mort, Paris,* Ed. L'Esprit du Temps, coll " Psychologie ", 1998; DOMENACH J., L'échange *symbolique et la mort, Paris, Ed.* (dir.), *La mort à vivre,* Paris, *Esprit,* n°3, March 3, 1976; ELIAS N., *La solitude des mourants,* Paris, Ed. Christian Bourgeois, coll. " Détroits ", 1987; FAIVRE D. (dir.), *La mort en question : approche anthropologiques de la mort et du mourir,* Paris, Ed. Eres, 2013; GODELIER M. (dir.), *La mort et ses au-delà,* Paris, Ed. Du C.N.R.S., coll. " Bibliothèque de l'anthropologie ", 2014; HANUS M., *La mort retrouvée,* Paris, Ed. Frison Roche, coll. "Face à la mort", 2000; ROUSSET B., *La mort aujourd'hui,* Paris, Ed. Anthropos, coll. "Publications du Centre universitaire de recherche sociologique", 1977; THOMAS L.-V., *Anthropologie de la mort,* Paris, Ed. Payot, 1975; THOMAS L.-V., *Rites of Death, Paris, Ed.* Fayard, 1985; VERGELY B., *La mort interdite, Paris,* Ed. Lattès, coll. "Philosphie dans la cité", 2001; VESPIEREN P., *Face à celui qui meurt,* Paris, Ed. Desclée de Brouwer, coll. " Temps et contretemps ", 1984; ZIEGLER J., *Les vivants et la Mort,* Paris, Ed. Points, 2008 – FREUND J., " La signification de la mort et le projet collectif ", *Archives de Sciences sociales des religions,* 1975, pp. 31 et seq.
For historical studies on death: For Egyptian, Greek and Roman antiquity: ASSMANN J., *Mort et au-delà dans l'Egypte ancienne,* translated by BAUM N., Monaco, Ed. Du Rocher, 2003; CHABOT J.-L., FERRAND J. and *MATHIEU M.,*

Furthermore, the end of life should not be considered as merely a private matter either. Beyond spiritual and philosophical questions, the question of caring for the terminally ill, with its considerable financial constraints, is eminently political. Moreover, the State is not just a receptacle of individual and collective projections on this subject. If judicial references are always a "universe of fiction"[11], this fiction influences reality, and by drawing the contours of end-of-life care, the State contributes to defining this notion.

Since the end of the Second World War, despite its many critics, increasing liberalisation and new challenges brought about by globalisation, European States continue to prevail when it comes to health initiatives and supporting individuals at the end of their lives. From the 1789 Declaration of Human Rights and of the Citizen to the European Convention on the Protection of Human Rights and Fundamental Freedoms, the individual has a right to the protection of his or her health and the appropriate means to live until his or her death. In recognising the power of civil society and its role in swaying authorities in the context of public health matters and respecting human dignity, end-of-life policies are now prone to public intervention. In the same way, questions are being raised about the role of

---

Les représentations de l'Antiquité, Paris, Ed. L'Harmattan, coll. " La librairie des humanités ", 2011; DUNAND F. and LICTHTENBERG R., *Les momies. Un voyage dans l'éternité,* Paris, Ed. Gallimard, coll. " Découvertes ", 2001; DONDIN- PAYE M., LE BOHEC Y., ETIENNE R., LASSERE J.-M., et BRIQUEL D. et a., *La mort, les morts et l'au-delà dans le monde romain,* Caen, Ed. Presses universitaires de Caen, 1987; LE BRIS A., *La mort et les conceptions de l'au-delà en Grèce ancienne à travers les épigrammes funéraires,* Paris, Ed. L'Harmattan, coll. " Etudes grecques ", 2003. For the period from the Middle Ages to the end of the Ancien Régime: ALEXANDRE-BIDON D. (ed.) and TREFFORT C., (ed.), *A réveiller les morts : la mort au quotidien dans l'Occident médiéval,* Paris, Ed. PUF, 1993; ALEXANDRE-BIDON D., *La mort au Moyen Âge (XIIIe-XVIe siècle), Paris, Ed.* Pluriel, 2011; ARIES P., *Essai sur l'Histoire de la mort en Occident du Moyen Age à nos jours, Paris,* Ed. du Seuil, coll. " Points/Histoire ", 1975; ARIES P., *Histoire des populations françaises et de leurs attitudes devant la vie depuis le XVIIIe siècle,* Paris, Ed. Self, 1948; ARIES P., *Images de l'homme devant la mort, Paris,* Ed. du Seuil, 1983; CHAUNU P., *La mort à Paris : XVIe, XVIIe et XVIIIe siècles,* Paris, Ed. Fayard, 1978; LAUWERS M., *La mémoire des ancêtres, le souci des morts. Morts, rites et société au Moyen-Age*, Paris, Ed. Beauchesne, coll " Théologie historique ", 1997; VOVELLE M., *L'heure du grand passage, chronique de la mort, Paris,* Ed. Gallimard, 1993; VOVELLE M., *La mort et l'Occident de 1300 à nos jours, Paris, Ed.* Gallimard, 1983. For the French Revolution: BIZIERE J.-M. et LIRIS E., *La Révolution et la mort,* Toulouse, Ed. Presse Universitaire du Mirail, 1991.

11 PADIOLEAU J. G., L'Etat au concret, Presses Universitaires de France, 1982, 222p.

health systems, public action and social ties. Thus, the palliative approach is at a crossroads of different social, economic, legal and budgetary choices, which reveal the concept of dying and old age in society. Social and territorial inequalities in the face of death cannot be resolved. In the same age groups, the risk of death is significantly different from one socio-professional category to another. Statistics show that age, marital status, and socio-professional status have an influence on death. Medical advances have simultaneously increased life expectancy, and more and more people have been living longer with serious illnesses or disabilities. The end-of-life stage has become a major political problem in the 21st century.

In addition to issues underlined from a medical perspective, it is important to note that the end of life concerns all social fields and should be broached through a multidisciplinary lens. Yet, the end of life appears all too often as a broad field, intensely cultivated in some places by the law and left fallow in others when studied by jurists. Thus, legal studies on subjects such as the subtle and controversial semantic variations between so-called passive euthanasia and so-called active euthanasia, the cessation of care, food, and hydration are no longer taken into account. Legal precedents are filled with life stories that have become textbook cases, such as the Vincent Humbert case, the Vincent Imbert case, and the Chantale Soubire case. The end of life, a multifaceted and complex subject, cannot be restricted solely to its medical posture. When taking into account the end of life of foreigners, of homeless people, of prisoners, of thousands of people who die each year on the road (because of cigarettes or sugar), of soldiers on external operation sites or of security agents in the context of law enforcement operations, and of the mentally disabled in psychiatric institutions, these are all issues often neglected by the rule of law. The question of managing the end of life in the context of the Covid-19 epidemic has demonstrably brought to light a sense of deep-seated close-mindedness as well as the difficulties present in legal doctrines; locked in the restricted epistemological field of medical decisions at the end of life and unable to anticipate other problems related to the confrontation of society with death.

While questions surrounding the "care" of the elderly were addressed as early as the thirteenth century, the question of end-of-life management appeared later in public debates in Europe. The identification of this specific problem did not come about spontaneously at the collective level. The process that led public authorities to include the end of life in the political agenda is, instead, the result of complex mechanisms. Understanding how the end of life became a political problem on its own by moving out from the private sphere and into the public sphere raises questions about the evolution of a social fact – death – and the evolution of social representations. The recognition of the collective need for end-of-life care results from a threefold movement in the societal field: the dramatisation of the relationship with death in modern society, the promotion of new representations of death, and the creation of militant movements.

Palliative care is often presented as a response to the degradation of the end of life and a devalued vision of "dying", marked by powerful medical advancements and therapeutic relentlessness. A time of passage and transmission in many cultures, the "act of dying" is seen in modern society as something unfair, accompanied by suffering, physical degradation, and loneliness. The rites performed for a person's final days in ancient times would no longer find their place in the current context of generalised medicalisation and scientific progress. Death is deliberately hidden in marginalised spaces in society. If the negative vision of the end of life can be found in medical realities, then perhaps the holistic vision results from intellectual discourse. Considerations on the over-medicalisation and evacuation of death in the most industrialised societies sometimes express a form of nostalgia for idealised traditional societies and have quickly become a recurring theme for analysis. These discourses constitute the breeding ground for militant speech. The reality of dying must be reinvented, and palliative care is a vehicle that can allow individuals to reappropriate their own death.

However, it is essential to be aware of false evidence of social issues. The end of life does not have a stabilised social and legal definition. It is a social construct derived from different schools of meaning. Indeed, claiming to carry out a policy not only means solving problems but also constructing them. The awareness of public action is not linked to any threshold of intensity of end-of-life issues. This is just a transformation of perceptions surrounding end-of-life situations. For a long time, the condition of dying did not arouse the interest of public opinion.

Like many other social facts, specific end-of-life issues might not have elicited any political response to this day. Palliative care could have remained an orphaned political issue. Still, instead, the emergence of palliative care as an important topic is the result of three waves: a medical wave based on new scientific expertise, a popular wave marked by associative engagement and a political wave, moulded by decision-makers in response to the demands of their citizens in a political democracy ruled by electoral laws. In an intellectual context marked by the affirmation of individual liberties and social movements to reappropriate the body, political demands have since emerged for dying patients' care. These demands are now part of a new medical context, marked by the development of new technological innovations that make it possible to prolong the longevity of populations significantly. Some medical practices are gradually being stigmatised by a group of health care professionals who are forming a specialised body of "end-of-life" professionals. The development of this movement was achieved by denouncing curative medicine and the construction of a particular medical sphere based on a holistic approach to understanding human beings (often at odds with a medico-technical model). It is also important to note that public opinion was impacted by the numerous deaths of young people with AIDS to date. Not only did many fear being infected, but they were equally distressed, as they were confronted with the end of their loved ones. At this point, end-of-life issues began to be monopolised by the medical discourse, mostly present in hospitals. On the one hand, initiatives to develop palliative care in hospitals were amplified during this period, many reports were produced, and adapted structures were created. Palliative care requires specific techniques, training, "life skills", and end-of-life policies in specific units with a high death rate (such as oncology) and intensive care and emergency units to help people who are young and dying. On the other hand, political debates about the end of life gradually became confined to the hospital space.

Around the world, many questions concerning the end of life in other regions and amongst specific demographics – foreigners, the mentally disabled, minors, prisoners, the elderly – are ignored by politics. The distinct evolution of palliative care concerning geriatrics and gerontology illustrates the relative lack of global insight when it comes to the end of life. The birth of end-of-life policies explains why the legal debate has been mostly built around medical questions. However, medical staff, scientists, politicians, and lawyers have not been making enough efforts to bring to light other related issues, to the detriment of a more all-encompassing and holistic mindset regarding the concrete difficulties posed by the "classic" end-of-life situations affecting the elderly population. The instrumentalisation of the debate by militant associations has long distracted public authorities from the overall difficulties of dealing with older people's death. By positioning themselves as ethical experimenters, the leading players in palliative care have affirmed their originality and maintained an autonomous sphere of power escaping bureaucratic technocracy. At the same time, they have helped isolate palliative care from the institutional phenomenon. The development of an authentic "palliative culture" for the elderly began late in France.

Florence Bellivier, Professor at the University Paris Nanterre, Co-director of the Centre for Criminal Law and Criminology, *The Influence of Bioethics on End-of-Life Legislation – Was Aldous Huxley a Visionary*

L'influence de la bioéthique sur la législation relative à la fin de vie – Aldous Huxley était-il visionnaire?
Presque 100 ans après la parution du Meilleur des mondes d'Aldous Huxley (1932), l'impression se dégage qu'il fut visionnaire mais davantage s'agissant de la fin de vie que du début. En effet, autant sa description de la production industrielle et hiérarchisée de la vie humaine relève encore de la science-fiction, autant la description de la mort de la mère du « sauvage », Linda, préfigure, à la façon d'un roman, bien sûr, la mort telle qu'elle se déroule souvent aujourd'hui à l'hôpital. Or ce parallèle, souvent dessiné, entre début et fin de vie, n'est pas pertinent quand on étudie les lois qui prennent respectivement pour objet ce qui entoure le début de la vie et ce qui précède la mort. En effet, le législateur français a choisi d'appréhender les deux questions (bioéthique, dont la matrice, en droit français est l'assistance médicale à la procréation, et fin de vie) dans deux corpus différents. Or si ce choix s'explique par différents rayons qu'il conviendra d'analyser (nature de la demande sociale ; rôle des médecins), les deux corpus n'évoluent pas parallèlement mais par un jeu d'influences réciproques.

Almost 100 years after the publication of Aldous Huxley's *Brave New World* (1932), the impression emerges that he was a visionary, but in a truncated way. As much as his description of human life's industrial and hierarchical production is still science fiction, so much the description of the death of the mother of the "savage", Linda, prefigures, in the manner of a novel of course, death as it often happens today in the hospital: the death, if not sweet, at least sweetened, a process which became the norm in Huxley's novel and which today is controversial.[12] Linda will die comfortably settled on the 17th floor of Park Lane Hospital for the Dying, in

12 See, in another vein, M. Houellebecq, *La carte et le territoire*, Flammarion, 2010, which can be put into perspective with the article that the writer devoted to the death of Vincent Lambert in *Le Monde* of July 11, 2019.

Room 81 (for galloping senility), stuffed with soma (the pill of happiness) and surrounded by raging twins, conditioned to death and coming to see the astonishing spectacle of a human-looking like an old lady. There is no question of euthanasia or assisted suicide in this chapter because there is no need for it. The soma is enough.[13]

However, this parallel, often drawn, between the beginning and end of life is not relevant when we study the laws about the beginning of life and what precedes death. Indeed, the French legislator has chosen to deal with the two issues (Bioethics, on the one hand, the matrix of which in French law is medically assisted procreation and end of life, on the other hand.) in two different law bodies. On the one hand, bioethics was regulated for the first time by the two laws of July 29, 1994, relating, for the first time, to respect for the human body (and modifying the civil code) and, for the second, to the donation and use of elements and products of the human body (and modifying the Public Health Code). On the other hand, the end of life was regulated by Law No. 2005–370 of April 22, 2005, relating to patients' rights and the end of life, known as Leonetti, supplementing the Kouchner Law relating to patients' rights, then amended by Law No. 2016–87 of February 2, 2016, creating new rights in favour of patients and people at the end of life. To put it schematically, but this distinction is lasting, the end of life is seen as falling under a particular corpus which is the corpus of laws applying to sick people; the law of bioethics is considered as a corpus of texts that transcends the ill/healthy distinction.

However, if we define bioethics as « a moral question (often informed by religious principles) in the face of advances in science in general and medicine in particular ("biomedicine"), whose interventions on human life are ever more advanced and technical»[14], the end of life should fall within this very open field. And this is not the only issue that conceptually falls within the scope of bioethics and is not included in the law on bioethics. One thinks, for example, of termination of pregnancy[15], sterilisation[16] or sex change in civil status[17], which are the subject of autonomous laws, even though they would have had their place in bioethics legislation. In this respect, the practice of sterilisation for contraceptive purposes is

13 A. Huxley, *Le meilleur des mondes*, édition Pocket, p. 247 et s.

14 F. Bellivier et S. Hennette-Vauchez, « Bioéthique », *Cahiers Droit, Sciences & Technologies*, 4 | 2014, p. 227.

15 Articles L. 2211–1 to L. 2223–2 of the Public Health Code.

16 Articles L2211–1 to L2223–2 of the Public Health Code.

17 Articles 61–5 to 61–8 of the Civil Code.

particularly revealing of the links between the different corpus since, to prepare for its inclusion in the law, it was necessary to modify the first paragraph of Article 16–3 of Law no. 94–653 of July 29 1994, thus the original corpus of bioethics, by replacing the adjective "therapeutic" by the adjective "medical".[18]

From the point of view of corpus articulation, three models can be distinguished. According to the first (model of exteriority), a question that conceptually falls within the scope of bioethics remains formally outside its scope, regardless of whether it has been the subject of earlier or later legislation (e.g. the termination of pregnancy or the change of sex in civil status). According to the second (migration model), an issue that had been dealt with elsewhere than in the bioethics law is fully or partially integrated into it (e.g. blood or *post-mortem* organ donation or medical termination of pregnancy). Finally, according to the last model that could be described as aspirational, a long-standing practice regulated by special and infra-legislative texts (the donation of one's body to science, for example) or emerging (such as brain imaging or the algorithmic processing of health data) is integrated into the law of bioethics as it is revised.

To stick to the links between the end of life and bioethics, it is advisable to keep an equal distance between two postures: one, formalist, considers that the questions are separate since two different laws frame them; the other, all-inclusive, obscures what is specific about the end of life (perhaps not for long). Between these two positions, we will see, on the one hand, why, conceptually, there was *a priori* no reason to exclude the end of life from the law of bioethics (I), and on the other hand, the reasons for this bias (II). In any case, the two corpora do not evolve in parallel but through a play of reciprocal influences (III).

I. The end of life, at the heart of questions relating to bioethics

For at least three reasons, it would have been conceivable that at the beginning 1990s, the French legislator would at the same time have taken

---

18 In its current version, the text reads as follows: « There may be no infringement of the integrity of the human body except in case of medical necessity for the person or exceptionally in the therapeutic interest of another » (for this translation, see D. Gruning, A. R. Levasseur, J. R. Trahan, E. Roy, « Traduction du Code civil français en anglais version bilingue », 2015. halshs-01385107

up the question of the end of life and the practices that have to be included in the corpus of bioethics in 1994.

First of all, those who invented the term and institutionalised bioethics have a broad understanding of it from the outset. If the paternity of the term is most often attributed to the American oncologist Potter who, in 1971, published *Bioethics: A Bridge to the Future*[19] and has a broad conception of bioethics that includes the protection of the ecosphere and focuses on multidisciplinarity, German pastor Fritz Jahr used the word as early as 1926 to include plants and animals.[20] Let's take the example of the Hastings Centre, an American research centre founded in 1969. We can see that its founders have from the outset focused on issues as diverse as population control, including the freedom to procreate, behavioural sciences, death and the process leading to it, as well as human genetics.

Second, in France, it was during the 1980s that, in parallel, questions arose concerning assisted reproduction, on the one hand, and end of life, on the other. In this respect, we can mention the creation, in 1980, of the Association for the Right to Die with Dignity (ADMD)[21], the birth, in 1982, of the first child born in France from an in vitro fertilisation technique, the publication, the same year, of the book *Suicide mode d'emploi*[22], and the creation, the following year, of the National Consultative Ethics Committee for Life and Health Sciences[23]. The two poles of life are disrupted, each in its own way, by an increasing technicization of hitherto natural processes, by the same eugenicist imaginary summoned (the creation of perfect children, the elimination of the sick at the end of life or of people who are physically or morally weak), by questions about the respective part that the different sources of law, in particular statutes and case-law, must take in these areas, by a tension between individual will and public order and, finally, a rise in the sphere of privacy. This is evidenced by the jurisprudence of the European Court of Human Rights, which, while remaining very cautious about claims relating to access to assisted reproduction and the alleviation of suffering at the end of life and

---

19 Van R. Potter, *Bioethics: Bridge to the future*, Englewood Cliffs, N. J. Prentice-Hall, 1971.

20 F. Jahr, *Wissenschaft vom Leben und Sittenlehre. Die Mittelschule Zeitschrift für das gesamte mittlere Schulwesen*, 1926, 40 :604, 15, Dezember 1926.

21 https://www.admd.net

22 C. Guillon et Y. Le Bonniec, *Suicide, mode d'emploi. Histoire, technique, actualité*, éd. Alain Moreau, 1982.

23 https://www.ccne-ethique.fr/en/pages/presenting-national-consultative-ethics-committee-health-and-life-sciences

hiding behind the national margin of appreciation of States, considers that these claims fall within the scope of Article 8 of the European Convention on Human Rights[24].

Lastly, with the tightening of bioethics on medical ethics in France in the 1980s, it is the same professional body primarily concerned with the beginning and end of life, i.e., physicians and, more generally, health professionals. Powerful and structured, this body is the object of very strong expectations and, correlatively, of sharp criticism, which will gradually lead to medical paternalism questioning. Whether at the beginning of life or the end, social demands are expressed for doctors to practice the technical gesture that alleviates the body's weaknesses (sterility) or accelerates a process (death) while not leaving doctors alone to decide on the legitimacy of these demands.

And yet, while these three factors could have led to the end of life being integrated, not only in the general reflection on bioethics but also in bioethics legislation, this was not the case.

II. Two separate paths

At first glance, one might be tempted to think that there would be old issues (e.g. abortion, euthanasia, sex change) on the one hand and radically new problems on the other (e.g.assisted reproductive technologies, embryo research). The reasoning behind this hypothesis would be the following: since antiquity, at least, women have had abortions, people have lived in sex other than the one assigned to them by society, and individuals have chosen to end their physical or moral suffering by killing themselves. On the other hand, it is only very recently that we have, by technical means, dissociated procreation and sexuality, not only to avoid the birth of children but, on the contrary, to make this birth possible when the couple is sterile. This distinction is not completely useless because it no doubt explains why the 1980s were the time of great effervescence around the reproductive technologies (which will become the piece of choice in bioethics) because in this field, one starts from nothing, which is not the case with euthanasia, which cannot be separated from the founding ban

24 See the research report "Bioethics and Jurisprudence of the European Court of Human Rights", by the Court's Research Division, updated in October 2016 and available at https://www.echr.coe.int/Documents/Research_report_bioethics_ENG.pdf

on giving death to others. But this distinction between classical and new questions is nevertheless not really satisfactory because if the question of a good death is old, the social demand for a shortening of life employing technology (disconnection of artificial respiration apparatus, lethal injection) is recent. It is, therefore, more plausible that if the two corpora have remained separate, it is because of the specificities of regulated practice.

In France, medically assisted procreation was conceived in 1994 as the response of law and medicine to the request of a heterosexual couple whose two members are alive. At the other end of life, the request is, by hypothesis, a request for death (and not life) and an individual request.

Then, given the role, as we have seen, of the medical profession in the satisfaction that is or is not given to the requests, this profession's attitude towards the appropriateness of legislation in this area is decisive. Although doctors have been very much in favour of legal regulation of practices since the 1980s, they have been, to say the least, circumspect concerning legislative intervention in the area of end-of-life care.

And yet, parallels have been drawn, notably by activists of the association for the right to die with dignity who criticise debates' compartmentalisation. Thus, in 2009, Jean-Luc Fichet, then Senator of Finistère, drew the attention of the Minister of Health and Sports, *via* a written question, to the absence of the end-of-life issue from the themes of the « Etats généraux de la bioétique » established for the revision of the 2010 bioethics laws. According to him, "Law No. 2005–370 of April 22, 2005, known as the Leonetti Law, has allowed for progress in terms of support and end of life, but clarifications could be made, in particular regarding requests for euthanasia. The debate cannot be closed. It is logical that this societal issue that affects medical research and ethics should be included ». The Minister responds by taking up the classic distinction between the field of bioethics, divided according to medical specialities, and that of the end of life, which comes under the right of patients: « centered on the revision of the Bioethics Law of August 6, 2004, and its themes, the mission letter addressed to the steering committee of the *Etats généraux* intended to focus the debate on the areas covered by the law, the Government, therefore, selected five major themes within this exclusive framework: stem cell and embryo research, predictive medicine, medically assisted procreation, sampling and transplantation, prenatal and pre-implantation diagnostics. The law of April 22, 2005, relating to the right of patients and the end of life, is more in line with the overall issue of patients' rights. Nevertheless, the subject has been debated, and many contributions have been collected on this point which, beyond the bioethical question, enrich the current reflection on the evaluation of the law of April 22 2005 ».[25]

III. Reciprocal interplay of influences

The enrichment of the reflection on the legislative corpus relating to end of life by the preparation of a revision of the law on bioethics is hardly surprising given the numerous points of intersection between these two fields, both of which presuppose a fine articulation between the rights and duties of individuals, the power of physicians and the prerogatives of the State. While it is not easy to determine whether these intersections are the result of a play of influences or more or less fortuitous convergences, it can be noted that the end of life, like the issues classically classified under the category "bioethics", are subject to the same tensions and developments, whether in terms of principles or actors.

First of all, regarding the principles, end of life and bioethics are both seeing a growing role given to the principle of individual autonomy, even if it is framed, particularly by the principles of dignity or respect for public order. The main developments in both bodies of work can be explained by the increasing autonomy, whether it be the opening of medically assisted procreation to couples and single women[26] or the legal possibility of deep sedation for people at the end of life[27]. It is one thing for some people to judge, in the name of their own convictions, that these developments are unfinished business. Still, the general meaning of the legislative changes towards more significant consideration of individual choices is indisputable. And this dynamic has been made possible by two features of bioethics that have undoubtedly influenced end-of-life law. On the one hand, the replacement, by the law of July 27, 1999, of the adjective "therapeutic" by the adjective "medical" in paragraph 1 of article 16–3 of the Civil Code has had considerable effects, for example, by paving the way for the law of July 4, 2001, authorising doctors to perform sterilisations for contraceptive purposes or by changing how we call terminations

25 See Written Question n° 09689 by Mr. Jean-Luc Fichet (Finistère – SOC) published in the JO Sénat of 23/07/2009 – page 1830 : https://www.senat.fr/questions/base/2009/qSEQ090709689.html

26 This opening is included in the bill on bioethics (Article 1) adopted by the Parliament on 29 June 2021.

27 Article L. 1110–5–2 of the Public Health Code.

of pregnancy intended to prevent the birth of a child suffering from an incurably serious disease ("medical" terminations of pregnancy, not "therapeutic"). All these acts are obviously not therapeutic, but they are medical because they are performed by a doctor in a medical setting and have a medical purpose in the broadest sense. Thus, one has become accustomed – and physicians in the first place – that the therapeutic aim does not exhaust the notion of the art of medicine. This is undoubtedly what convinced parliamentarians to conditionally decriminalise the performance, by physicians, of acts that accelerate the coming of death. On the other hand, the law of bioethics is from the outset a finalist law in the sense that it was elaborated precisely to permit the use of the elements and products of the human body, as the very title of the second law of July 29, 1994 shows[28]. From then on, bioethics law's framework consists of making the departure between legitimate and illegitimate ends, which leads to perpetual adjustments. For example, to bring organ removal within the framework justifying the violation of the integrity of the human body, it has been necessary to add, exceptionally, to "a medical necessity for the person", "the therapeutic interest of another"[29]. It is also a finalist type of reasoning that makes it possible to reconcile deep sedation with the prohibition of killing: the lethal gesture is not intended to cause the person to die at the end of life, but to relieve his or her suffering, even if death would follow[30]. Secondly, in both fields (end of life and bioethics), we observe mutations concerning the actors. First of all, although medical power has not disappeared, it is exercised in a less solitary way than thirty years ago: collegiality is now an obligation for a whole series of medical decisions, both in the field of bioethics *stricto sensu*, for example, in the realm of medical termination of pregnancy[31], and in the field of end-of-life[32]. Then, the role of the family or close relations undergoes -at the stage of decisions – the same phenomenon of relative effacement favouring the will of the individual concerned. The comparison of the evolution of post-mortem organ retrieval with that of the end of life is revealing in this respect in that, in both cases, the legislator promotes, without making them mandatory, mechanisms for expressing individual will (registration of op-

28 See the very title of the second law of July 29 1999: law n° 94–654 of July 29, 1994, relating to the donation and use of elements and products of the human body, medical assistance for procreation and prenatal diagnosis.

29 See above footnote 7.

30 See articles L. 1110–5–1 and L. 1110–5–2 of the Public Health Code.

31 See article L. 2213–1 of the Public Health Code.

32 See articles L. 1110–5–1 and L. 1110–5–2 of the Public Health Code.

position to organ donation in an automated national register[33], advance directives[34]) intended, in particular, to avoid, as far as possible, possible conflicts between relatives or friends of the deceased or the opposition of these persons to the removal of lethal gesture.

The revised bioethics law was finally promulgated on 2 August 2021, after a discussion that had started in 2018. Conversely, the Covid crisis has accelerated reflection on the end of life elsewhere than in hospitals, retirement homes or homes, places where the collegiality of decisions and guarantees relating to the rights of patients at the end of life may be blurred[35]. Nevertheless, the probability that these two fields' intellectual connections will intensify is high, thanks to three phenomena.

Firstly, in assessing the legitimacy of this or that request, the medical criterion seems to be losing speed. Thus, with the opening of medical assistance for procreation to single women or same-sex female couples, the medical criterion of infertility has been abandoned; as for the procedure of sex change in civil status, it has been demedicalized since the law of November 18, 2016, which means that the bodily transformation of the claimant is no longer a condition set by the judge to assess the legitimacy of the claim[36]. Secondly, while the question of the cost of the practices in question is little highlighted in a health system that, like that of a country such as France, socialises risks, it does come to the fore here and there, particularly concerning the reimbursement of medical assistance for procreation to women who are not medically sterile[37]. It is possible that the more the medical will detach itself from the pathological, the more these questions will arise, which does not mean that they would have the same effects. One can thus imagine that the high cost of medically assisted procreation will eventually lead to a partial or total delisting of the acts or the opening of this activity to the lucrative private sector, but that, conversely, concerning the end of life, it is not the cost of euthanasia or assisted suicide that is a factor of evolution but that of the management of

33 See article L. 1232–1 of the Public Health Code.

34 See articles L. 1111–11 and article L. 1111–12 of the Public Health Code.

35 See S. Hennette-Vauchez and L. Marguet, *Cahiers Droit, Sciences & Technologies*, 11 | 2020, p. 173 and pp. 181–183.

36 See article 61–5 of the Civil Code.

37 See on this subject the opposition between the Senate (in favour of limiting health insurance coverage to claims based on medical indications) and the National Assembly (against this distinction) during the parliamentary debates on the bioethics law currently being revised. *Adde* : S. Hennette-Vauchez and L. Marguet, *Cahiers Droit, Sciences & Technologies*, 11 | 2020, pp. 192–196.

the pathologies of the persons before death. Finally, it can be observed that social demands are now less formulated in terms of the "right to" (a child, a gentle death, etc.) but in terms of the right to access to a technique, a double mediation (access and technique) that erases asperities. In Huxley's imagination, the beginning of life was highly technical, the end of life weak. It is decidedly not sure that this difference will last in the 21st century.

Michael Eichberger, Richter Bundesverfassungsgericht a.D., Honorarprofessor Eberhard Karls University Tübingen, *Judgment of the Federal Constitutional Court of February 26, 2020, on the Criminalisation of Assisted Suicide Services*

Almost exactly two weeks ago, the Second Senate of the German Federal Constitutional Court published a judgment in which it declared a penal law criminalising assisted suicide services unconstitutional. During my presentation, I would like to talk about the German legal framework on suicide in itself and assisted suicide and explain the principles underlying the recent decision of the Federal Constitutional Court.

A. Previous Legal Framework

Suicide was not and is not criminalised under German law. Accordingly, aiding and inducing suicide – the two relevant modes of participation under German criminal law – are not criminalised. The decisive characteristic of suicide is that the person wanting to end their life carries out the decisive act of killing him- or herself – for example, taking a deadly substance. Physicians and other third persons are not obliged to help individuals wanting to end their life. They neither have to provide them with lethal substances nor physically help them consuming them. In several binding professional codes of conduct for doctors that the German Federal States' medical profession gives itself, providing aid to commit suicide is even expressly prohibited. Apart from such prohibitions, doctors and other third parties may voluntarily aid in committing suicide – used narrowly within the criminal law sense of the term without violating German law.

One has to distinguish a suicide, so the act of ending one's life oneself, from assisted suicide. Assisted suicide means different forms of ending the life of a terminally ill person, where a third person takes the decisive action to end this life according to the will or supposed will of the ill person.

In this regard, the legal framework in Germany is considerably more complicated. Killing on request is expressly punishable under section 216 of the Criminal Code. On the other hand, the courts exempt cases of indirectly assisted suicide therapy from punishment, such as an earlier death of a dying or terminally ill person due to medically indicated pain-reducing therapy. The same applies to the so-called discontinuation of treatment – i.e. any active or passive limitation or termination of a life-sustaining or life-prolonging medical measures, provided that it is accordingly to with the actual or presumed will of the patient. Beyond this, however, much is unclear and controversial.

B. Subject matter of the decision of the Federal Constitutional Court: Section 217 Criminal Code

The question of whether the supportive participation of third parties in suicides should be made a punishable offence has repeatedly been the subject of academic and societal debate in recent decades. The considerable increase in publicly accessible suicide assistance services offered by organisations or individuals and the perceived danger by civil society and politicians of normalisation of suicide, especially regarding vulnerable members of society, has prompted the legislator to act.

Following an intensive public and parliamentary debate, a large majority of the German Bundestag voted in favour of the new version of section 217 StGB in 2015. This provision (prohibition of assisted suicide services – geschäftsmäßige Förderung der Selbsttötung) imposes criminal punishment on anyone who, with the intention of assisting another person to commit suicide, provides, procures or arranges the opportunity for that person to do so as a professionalised service.

This provision was challenged in constitutional complaints proceedings by, among others, associations offering suicide assistance based in Germany and Switzerland, persons with serious illnesses seeking to end their lives with the assistance of such an association, physicians working in outpatient or inpatient care, and lawyers advising on suicide-related matters.

C. The Judgment of the Federal Constitutional Court of February 26 2020

In this ruling, the Federal Constitutional Court deals for the first time head-on with the constitutional basis and limits of suicide and the possibilities of its legal regulation. In clarity and sharpness of argument that surprised many observers, the Court emphasises every human being's autonomy, which is rooted in fundamental rights and essentially based on human dignity. From this autonomy, it derives a far-reaching inviolability of the decision to end one's life voluntarily.

I Basis of human rights

In a first step, the Court substantiated in a fundamental way the guarantee of self-determined and autonomous decisions of the individual about his or her own living conditions and ultimately own life, derived from the liberty rights and human dignity. The essential considerations of the Court in this regard are as follows (Quotation of the press release):

> "(a) The general right of personality guarantees the right to choose, in self-determination, to take one's own life based on an informed and deliberate decision.
>
> (aa) Respect for and protection of human dignity and freedom are fundamental principles of the constitutional order, informed by the central notion that human beings are capable of self-determination and personal responsibility. Rooted in the belief that personal autonomy and development of one's personality are integral to human freedom, the guarantee of human dignity encompasses, in particular, the protection of one's individuality, identity and integrity. (...) The specific guarantees deriving from the general right of personality give effect to this notion of personal autonomy and self-determination. They safeguard the basic conditions that allow the individual to find, develop and maintain their identity and individuality in self-determination.
>
> Maintaining one's personality in self-determination requires that individuals control their lives on their own terms and are not forced into ways of living that are fundamentally irreconcilable with their ideas of self and personal identity. In terms of human personality, the decision to end one's own life is of the most fundamental significance to one's existence. For the individual, the purpose of life, and whether and for what reasons they might consider ending their own life, is subject to highly personal beliefs and convictions. The decision to commit

suicide concerns basic questions of human existence and bears on the identity and individuality of that person like no other decision. Therefore, the right to a self-determined death is not limited to the right to refuse, of one's own free will, life-sustaining treatments. It also extends to cases where the individual decides to take their own life actively.

(bb) The right to a self-determined death is not limited to situations defined by external causes like serious or incurable illnesses, nor does it only apply in certain life stages or diseases. Rather, this right is guaranteed in all phases of a person's existence. Restricting the scope of protection to specific causes or motives would essentially amount to a substantive evaluation, and thereby predetermination, of the reasons of the person seeking to end their own life, which is alien to the Basic Law's notion of freedom. The individual's decision to end their own life, based on how they define the quality of life and meaningful existence, eludes any evaluation based on general values, religious dogmas, societal norms for dealing with life and death, or considerations of objective rationality. Thus, it is not incumbent upon the individual to further explain or justify their decision; rather, their decision must, in principle, be respected by the State and society as an act of autonomous self-determination.

(cc) The right to commit suicide may not be denied because a person committing suicide forfeits their dignity given that, by ending their life, they also give up the very basis of self-determination. Instead, the self-determined act of ending one's life is a direct, albeit final, expression of the pursuit of personal autonomy inherent in human dignity.

(b) The right to take one's own life also encompasses the freedom to seek and, if offered, utilise assistance provided by third parties for this purpose. The free development of one's personality, as guaranteed by the Basic Law, also protects the freedom to engage with others who, for their part, are also acting freely. Where the exercise of a fundamental right depends on the involvement of third parties, and the free development of one's personality is dependent on the participation of another, that fundamental right also protects from restrictions that take the form of prohibiting those third parties from offering, in the exercise of their own freedom, such necessary assistance."

II. Based on these arguments, the Federal Constitutional Court argues – in a second step – that § 217 StGB violates these fundamental rights.

1. First, it detects, § 217 StGB interferes with the general right of personality of persons wishing to die, even though the provision does not directly address them. The criminalisation of assisted suicide services in § 217(1) StGB objectively has the effect of restricting the freedom to commit suicide. It makes it factually impossible for individuals to receive suicide assistance.

2. Second, the Court rules that the interference is not justified. The prohibition of assisted suicide services must be measured against the standard of strict proportionality. A law restricting fundamental rights only satisfies this standard if it has a legitimate purpose, is suitable and necessary for achieving that purpose, and strikes an appropriate balance between the purpose pursued and the resulting restrictions.

a. However, the Federal Constitutional Court accepts that the legislator pursues a legitimate purpose prohibiting assisted suicide services.

Aiming to protect autonomy and life, the prohibition in § 217 StGB serves to fulfil the State's duty of protection under constitutional law and thus pursues a legitimate purpose. The State has a duty to protect the individual's autonomy in deciding whether to end their own lives and protect life as such. In discharging this duty of protection, the legislator may not only act to protect personal autonomy against specific and impending dangers arising from the conduct of third parties. It may also pursue, as a legitimate purpose, the aim of preventing assisted suicide from becoming recognised within society as a normal way of ending life. In this regard, the legislator may intervene to counteract developments that potentially create social expectations pressuring individuals in certain situations to take their own life, especially based on considerations of usefulness.

The oral hearing confirmed that it was at least tenable for the legislator to consider the existing practice of assisted suicide services in Germany as unsuitable for ensuring free will and thus protecting free self-determination in every case. In practice, the assessment of whether a resolution to commit suicide was based on the person's free will was often limited to plausibility considerations that were not based on comprehensible criteria. Notably, assisted suicide organisations were found to have provided suicide assistance to persons with physical or psychological conditions without consulting the affected person's medical files or ensuring that a medical examination, consultation and information had been provided by a specialised practitioner. Accordingly, it was plausible for the legislator to assume that where suicide assistance is offered as a professionalised service, the focus is mainly on assisting persons in carrying out the suicide. The free will and free decision-making of the individual are not therefore sufficiently ensured.

Further, the legislator's assessment is comprehensible in that assisted suicide services could lead to a 'societal normalisation' of suicide assistance and that assisted suicide could become recognised as a normal way of ending life, especially for elderly and ill persons, which might create social expectations and pressure endangering personal autonomy. Countries with liberal laws on suicide assistance and assisted dying have experienced a continuous increase in assisted suicide and killing 'at the victim's request' (Tötung auf Verlangen). As confirmed by domestic and foreign studies, a common motive for seeking suicide assistance is the desire not to burden relatives or third parties.

b. The restriction of the right to a self-determined death by § 217 StGB, however, is in any case not appropriate.

Criminal law exceeds the limits of what constitutes legitimate means for protecting personal autonomy in the decision on ending one's life where it no longer protects free decisions of the individual but renders such decisions impossible. The exemption of suicide and assistance rendered in this regard from criminal liability reflects the – constitutionally mandated – recognition of individual self-determination; thus, it is not at the legislator's free disposal. At the heart of the Basic Law's constitutional order lies a central notion of human beings informed by dignity and the free development of one's personality through self-determination and personal responsibility. This notion must be the starting point for any normative framework. It follows that the State's duty to protect self-determination and life can only take precedence over the individual's freedom where the individual is exposed to influences that endanger the self-determination of their own life. The legal order may counteract these influences through preventive measures and safeguards. Beyond this, however, an individual's decision to end their life, based on their personal understanding of what constitutes a meaningful existence, must be recognised as an act of autonomous self-determination.

Therefore, recognising the right to a self-determined death does not bar the legislator from taking measures of general suicide prevention. In particular, the legislator may take measures to expand and strengthen palliative care to curb desires to commit suicide born out of illness. It also has to counter dangers to autonomy and life arising from current and foreseeable liv-ing conditions capable of influencing the individual's decision by encouraging them to choose suicide and deter them from choosing life. Yet, the legislator cannot evade this responsibility in social policy by eliminating the constitutionally protected right to self-determination altogether. However, where the protection of life runs counter to the protection of autonomy, it contradicts the central understanding of a community that places human dignity at the core of its order of values and thus commits itself to respecting and protecting the freedom of human personality as the highest value of its Constitution.

The prohibition of assisted suicide services violates constitutional law insofar as it fails to leave sufficient space to pursue autonomous self-determination. As the law stands, the introduction of the provision criminalising assisted suicide services effectively causes the right to suicide to be largely vitiated. It is true that the prohibition set out in § 217 StGB is limited to assisted suicide services, i.e. a particular form of suicide assistance. However, the resulting loss of autonomy is disproportionate to the extent that, and as long as, the remaining options available to the individual provide only a theoretical but no actual prospect of self-determination.

The detrimental effects on personal autonomy stemming from § 217 StGB are further aggravated precisely because, in many situations, individuals are left with no actual, reliable options other than seeking suicide assistance to carry out a decision to commit suicide. The legislator's tacit assumption that options for suicide assistance other than assisted suicide services are actually available fails to consider the legal order as a whole. Suppose the legislator excludes specific ways of exercising freedoms concerning remaining alternatives. In that case, these remaining courses of action must be suitable for ensuring the effective exercise of the fundamental rights in question.

Without the availability of assisted suicide services, the individual is mainly reliant on physicians' willingness to assist, at least in the form of prescribing the substances necessary to commit suicide. Realistically, such individual will on the part of a physician can only be expected in exceptional cases. To date, physicians have shown little willingness to provide suicide assistance and cannot be obligated to do so; the right to a self-determined death does not entitle the individual to request suicide assistance from third parties. As long as this situation persists, it creates a factual need for assisted suicide services.

Improving palliative care is, by itself, also not suitable to compensate for the disproportionate restriction of individual self-determination. Improvements in palliative care might rectify existing deficiencies in care services and thus be a suitable means for reducing the number of cases where terminally-ill patients wish to die because of such deficiencies.

The State may also not simply refer the individual to the option of using suicide assistance offered abroad. The State must guarantee the protection of fundamental rights required under Art. 1(3) GG within its own legal order.

III. After all, the Federal Constitutional Court concludes that § 217 StGB, due to the violations of the Constitution set out above, must be declared void.

Finally, the Federal Constitutional Court gives guidelines and points out options for the legislator to renew the voided regulation according to the Constitution. As the FCC emphasises, it does not follow that the legislator is completely barred from regulating suicide assistance. But any legislation on this subject must be guided by the notion of humans as intellectual-moral beings capable of pursuing and exercising their freedom in self-determination. In the context of organised suicide assistance, a broad spectrum of options is available to the legislator for ensuring the protection of self-determination in decisions regarding one's own life. These include procedural safeguards such as statutory obligations to provide information or observe waiting periods; requirements to obtain administrative approval, which ensure the reliability of the assisted suicide services offered; as well as the prohibition of hazardous forms of suicide assistance. The legislator may also resort to the use of criminal law in that regard, at least to secure compliance by means of criminal sanctions. However, the right to suicide does, which is a new and unexpected aspect in the decision of the Court, prohibit linking the permissibility of suicide assistance to specific substantive criteria, e.g. by requiring a diagnosis of an incurable illness. Nonetheless, different requirements may be set, depending on the relevant circumstances, concerning establishing that the individual's resolution to commit suicide is sincere and final. Simultaneously, sufficient space must remain in practice for the individual to exercise the right to depart this life and, based on their free will and the support of third parties, to carry out this decision on their own terms.

The decision finally concludes with the enhancement that in any case, there can never be an obligation, on anyone, to assist in another person's suicide.

D. Conclusion

Shortly after the Federal Constitutional Court's decision, the German Minister of Justice announced that Government and Parliament would try to give a new law according to the Court's standards till the end of the year 2020. We will be curious about the results of these efforts.

Birgit Daiber, LL.M., Professor Seoul National University, South Korea*,
Human dignity in German civilisation

Résumé

La loi fondamentale, la constitution allemande de 1949, commence en son article 1, paragraphe 1, première phrase, en statuant que la dignité de l'homme est intangible. Parler de cette dignité humaine dans la civilisation allemande veut dire qu'on ne se restreint pas au droit seulement, mais plutôt qu'on suit une approche plus large, une telle approche se justifiant par l'histoire d'origine de l'inclusion de la dignité humaine dans cette constitution en ce qu'une telle protection ne connaissait pas de prédécesseur dans l'histoire constitutionnelle allemande de sorte qu'une notion juridique de la dignité humaine n'existait pas encore en ce moment. Afin de développer cette notion, l'histoire, la philosophie, et la religion se sont prêtées comme sources de compréhension. La contribution détaille les idées découlant de ces sources et démontre qu'on peut les trouver dans la jurisprudence de la Cour constitutionnelle fédérale allemande concernant la dignité humaine.

* This article was funded by the 2021 Research Fund of the Seoul National University Asia-Pacific Law Institute, donated by the Seoul National University Law Foundation.

I. Introduction

The Basic Law (Grundgesetz [GG])—the German constitution entered in force in 1949[38], starts in its Article 1 Paragraph 1 Sentence 1 by stating that "human dignity shall be inviolable" ("Die Würde des Menschen ist unantastbar."). Talking about human dignity in the wider landscape of German civilisation means that we do not restrict ourselves to law, but rather follow a broader approach—which is justified by the history of origin of its inclusion in the Constitution in 1949 because such protection did not have a predecessor in German constitutional history; a *legal* notion of human dignity therefore did not yet exist at that time.

Admittedly, the Constitution of the Weimar Republic dating from 1919 (Weimarer Reichsverfassung)[39] provided in Article 151 Paragraph 1 Sentence 1 that the "regulation of economic life must be compatible with the principles of justice, aiming at the attainment of human conditions of existence for all" ("Die Ordnung des Wirtschaftslebens muß den Grundsätzen der Gerechtigkeit mit dem Ziele der Gewährleistung eines menschenwürdigen Daseins für alle entsprechen."). In that the new Constitution took human dignity out of the economic context and made it a generally protected principle, it became necessary to develop a similarly general understanding. The question that arose, therefore, was which fields to consult

38 BGBl. I, p. 1 et seqq. An English translation can be found here: http://www.gesetze-im-internet.de/englisch_gg/englisch_gg.html.

39 RGBl., p. 1383 et seqq. An English translation can be found here: reader.library.cornell.edu/docviewer/digital?id=nur: 01840#mode/1up.

in order to develop this perception. In this regard, history[40], philosophy[41], and religion[42] have lent themselves as sources of understanding.[43]

II. Sources of understanding

1. History

The first source of understanding consists in the experience shared by all members of the Parliamentary Council (Parlamentarischer Rat) responsible for elaborating the Basic Law: National Socialism which was defeated only three to four years previously. After the exclusion of Jews from citizenship[44] and the attempt at their extinction, after total control of the population and the persecution of all those who were considered enemies

---

40 *J. Isensee*, Würde des Menschen, in: D. Merten/H.-J. Papier (eds.), Handbuch der Grundrechte in Deutschland und Europa, volume IV/1, Heidelberg 2011, § 87, para. 29; *K. Stern*, Das Staatsrecht der Bundesrepublik Deutschland, volume IV/1, München 2006, § 97 II.2.a.

41 *H. Dreier*, in: id. (ed.), Grundgesetz, Kommentar, volume I, 2nd ed., Tübingen 2004, Article 1 Paragraph 1, para. 1 et seq., 9, 11; *P. Häberle*, Die Menschenwürde als Grundlage der staatlichen Gemeinschaft, in: J. Isensee/P. Kirchhof (eds.), Handbuch des Staatsrechts der Bundesrepublik Deutschland, volume II, 3rd ed., Heidelberg 2004, § 22, para. 33, 37; *M. Herdegen*, in: Th. Maunz/G. Dürig/R. Herzog/R. Scholz (eds.), GG, Article 1 Paragraph 1, para. 7, 20; *J. Isensee* (l.c., footnote 40), para. 6 et seq., 55, 85; *Chr. Starck*, in: H. v. Mangoldt/Fr. Klein/id. (eds.), Kommentar zum Grundgesetz, volume 1, 6th ed., München 2010, Article 1 Paragraph 1, para. 6 et seq., 17; *K. Stern* (l.c., footnote 40), § 97 I.1., 3., II.1.

42 *P. Häberle* (l.c., footnote 41), para. 33; *M. Herdegen* (l.c., footnote 41), para. 7, 19 et seq.; *J. Isensee* (l.c., footnote 40), para. 6 et seq., 55 et seqq., 85 et seq.; *W. Pannenberg*, in: W. Kerber (ed.), Menschenrechte und kulturelle Identität, München 1991, p. 61 et seqq.; *Chr. Starck* (l.c., footnote 41), para. 5 et seqq.; *K. Stern* (l.c., footnote 40), § 97 I.1.a., c., 3, II.1.

43 See also *C. Ruiz Miguel*, Human Dignity: History of an Idea, JöR 50 (2002), p. 281 et seqq.
Concerning the constitutions of other states, of the Länder et other documents of Public International Law, see *H. Dreier* (l.c., footnote 41), para. 19, 26, 34; *M. Herdegen* (l.c., footnote 41), para. 15 et seq.; *J. Isensee* (l.c., footnote 40), para. 10 et seqq.; *Chr. Starck* (l.c., footnote 41), para. 2; *K. Stern* (l.c., footnote 40), § 97 I.2.
As to the question whether Public International Law can serve as a source of understanding, see *M. Herdegen* (l.c., footnote 41), para. 42; *J. Isensee* (l.c., footnote 40), para. 44.

44 § 2 of the Reich Citizens Act (Reichsbürgergesetz) of 15 September 1935, RGBl. I, p. 1146.

or anti-social by the National Socialist regime, the members of the Parliamentary Council were determined to build a new order that would ensure that such tyranny could not reoccur.[45]

2. Philosophy

A second tool used to develop a legal notion of human dignity can be found in philosophy, more precisely that of Immanuel Kant, in that he demanded that a person can never only be a means; rather, they should be the purpose, an intrinsic goal ("Denn vernünftige Wesen [Menschen[46]] stehen alle unter dem Gesetz, daß jedes derselben sich selbst und alle andere niemals bloß als Mittel, sondern jederzeit zugleich als Zweck an sich selbst behandeln solle.")[47], naming the qualification of being the purpose and intrinsic goal "dignity" (Würde)[48]. According to Kant, human beings should therefore not be considered mere instruments for others to reach their aims ("der Mensch ... ist nicht bloß als Mittel zu anderer ihren ... Zwecken ... zu schätzen")[49].[50]

3. Religion

If we speak of religion as the third source of understanding for human dignity, we are referring to Christianity and its concept that human beings

---

45 For the whole paragraph, see *H. Dreier* (l.c., footnote 41), para. 40; *P. Häberle* (l.c., footnote 41), para. 36; *M. Herdegen* (l.c., footnote 41), para. 16, 25, 39; *J. Isensee* (l.c., footnote 40), para. 29; *Chr. Starck* (l.c., footnote 41), para. 1, 10, 17; *K. Stern* (l.c., footnote 40), § 97 I.3.

46 See *I. Kant*, Die Metaphysik der Sitten, Frankfurt a.M., 10th ed. 1993, p. 550. The fact that he is talking of human beings can be seen from page 569, 600.

47 Kritik der praktischen Vernunft, Grundlegung zur Metaphysik der Sitten, Frankfurt a.M. 1995, p. 66. See also Die Metaphysik der Sitten (l.c., footnote 46), p. 600.

48 Kritik der praktischen Vernunft, Grundlegung zur Metaphysik der Sitten (l.c., footnote 47), p. 68; Die Metaphysik der Sitten (l.c., footnote 46), p. 569, 600.

49 L.c., footnote 46, p. 569.

50 For the whole paragraph, see *H. Dreier* (l.c., footnote 41), para. 12; *M. Herdegen* (l.c., footnote 41), para. 12; *J. Isensee* (l.c., footnote 40), para. 79 et seqq.; *W. Pannenberg* (l.c., footnote 42), p. 62 et seq.; *Chr. Starck* (l.c., footnote 41), para. 6; *K. Stern* (l.c., footnote 40), § 97 I.1.b.

are created in the likeness of God[51].[52] However, there is no unanimity on whether religion could even serve as a source of understanding. Since the Basic Law is a secular constitution, it is at least clear that a religious conviction cannot play a role in developing a legal understanding of human dignity.[53] Therefore, the proponents of drawing on religion for that purpose rather base their arguments on the aforementioned idea of human beings, the origins of which they find in Christendom.[54] On the contrary, those against referring to religion point to the fact that the church in its history has not been at the forefront of the development of the recognition of human dignity.[55] However, inasmuch as even the latter concede that the actual evolution in no way changes the relevance or the importance of the concept itself[56], we can conclude that there is a point shared by all: the aforementioned idea that human beings are created in the likeness of God. As such, they are perceived as being endowed with reason[57] and capable of self-determination[58].

III. Case law of the German Federal Constitutional Court

If we look at the case-law of the German Federal Constitutional Court on human dignity, we can find all aspects described so far:

1. Influence of history

a. First, the idea of human existence as it was stipulated in the Constitution of the Weimar Republic resurfaces: To also ensure that standard under the new Constitution, the Court combines the human dignity in Article 1 with the social state principle stated in Article 20 Paragraph 1. The Court deduces that everyone must be able to dispose of the

---

51 See *J. Isensee* (l.c., footnote 40), para. 58 et seqq.

52 See *M. Herdegen* (l.c., footnote 41), para. 7; *J. Isensee* (l.c., footnote 40), para. 56; *W. Pannenberg* (l.c., footnote 42), p. 64 et seqq.; *Chr. Starck* (l.c., footnote 41), para. 5; *K. Stern* (l.c., footnote 40), § 97 I.1.a.

53 *J. Isensee* (l.c., footnote 40), para. 9, 87.

54 *J. Isensee* (l.c., footnote 40), para. 9, 87.

55 *H. Dreier* (l.c., footnote 41), para. 7.

56 *H. Dreier* (l.c., footnote 41), para. 8.

57 *J. Isensee* (l.c., footnote 40), para. 62; *W. Pannenberg* (l.c., footnote 42), p. 65; *Chr. Starck* (l.c., footnote 41), para. 6.

58 *J. Isensee* (l.c., footnote 40), para. 62.

minimum conditions for such an existence. As a consequence, the State must pay social benefits when needed. Additionally, those who have enough means themselves must not see the necessary sum taxed.[59] The income tax law, therefore, exempts the amount of 9,408 euros per year from taxation.[60]

b. Further, the Court, already in one of its first judgments, qualified humiliation, stigmatisation, persecution, and ostracism ("Erniedrigung, Brandmarkung, Verfolgung, Ächtung")—actions which took place during National Socialism[61]—as violations of human dignity.[62]
c. Even recently, one can find ideas reminiscent of this dark time in German history: In its judgment of 17 January 2017, not to ban the Nationaldemokratische Partei Deutschlands (NPD)[63], a far-right party, the Court states that the unconditional subordination of the individual under a collective constitutes a violation of human dignity.[64] It is not difficult to remind oneself in this context of the saying of the National Socialists that the individual does not count, but only the people ("Du bist nichts; Dein Volk ist alles.").
d. In the same judgment, there is another embodiment of human dignity that can also be linked to National Socialism's experience: The Court underlines the importance of equality before the law. Of course, simple differences in treatment are not ruled out, but human dignity is opposed to the general refusal of recognising rights to a group[65] as was done to Jews during the Third Reich. The Court, therefore, expressly mentions anti-Semitism and racism in this context.[66]

---

59 For the whole paragraph, see BVerfGE 82, 60, 85. Concerning the possibility to reduce the benefits in cases where the beneficiaries do not conform to their obligation to make efforts to overcome their situation, see the ruling of 5 November 2019, in the case 1 BvL 7/16, available here: https://www.bundesverfassungsgericht.de/SharedDocs/Entscheidungen/EN/2019/11/ls20191105_1bvl000716en.html.

60 Article 32a Paragraph 1 Sentence 2 of the Income Tax Act (Einkommenssteuergesetz [EStG]).

61 Concerning the link to National Socialism, see BVerfGE 109, 279, 312.

62 See only BVerfGE 1, 97, 104.

63 This ruling has already been analysed in *S. Lee/B.Daiber*, Neue Entscheidungen zum Verbot politischer Parteien in Korea und Deutschland—eine rechtsvergleichende Untersuchung, Zeitschrift der Koreanisch-Deutschen Gesellschaft für Sozialwissenschaften, 27(4), 2017, p. 143–181.

64 BVerfGE 144, 20, para. 540.

65 L.c., para. 646 in connection with para. 638.

66 L.c., para. 541.

e. Finally, human dignity cannot be reconciled with a totalitarian regime that wants to cover all aspects of life and wants to determine everything and control everything, as was, for example, expressed by Adolf Hitler when he declared during a speech that (young) Germans would not become free again for the rest of their lives ("Sie werden nicht mehr frei, ihr ganzes Leben.").

aa. Thus, state jurisdiction does not include the political and religious beliefs of the citizens.[67] In particular, the state must not endanger or violate their physical integrity, their lives, or their freedom because of these beliefs ("kein Staat... [hat] das Recht, Leib, Leben oder persönliche Freiheit aus Gründen zu gefährden oder zu verletzen, die allein in der politischen Überzeugung, in der religiösen Grundentscheidung oder in unverfügbaren Merkmalen" liegen). This also entails consequences for the right of asylum included in the constitution as early as 1949. As provided for in Article 79 Paragraph 3 GG, a constitutional amendment must not affect human dignity. The possibility of restricting the right of asylum is therefore limited.[68]

bb. In addition, the State has no competence in the area of development in strictly personal matters ("Entfaltung in ... höchstpersönlichen Angelegenheiten"). The core area of private life is therefore absolutely protected ("unantastbarer/absolut geschützter Kernbereich privater Lebensgestaltung"). In this regard, the Court mentions sensations and feelings, reflections, views, and experiences of a strictly personal manner ("Empfindungen und Gefühle sowie Überlegungen, Ansichten und Erlebnisse höchstpersönlicher Art") in addition to confidential conversations with family or other close and intimate friends.[69] As a result, the acoustic surveillance of residences[70] and online searches[71] are restricted by human dignity. Admittedly, the Court did not declare these measures unconstitutional, but it demanded guarantees in order that the absolute protection of the core area of private life remains assured.[72]

cc. Finally, human dignity is also opposed to a totalitarian approach in that it prohibits the state from registering and indexing all aspects of

---

67 The limits of state jurisdiction have already been treated in *B. Daiber*, Grenzen staatlicher Zuständigkeit, Berlin 2006.

68 For the whole paragraph, see BVerfGE 94, 49, 103.

69 For the whole paragraph, see BVerfGE 109, 279, 313 et seq., 319.

70 BVerfGE 109, 279.

71 BVerfGE 120, 274.

72 BVerfGE 109, 279, 311, 314 and BVerfGE 120, 274, 335 et seqq., respectively.

the personality ("den Menschen ... in seiner gesamten Persönlichkeit zu registrieren und zu katalogisieren")[73] and from establishing a personality profile (Persönlichkeitsprofil)[74].

2. Influence of Kant's philosophy

With regard to Kant's philosophy, we can recognise it in the right—coming from human dignity—to see one's value recognised and to be respected ("sozialer Wert- und Achtungsanspruch"), which prohibits anyone being debased by being perceived only as an object of State action ("bloßes Objekt")[75].[76] This right derives from the fact that every human being has to be qualified as a subject (Subjektqualität)[77] and said right is therefore independent of skills, physical or mental situation, performance, or social status ("Ohne Rücksicht auf seine Eigenschaften, seinen körperlichen oder geistigen Zustand, seine Leistungen und seinen sozialen Status")[78].

a. The consequences of this right are manifested in particular in criminal law[79], beginning already at the investigative stage, where some measures are prohibited, namely those that reduce suspects to a means of establishing the truth by no longer allowing them to freely form their will (Willensentschließungsfreiheit) on whether to remain silent or to exercise that will freely (Willensbetätigungsfreiheit), in particular by means of ill-treatment.[80]

---

73 BVerfGE 27, 1, 6.

74 BVerfGE 109, 279, 323.

75 See only BVerfGE 144, 20, para. 539.

76 *H. Dreier* (l.c., footnote 41), para. 53.

77 See only BVerfGE 144, 20, para. 539.

78 See only BVerfGE 115, 118, 152.

79 Concerning the jurisprudence of the German Federal Constitutional Court on the implications of Article 1 Paragraph 1 GG on criminal law, see also *D. Hömig*, Menschenwürdeschutz in der Rechtsprechung des Bundesverfassungsgerichts, in: R. Gröschner/O. Lembcke (eds.), Das Dogma der Unantastbarkeit, Eine Auseinandersetzung mit dem Absolutheitsanspruch der Würde, Tübingen 2009, p. 25, 29.

80 BVerfG, NJW 1998, p. 1938, 1939 (concerning the use of a lie detector). See also Article 136a of the Code of Criminal Procedure (Strafprozeßordnung [StPO]): Die Freiheit der Willensentschließung und der Willensbetätigung des Beschuldigten darf nicht beeinträchtigt werden durch Mißhandlung, durch Ermüdung, durch körperlichen Eingriff, durch Verabreichung von Mitteln, durch Quälerei, durch Täuschung oder durch Hypnose.

b. For the same reason that a suspect must always be more than the mere object of the authorities' efforts to establish the truth, it follows from human dignity that no one can be criminally compelled to incriminate oneself. Of course, the law may impose the duty to provide information (kein Erhebungsverbot), and this applies even if the information is self-incriminating. However, the information gathered may only be used for purposes other than punishment, such as protecting consumers from the dangers of defective products for which the person can be held responsible. The use of said information in a criminal trial, though, is excluded (Verwertungsverbot).[81]
c. With regard to the substantive part of criminal law, the principle that no penalty can be imposed against someone who is not guilty is an integral part of human dignity.[82] Indeed, without guilt, the person did not actively contribute to the violation and can, therefore, not be blamed. Without being guilty, the person would hence only be the object of state measures aiming at crime prevention.
d. Finally, the right to see one's value recognised and to be respected also influences the execution of prison sentences[83] and other custodial measures such as preventive detention (Sicherungsverwahrung)[84]. As a consequence, no one must become just the object of the prison regime, and even prisoners must be treated as human beings capable of development. The prison regime must therefore be oriented towards the reintegration (Resozialisierung) of prisoners. This implies that all prisoners, including those sentenced to life imprisonment, should have the chance to be freed.[85]
e. Beyond criminal law, the Court also applied said right when it was required to examine a bill authorising the shooting of a kidnapped plane to prevent an incident like the one in the United States on 11

81 For the whole paragraph, see BVerfGE 56, 37, 49.

82 BVerfGE 123, 267, 413.

83 For the whole paragraph, see BVerfGE 45, 187, 238 et seq.

84 For the whole paragraph, see BVerfGE 109, 133, 151.

85 See Article 57a of the Criminal Code (Strafgesetzbuch [StGB]). For the unconstitutionality of a refusal to allow a prisoner to leave the prison for some hours while being accompanied by a security guard, see the ruling of 18 September 2019, in case 2 BvR 681/19, available here: https://www.bundesverfassungsgericht.de/SharedDocs/Entscheidungen/DE/2019/09/rk20190918_2bvr068119.html. Concerning the jurisprudence of the European Court of Human Rights see the ruling of 13 June 2019, in the case 77633/16—Marcello Viola c. Italie (No 2), para. 113.

September 2001. To reach its decision, the Court established a difference between the kidnappers on the one side and the passengers as their victims on the other: In this regard, it pointed to the fact that the kidnappers, as the ones responsible for the danger, contribute actively to the situation. Therefore, a link can be established between their behaviour and the actions of the police. Hence, they are not simply the objects of the latter's approach. By contrast, the passengers do not have a share in the situation. If their lives could be sacrificed by the authorities' attempt to down the plane, they would have no chance to act. They would only be the objects of the measure to save the lives of other possible victims. Therefore, it cannot matter whether these other potential victims are more numerous, as human dignity and the right to have one's value recognised and to be respected prohibit simply contrasting the figures.[86]

3. Influence of religion

a. As for the influence of religion, the idea of self-determination can also be found in the case law of the Court's in that this idea is opposed to totalitarianism, as the latter does not leave any space for carrying one's life in one's own hands.[87] The aspects which have been evoked above with respect to the exclusion of a totalitarian regime[88]—namely the protection of political and religious beliefs, the idea of development in strictly personal matters and the resulting protection of the core area of private life, and, finally, the prohibition of registering and indexing all aspects of the personality—can therefore also be linked to the idea of self-determination and hence to religion.

b. Regarding, finally, endowment with reason, we discover a particular attention in the jurisprudence of the Court for the protection of the will: If, as already mentioned above[89], the methods of investigation within the framework of a criminal procedure must not touch the possibility of forming and exercising the will freely, the case law concerning human dignity shows an appreciation of the said endowment with reason. The same is true of the principle that no penalty can be imposed on someone who is not guilty: Since, according to this principle, the

86 For the whole paragraph, see BVerfGE 115, 118, 153 et seqq.

87 See also *W. Pannenberg* (l.c., footnote 42), p. 67 et seq.

88 See p. 43 et seq.

89 See p. 44.

objective result of a violation is not sufficient for punishment, with punishment also depending on the intellectual capacity to foresee the outcome and even the will to achieve it, the principle finds its raison d'être in the perception of human beings as being capable of envisaging and, consequently, being endowed with reason.

IV. Conclusion

These remarks demonstrate that one can find ideas deriving from history, the philosophy of Immanuel Kant, and the concept of human beings in Christianity in the jurisprudence of the German Federal Constitutional Court concerning human dignity. These sources can perhaps even explain why the approach is negative in some cases in that the violation of human dignity is described[90] rather than its content, while it is positive in others: If one refers to history, especially to National Socialism, repetition should be avoided, and therefore, negative examples are put forward.[91] If, on the other hand, we refer to Kant's philosophy and to religion, we can invoke positive points, namely human beings as a purpose and intrinsic goal, their right to see their value recognised and to be respected, and the Christian conception of them as being created in the likeness of God, endowed with reason and capable of self-determination.[92]

90 BVerfGE 109, 279, 312; *H. Dreier* (l.c., footnote 41), para. 50 et seq.; *M. Herdegen* (l.c., footnote 41), para. 36; *J. Isensee* (l.c., footnote 40), para. 162; *K. Stern* (l.c., footnote 40), § 97 II.1.

91 See also *H. Dreier* (l.c., footnote 41), para. 50; *D. Hömig* (l.c. footnote 79), p. 40; *J. Isensee* (l.c., footnote 40), para. 162.

92 Concerning the positive aspects, see also *D. Hömig* (l.c., footnote 79), p. 39 et seq.

CHAPTER II: Treatment of dying patients: Treatment waiver, treatment discontinuation, palliative care, sedation

Prof. Dr. Tobias Lettl, LL.M. (EUR), University of Potsdam, *Patient decree and help for dying (Euthanasia) in German law.*

Der folgende Artikel befasst sich mit der Frage, unter welchen Voraussetzungen eine Patientenverfügung im deutschen Recht möglich ist. Eine Patientenverfügung kann innerhalb gewisser Grenzen den Willen des Patienten im Stadium der Rechts-fähigkeit festlegen, was in bestimmten Situationen geschehen soll, wenn der Patient später in Pflege ist und daher eine Pflegekraft seine Vertretung bei bestimmten Entscheidungen übernimmt. Dies gilt insbesondere für die Beendigung von lebenserhaltenden Maßnahmen im Krankheitsfall.

The following article deals with the question under which conditions a patient decree is possible in German law. A patient decree can, within certain limits, define the will of the patient at the stage of legal capacity to determine what should happen in certain situations when the patient is later under care and a caregiver there-fore takes over his or her representation in certain decisions. This applies in particular to the termination of life-sustaining measures in case of illness.

A. Introduction

Many people are afraid of being perceived as a burden in old age, especially in illness, of being completely dependent on others' help and losing their autonomy in the process. Added to this are fears of being poorly and undignifiedly cared for or having to endure severe pain.[93] In particular, the existential question arises for them whether, how, and, if necessary, to what extent they are allowed to make legally binding decisions about the end of their lives. This is all the more true as the in-dividual is often no longer legally allowed to make sure and particularly far-reaching decisions himself because of mental restrictions such as dementia. Instead, a

93 E. g. *Klostermann/Schneider*: „So ist kein Leben“, 2004, S. 35 – 40.

representative must then act on his or her behalf. For if an adult cannot manage his affairs in whole or in part because of a mental illness or a physical, mental or psychological disability, the guardianship court appoints a guardian for him (§ 1896 p. 1 s. 1 BGB).

The necessity that the person being cared for should be able to make decisions about his death when he can still form his own will freely and self-determinedly is shown by the case of the US American Theresa Schiavo. Her case was also heavily covered in the media in Germany at the time. She had been in a persistent vegetative state for years and had not decided for this situation. Her death on 31 March, 2005, which occurred due to the removal of a stomach tube, ended a 15-year legal dispute between Schiavo's husband and her parents. After the husband demanded the termination of life support, the parents opposed this request. The reactions to Schiavo's death varied according to different world views and were emotionally charged. This already shows the tensions in which the subject under investigation moves. In the following, it will be shown which possibilities German law provides for the individual to determine his will in a legally binding manner for third parties even before the occurrence of a situation of inability to decide. For this purpose, the German legislator introduced the possibility of a patient decree into the law of care in 2009 with § 1901a of the German Civil Code (BGB).

B. Patient decree (§ 1901a p. 1 s. 1 BGB)

I. Term

Even in the cases of care, the person being cared for can realise his right to self-determination at a time when there was no mental impairment. German law has provided in § 1901a p. 1 s. 2, 3 BGB that the caregiver must give expression and validity to the will of the person being cared for if

1.

a. consenting adult

b. for the case of his incapacity to consent

c. set out in writing (§ 126 BGB; warning and clarification function)

d. whether he is involved in specific medical examinations, treatment or medical interventions which are not immediately forthcoming at the time of the determination

e. consents or prohibits it (legal definition of patient decree) and

2. these specifications apply to the current living and treatment situation (so-called congruence between the written specification and the current living and treatment situation, to be checked by the caregiver).

This applies regardless of the type and stage of the person's illness being cared for (§ 1901a p. 3 BGB).

Therefore, with a patient decree, a person who is capable of making decisions in the legal sense can – just as for his assets by will – exercise his right of self-determination in the area of medical care for a later point in time in time in a forward-looking manner. The person's own decision then continues to affect a later point in time of his care. The consent of the caregiver or even of the Court of custody is then not required because the person being cared for has made this decision himself in a manner binding on all parties involved.[94]

The question of the individual's right to self-determination arises in particular concerning assistance by others in the event of one's own death, for example, by discontinuing treatment or renouncing life-supporting measures. Therefore, according to § 1901a p. 1 s. 1, BGB, a living will also is and especially for physicians of great practical importance when questioning whether and, if so, which treatment measures are to be carried out or omitted. However, the question remains whether and under what circumstances and for what situations the anticipated decision, for example, to discontinue life-supporting measures, is legally permissible.

II. Purpose

The purpose of the statutory provisions on patient decree is to create legal and behavioural certainty[95] concerning the right of self-determination guaranteed under Article 1 p. 1, 2 p. 1 of the German Constitution and the protection of human life, also constitutionally required under these provisions. The resulting general right of personality resulting from this also grants a person the right to decide how and at what time his life is to end, as long as he is still free to form his will, choose accordingly, and,

94 BT-Drucks. 16/8442, S. 11 f.; BGH FamRZ 2003, 748, 750; BGH FamRZ 2014, 1909 Rn. 14.

95 BT-Drucks. 16/13314, S. 3f. u. 7f.

if necessary, act.[96] Thus, if a person capable of giving consent has declared in writing that he does not wish to be treated any further, this is binding on third parties, in particular physicians, even if the person concerned can no longer decide freely and independently at the time of the treatment termination (see also § 630d p. 1 s. 2 BGB). Further treatment against the free will of the person affected, once declared, is then prohibited by the constitution, even if non-treatment leads to death.[97] The general right of personality is protected under civil law by the tort rule of § 823 p. 1 BGB.

III. Sufficient certainty

A patient decree must be sufficiently specific. Therefore, it must contain concrete decisions by the person concerned as to which medical treatment should be carried out or not carried out in which specific situation.[98] General instructions such as enabling a dignified death are not sufficient.[99] The same applies to the mere statement that no life-sustaining measures are desired.[100] Rather, the person concerned must describe what they want and do not want in a particular situation.[101] Thus, the person concerned could give the necessary concrete expression to the statement that he does not want life-sustaining measures by naming specific medical means or referring to sufficiently specified diseases or situations.[102] According to this, a patient decree is sufficiently specified about medical measures such as information on pain and symptom treatment, artificial nutrition and fluid intake, re-suscitation, artificial respiration, antibiotic delivery or dialysis.[103] The patient decree may also stipulate that, despite specific decisions, it should not be directly applicable. The treatment decision should always be made by the caregiver and the discretionary power of the caregiver.[104]

On the other hand, there is a lack of sufficient certainty, e.g. if a person later suffering from dementia and suffering from pneumonia merely states

96 BT-Drucks. 18/5373, S. 10; BVerwGE 158, 142 Rn. 23f.; BVerwG FamRZ 2019, 1455 Rn. 18 with comment *Schwab*.

97 BT-Drucks. 16/13314, S. 10.

98 BGH FamRZ 2016, 1671 Rn. 46; BGH FamRZ 2017, 748 Rn. 17.

99 BGH FamRZ 2016, 1671 Rn. 46; BGH FamRZ 2017, 748 Rn. 19.

100 BGH FamRZ 2016, 1671 Rn. 47.

101 BGH FamRZ 2016, 1671 Rn. 46; BGH FamRZ 2017, 748 Rn. 18.

102 BGH FamRZ 2016, 1671 Rn. 47.

103 BGH FamRZ 2017, 748 Rn. 48.

104 BT Drucks. 16/8442, S. 15.

in his patient decree: "Once I am demented, I do not want any life-sustaining measures".[105]

IV. Significance for criminal law

According to § 1901a p. 1, s. 1 BGB, a patient decree must also be taken into account for criminal law when determining the limit of a possible justification of causally life-ending measures.[106]

C. Help for dying (= Euthanasia)

I. Term

The concept of help for dying (= Euthanasia) in a sense to be taken as a basis here, covers four cases, namely

1. Non-treatment ("passive euthanasia"): renunciation of medically appropriate treatment to maintain or prolong life in the case of a life-threatening illness (while maintaining primary care and pain-relieving treatment), as well as the discontinuation of such a life-prolonging measure,
2. indirect help for dying: pain-relieving, palliative treatment at the risk of (unintended) shortening of life,
3. assisted suicide (suicide assistance): assistance to commit suicide, for example, by procuring and providing the lethal drug; and
4. active help for dying: intentional and active acceleration or induction of death.

The term "help for dying" is distinct from "help while dying". The latter refers to medical and nursing measures that alleviate pain without the aim of shortening life.

105 BT Drucks. 16/8442, S. 15.
106 BGH FamRZ 2011, 108 Rn. 12.

II. Legal limits

1. No distinction between action and omission

Concerning "help for dying", the Federal Court of Justice rightly does not distinguish between doing and omission, as it regularly involves a variety of activity and passivity (e.g. cutting a supply tube).[107] Rather, the "help for dying" is to be summarised in a normative and evaluative way. According to this, non-treatment covers both objective and subjective elements of action, which aim to terminate a medical treatment measure that has already begun, either wholly or partially, at the patient's will.[108]

2. Binding effect of the patient decree

As already shown, certain decisions made in writing by the caregiver before the time of care are binding on third parties and, in particular, the caregiver if they are sufficiently defined and, in particular, if they contain a concrete treatment decision for a specific disease situation. Of course, further investigation is required as to what sufficiently specific decisions made by the subsequently cared for a person in connection with the dying process may be directed at all.

The right of self-determination derived from Articles 1 p. 1, 2 p. 1 of the German Constitution grants the person the right to defend himself against unintentional interference with his physical integrity and the uninfluenced course of his life and death.[109] Thus, medical measures necessary to preserve life constitute interventions in a person's physical integrity and require consent. Conversely, the will of the person concerned is also decisive if the refusal of treatment is life-threatening.[110] Since the caregiver does not make a decision of his own but only implements the previously expressed, highly personal will of the person being cared for, the requirement of highly personalised will does not prevent the caregiver from deciding on behalf of the patient in connection with the dying process.[111]

---

107 BGH FamRZ 2010, 1551 Rn. 31.
108 BGH FamRZ 2010, 1551 Rn. 31.
109 BGH FamRZ 2010, 1551 Rn. 35.
110 Palandt/*Götz*, BGB, 79. Aufl. 2020, § 1901a BGB Rn. 6.
111 BGH FamRZ 2003, 748 Rn. 37f.

Help in the event of death by non-treatment is therefore justified if it is according to the patient's free will and allows a process of illness that, without treatment, leads to death to take its course.[112] Therefore, in the event of an irreversible fatal course of a simple illness of the patient, life-preserving or life-prolonging measures must be omitted if this is his will, previously expressed, for example, by a patient decree, and which has not been revoked.[113] This results from the dignity of the human being, according to which a right of self-determination exercised in a state capable of giving consent must also be respected at a later point in time of incapacity to give consent.[114] The illness is no longer treated, and the patient is left to die.[115] Intermediate treatments are then in-admissible, even if they are life-sustaining. A patient decree can also be issued to terminate artificial feeding.[116] The dying process does not have to have begun yet.[117] For this reason, the legal admissibility of non-treatment based on a patient decree does not require that a disease with an irreversible fatal course is present. Therefore, the refusal of curative treatment is also admissible if this treatment could defeat a disease that leads to death or further postpone the onset of death.[118] Indirect help for dying is also eligible for consent.[119]

Suppose a patient decree for a particular case provides for non-treatment. In that case, a special feature is added if the patient has consented to organ donation – in Germany, the consent and not the objection solution applies to organ donation. For the purpose of organ donation, the patient must continue to be kept artificially alive for at least a few days and, therefore, cannot be left to die alone. The patient decree will must then also refer to this.

However, the constitutionally guaranteed right of self-determination does not grant any right or even entitlement to third parties to independently intervene in life without connection with medical treatment of a life-threatening illness (active help for dying).[120] The person's consent to deliberate, i.e. deliberately life-ending actions outside such a context (e.g. administration of a lethal dose with food when the person enters a

---

112 BGH FamRZ 2010, 1551 Rn. 35.
113 BGH FamRZ 2003, 748 Rn. 31.
114 BGH FamRZ 2003, 748 Rn. 31.
115 BGH FamRZ 2010, 1551 Rn. 35.
116 Palandt/*Götz*, BGB, 79. Aufl. 2020, § 1901a BGB Rn. 6.
117 Palandt/*Götz*, BGB, 79. Aufl. 2020, § 1901a BGB Rn. 6.
118 BGH FamRZ 2014, 1909 Rn. 22.
119 BT-Drucks. 16/13314, S. 10.
120 BGH FamRZ 2010, 1551 Rn. 35.

particular state of health) is therefore not legally permissible. Hence, the question of the ability to consent is not relevant in this respect.[121]

The question of so-called suicide assistance, i.e. assistance in self-determined suicide, is also irrelevant to a patient decree by obtaining a lethal dose of tablets. This is because a person under care at the time of a living's validity will can regularly make hardly any self-determined decisions and indeed not decisions as far-reaching as those about life and death. The appointment of a caregiver is only made to the extent necessary. However, care for health care is regularly ordered, which also includes deciding whether to consent to the termination of life-prolonging measures without an explicit addition.

However, the caregiver cannot decide about assisted suicide of the person being cared for. In this respect, the question of the person concerned's free will must depend solely on the time of the life-ending act to be performed by the person himself so that an anticipated decision by patient decree on assisted suicide is not possible.

If the conditions under which non-treatment is desired in a patient decree are lack-ing, life-prolonging measures must be taken as long as the situation is not hopeless from a medical point of view.[122]

D. Summary

1. Even in cases of care, the patient can use his right of self-determination at a time when there was no mental restriction, under the conditions of § 1901a BGB (German Civil Code) using a patient decree. Third parties, in particular carers and physicians, are bound by this will of the patient. Further treatment against the affected person's free will, once declared, is prohibited, even if the failure to treat leads to death.
2. A patient decree must be sufficiently specified. It must contain concrete decisions by the person concerned about which medical treatment should be carried out or not carried out in which specific situation.
3. Assistance in dying by non-treatment is permissible if it corresponds to the patient's free will and allows a disease process that leads to death without treatment to take its course.
4. Indirect help for dying is also permitted if the patient decree says so.

121 BGH FamRZ 2010, 1551 Rn. 35; zur Unterscheidung auch *Höfling*, JuS 2000, 111, 113 u. *Verrel*, Gutachten zum 66. DJT, 2006, C 64.
122 Palandt/*Götz*, BGB, 79. Aufl. 2020, § 1901a BGB Rn. 6.

5. However, the constitutionally guaranteed right of self-determination does not grant a right or even a claim to third parties independently intervening in life with-out connection with medical treatment of a life-threatening illness (active help for dying).
6. The question of so-called suicide assistance is irrelevant to a patient decree.

Louis-Charles Viossat, Lecturer Global Social Policy, Sciences Po, *Palliative Care Strategy in France: What Lessons?*

Abstract

La politique de prise en charge de la fin de vie et des soins palliatifs est l'un des enjeux majeurs de notre époque, en France comme à l'étranger. Après avoir émergé en France dans les années 1980, cette politique publique a été progressivement mise en œuvre avec des spécificités par rapport au Royaume-Uni ou aux Etats-Unis, ce dont rend compte le présent article. 35 ans après la circulaire Laroque, il est temps de repenser la stratégie française.

End-of-life and palliative care are among key medical, ethical, societal and policy challenges of our times in France as well in other European countries.

Palliative care policies have emerged in France in the 1980s, a few years after the UK and the USA. Key milestones include the « circulaire Laroque » (Laroque decree), which set up the current palliative care architecture, the creation of the first palliative care unit (« USP ») by Doctor Abiven in 1987, the creation of the first hospital mobile unit (« EMSP ») at Hotel Dieu hospital in 1989, and the foundation of the French palliative care professional society (« SFAP ») during the same year. The 1990s have been a decade of consolidation and expansion: the 1991 hospital law established palliative care as a mission of hospitals; the 1999 palliative care law established the current definition of palliative care, a right of patients to palliative care and a legal status for caregivers and volunteers. Eventually, in the years 2000 and 2010, palliative care services have rapidly grown, and the legal framework has been finalised through three key pieces of legislation, in 2002, in 2005 and finally in 2016.

Moreover, since 1999, four national multi-year palliative care framework strategies, or plans, have been elaborated and implemented. The first plan (1999–2001) stressed that palliative care was a right. The second plan (2002–2005) put in place the graduated organisation, which is the core of palliative care services in France. It was supplemented by the first Cancer Plan 2003–2007, which included an essential palliative care component. The third plan (2008–2012) was focused on the expansion of palliative care services, training and research, as well as pediatric palliative care. The last plan (2015–2018) has developed and expanded these orientations.

French palliative care services are not based on hospices such as in the UK or the US but on a quite complex and diversified « graduated system of care », including three layers of hospital services. Level 1, the basic layer, is handled, on a standard basis, by all hospital services: in particular neurology and oncology as well as rehabilitation care services (« SSR ») and long-term hospital units (« USLD »), which specialise in geriatrics. Level 2 is a French exception: identified palliative care beds (« LISP ») in the hospital services, often in oncology and pneumology, which treat the highest number of patients in palliative care. LISP bring more staff, better rooms and more financing with them. Level 3 includes specialised and dedicated palliative units (« USP »), which have at least ten beds and 2,5 staff.

These three layers of hospital palliative care services are supplemented by specialised mobile teams (« ESMP »), which are generally handled by USP members and which support all other hospital services for taking care of their palliative care patients. They include around 3 or 4 staff: typically one doctor, one nurse and other health professionals.

In ambulatory care, palliative care services rely on all medical doctors, particularly GPs, and on specialised services of nurses, which are supported by home hospitalisation services (« HAD »). Around 50 % of EMSP also cover part of the geography outside their hospitals. And palliative care networks provide their expertise but not care. There are also 22 hospital-based dedicated regional teams for children in palliative care.

In total, palliative care services treat around 200,000 patients in hospitals and 70,000 patients in an ambulatory setting per year … They are staffed by 800 palliative care doctors, including 260 in USP.

From an international perspective, according to the 2019 EAPC Atlas, France is in the second quartile of European countries in terms of palliative care services density, below countries like the UK, Belgium or Sweden, even though there has been some progress since the early 2010s. According to the Economist Quality of Death Index, France was ranked at the 10th level in 2015, below the UK, Belgium and Germany. But this index methodology is not totally sound. And progress may have been made since 2015 due to the latest strategic plan.

The 4th strategic plan for the years 2015–2018 is in continuity with previous plans. One does not note striking differences with other strategic plans in Australia, Canada, Ireland or the UK. The 4th strategic plan includes four orientations, 14 measures and 41 activities. Strategic orientations are as follows: to inform patients on end-of-life and empower them, to train professional, support research and disseminate information on palliative care, to grow palliative care in ambulatory settings, in particular for residents of nursing homes, and finally to reduce inequalities of access to palliative care. According to a recent official evaluation report, the plan's implementation has been satisfactory overall but with too limited concrete impacts for patients yet. For example, the creation of a dedicated national centre for palliative care has been a progress in terms of patient empowerment, and communication campaigns have been a success too. However, objectives in terms of access, except early detection, have not been met, and palliative care supply has increased but not enough.

Thirty-five years after the Laroque circulaire, time may have come for a strategic (re)thinking and a reset of the French palliative care strategy. Solutions put in place so far have had only partial and too limited concrete impacts on the quality of end-of-life and access to palliative care services. In particular, clarification is needed around several key issues and questions: what are the priority population groups for palliative care services? Are LISPs an effective tool for palliative care services? What should be the role of home hospitalisation services versus palliative care mobile teams? Should France move towards a hospice-based system such as in the UK? Finally, in light of rapid innovations in healthcare and IT, what could and will be the impacts of innovative technologies on palliative care?

Kerstin Peglow, Professor, Université Paris Nanterre, *Palliative care in Germany in the light of the decision of the Federal Constitutional Court of 26 February 2020*

Abstract

Die Palliativversorgung wurde 2015 in Deutschland umfassend gesetzlich geregelt. Zielsetzung des Gesetzgebers war es, durch das Gesetz zur Verbesserung der Hospiz- und Palliativversorgung finanziell ein breites Spektrum an Maßnahmen bereitzustellen, die die medizinische, pflegerische, psychologische und seelsorgerische Unterstützung von Menschen in der letzten Lebensphase verbessern. Aus ethischer Sicht ging es dem Gesetzgeber bei Verabschiedung des HPG darum, die gewerbsmäßige Hilfe zum Selbstmord zu unterbinden, die fast gleichzeitig als Straftatbestand in § 217 des Strafgesetzbuches aufgenommen wurde. Diese äußerst umstrittene Vorschrift wurde jedoch am 26. Februar 2020 in einem aufsehenerregenden Urteil des Bundesverfassungsgerichts für nichtig erklärt. In der Entscheidung wird Palliativversorgung als Alternative zur gewerbsmäßigen Suizidhilfe angesprochen. Im vorliegenden Beitrag soll daher untersucht werden, ob und inwiefern das höchstrichterliche Urteil Einfluss auf die Palliativversorgung in Deutschland haben könnte.

Palliative care was comprehensively regulated by law in Germany in 2015. The legislator's goal was to fund a wide range of measures through a law on palliative and hospice care, which seeks to improve the medical, nursing, psychological and pastoral care for people during the last phase of life. From an ethical perspective, the legislator was determined to prevent the recurrent pursuit of assisted suicide services. Therefore, "business-like" suicide assistance was almost simultaneously included as a punishable offence in section 217 of the German Criminal Code. But this highly controversial provision was declared null and void in a landmark ruling by the Federal Constitutional Court on 26 February 2020. In the judgement, palliative care is mentioned as an alternative to "business-like" suicide services. The article will examine whether and to what extent this significant court decision will impact palliative care in Germany.

I. Introduction

In Germany, palliative care was comprehensively regulated by law in December 2015. The Hospice and Palliative Care Act (HPCA)[123] was the latest of a series of laws passed by the German *Bundestag* in the area of civil legislation on terminal care. From an ethical point of view, the legislator's clear intention in 2015 with the HPCA was to prevent "business-like" assisted suicide.[124] Indeed, the law which made assisted suicide by business-like operating associations and individuals a punishable offence was integrated into section 217 of the German Criminal Code on 3 December 2015, almost simultaneously with the adoption of the HPCA. Section 217,

123 *Gesetz zur Verbesserung der Hospiz- und Palliativversorgung*, promulgated on 1 December 2015 (*Bundesgesetzblatt* [Federal Law Gazette] 2015 I, n° 48, 7 December 2015, 2114).

124 Cf. *Peglow*, End of Life legislation under German Civil Law, in: *Rohlfing-Dijoux/ Hellmann*, Perspectives of law and culture on the end of life legislations in France, Germany, India, Italy and United Kingdom, Baden-Baden 2019, 187–196.

a highly controversial provision, was declared void by the Federal Constitutional Court on 26 February 2020.[125] In the judgment, as mentioned above, the Court deals with palliative care as a so-called alternative to suicide assistance. In this paper, after an overview of the HPCA, we will discuss palliative care in light of the Federal Constitutional Court's decision. Does the decision have a particular impact on palliative and hospice care, and what are the future prospects for the coexistence of palliative terminal care and "business-like" assisted suicide?

II. Major elements of the Hospice and Palliative Care Act

The Hospice and Palliative Care Act has officially been part of the German health care system since it entered into force on 8 December 2015. The vast majority of the population is insured by this system, consisting of a mix of different statutory health insurers. In Germany, statutory health insurance is part of the social insurance system along with pension insurance, unemployment insurance, occupational accidents and disease insurance and long-time care, which are all regulated in the Social Code-Books I – XII[126]. The HPCA was inserted into the Social Code-Books V and XI and involve statutory health and social care insurance funds in hospice and palliative care to a greater extent than before. Although there was already a legislative regulation before this, it only concerned the statutory entitlement to outpatient palliative care.[127] The following sections of the Social Book-Code V define palliative and hospice care as treatment measures covered by the social insurance system more than ever: section 27 I 3 SGB V (*health care also includes palliative care of insured persons*), section 37 (*palliative care in the context of home nursing care*), section 37b in conjunction with section 132d (*entitlement to specialised outpatient palliative care*), section 39a (*financing of inpatient, semi-inpatient and outpatient hospice services*), section 39b (*entitlement to palliative counselling by the health insurance funds*). Thus, the HPCA provides financial support for a wide range of measures that improve the medical, nursing, psychological, and pastoral

125 BVerfG (*Bundesverfassungsgericht*), 26 February 2020, Az.: BVR 2347/15 u.a.
German version: https://www.bundesverfassungsgericht.de/e/rs20200226_2bvr234715.html
English version: https://www.bundesverfassungsgericht.de/e/rs20200226_2bvr234715en.html

126 *Sozialgesetzbücher (SGB)* I – XII.

127 SGB V Section 37b.

support to people in the last phase of their lives, promoting a nationwide expansion of palliative and hospice care. Care for the terminally ill may take place in hospitals, nursing homes, hospices or at home.[128] Palliative and hospice care intend to alleviate an illness's consequences, such as physical pain, social isolation or depression, when there is no prospect of recovery anymore.

Apart from the general intention to guarantee a patient more financial security in the field of palliative care, the HPCA also tries to create incentives for advanced healthcare and treatment planning during the last phase of life (*gesundheitliche Versorgungsplanung für die letzte Lebensphase*). Advanced care planning is a relatively new approach within the German health care system. Experiences in Anglo-American countries inspired the legislator to establish a similar offer in Germany. Nowadays, many people are afraid of the last phase of life because they fear pain, unwanted treatments, or self-determination loss. Therefore, the HPCA tries to respond to these fears and inform people about ways to help them early and plan care in advance. According to section 132g of the Social Code-Book V, a person can now foresee which palliative measures they would like to have for the last phase of their life. They can do so in advance and detail, and with the help of medical professionals and their relatives. This is especially important in a situation where the person is no longer able to give their consent to palliative care on their own. The aim is to ensure that curative treatment is avoided when there is no longer any chance of recovery. The dreaded artificial extension of life that causes physical, psychological and social suffering can be overcome with the help of palliative or hospice care.

The HPCA uses two different terms explicitly: "palliative" and "hospice" care. These terms are not employed homogeneously in legal texts, expert statements and documents of specialised organisations. Besides, different terminologies in different countries can be traced back to various cultural backgrounds. Definitions given by the German Association for Palliative Medicine (*Deutsche Gesellschaft für Palliativmedizin*) are based on the recommendations of the European Association for Palliative Care (EAPC).[129] According to the EAPC, "palliative care is active, comprehensive care of

---

128 https://www.bundesgesundheitsministerium.de/service/begriffe-von-a-z/h/hospiz-und-palliativgesetz.html

129 Deutsche Gesellschaft für Palliativmedizin: Definitionen zur Hospiz- und Palliativversorgung (14 October 2016), with references to the "White papers on standards and norms for hospice and palliative care in Europe – recommendations from the EAPC", in: European Journal of Palliative Care 2009 and 2010. https://www.dgpalliativmedizin.de/images/DGP_GLOSSAR.pdf

a patient whose disease does not respond to curative treatment. Control or relief of pain and other symptoms, as well as social, psychological and spiritual problems, are the primary goal. Palliative care is interdisciplinary in its approach and includes the patient and their relatives. In this sense, palliative care offers the most basic concept of care – the one that is oriented towards the patient's needs wherever he or she is cared for, whether at home or in hospital. Palliative care values life and sees death as a normal process: it neither accelerates nor prevents death. It strives to maintain the best possible quality of life until death".[130] This definition is also essentially in line with that of the IAHPC defining palliative care as "the active, holistic care of individuals across all ages with serious health-related suffering due to severe illness, and especially of those near the end of life. It aims to improve the quality of life of patients, their families and their caregivers".[131]

In German-speaking countries, a distinction is traditionally made between palliative and hospice care. *Palliative* care is based on a medical approach; it is an independent medical discipline emphasising professionalism.[132] *Hospice* care is deeply rooted in a culture of civic commitment and social solidarity. It focuses on seriously ill and dying persons with their wishes and needs and their relatives and loved ones. But despite historically different developments in Germany, palliative care and hospice care are understood as a common approach and attitude. Full-time staff and volunteers work together in multi-professional teams. They aim to offer care oriented towards individuals' needs and decisions. Also, hospice care aspires to dignity, peace and quietness.[133]

Despite the increased supply of palliative and hospice care since 2015, patients who, because of their individual situation, which they perceive as unbearable, would prefer to end their life prematurely with professional help. The judgment of the Federal Constitutional Court addressed these concerns legally.

---

130 Deutsche Gesellschaft für Palliativmedizin: Definitionen zur Hospiz- und Palliativversorgung, 2.

131 International Association for Hospice and Palliative Care https://hospicecare.com/what-we-do/projects/consensus-based-definition-of-palliative-care/

132 *Maier/Sitte*, in: *Thöns/Sitte*, Repetitorium Palliativmedizin, 3 ed., Berlin, 2015, 11.

133 Deutsche Gesellschaft für Palliativmedizin: Definitionen zur Hospiz- und Palliativversorgung, 2 et seq.

III. Palliative care in the decision of the Federal Constitutional Court

Section 217 of the Criminal Code, which was declared void by the Federal Constitutional Court, read as follows: "(1) Whoever, with the intention of assisting another person to commit suicide, provides, procures or arranges the opportunity for that person to do so and whose actions are intended as a recurring pursuit incurs a penalty of imprisonment for a term not exceeding three years or a fine. (2) A participant whose actions are not intended as a recurring pursuit and who is either a relative of or is close to the person referred to in subsection (1) is exempt from punishment."

This provision was intended to prevent suicide support associations from expanding their field of activity and to keep suicide assistance from becoming a form of health care service for the seriously ill and elderly people.[134] Assisted suicide continued to go unpunished in individual cases only, as suicide itself is not a punishable act. The explanatory memorandum to the law pointed out that respect for life should be a model for a caring society because life includes suffering, severe diseases and disabilities. The fear of being only a burden to society had to be counteracted. Suicide assistance should not become the norm;[135] the patients' fundamental rights that the legislator has to protect are human life and individual freedom of decision.[136]

Regarding palliative care in end of life situations and its role as a "counterpart" of section 217, the Federal Constitutional Court held that the legal expansion of palliative medicine, hospice services and abroad assisted suicide offers cannot compensate for the prohibition of suicide assistance.[137] The prohibition of assisted suicide services violates the general right of personality of Art. 2(1) in conjunction with Art. 1(1) of the German Constitution[138], which guarantees the right to a self-determined death for persons determined to end their own lives. Self-determination as a constitutional right and the freedom to commit suicide also encompasses the right to seek and – if offered – make use of assistance voluntarily provided by third parties to this purpose.[139] The HPCA might be suitable

134 *Bundestagsdrucksache [Bt.-Dr.]* (*Bundestag* Printed paper), 18/5373, 2.
135 *Ibid.* 18/5373, 8.
136 *Ibid.* 18/5373, 10.
137 BVerfG, *op. cit.*, n° 278.
138 German Constitution: known as Basic Law (*Grundgesetz*).
139 BVerfG, *op. cit.*, *Leitsätze* (headnotes). According to the Court, legally authorised suicide services are not limited to particular criteria like incurable or terminal illness of the person looking for suicide assistance (BVerfG n° 340). Every indi-

to eliminate existing deficits in quantitative and qualitative palliative care. However, it cannot be a corrective to the restriction of suicide decisions made in free self-determination. Moreover, there is no obligation of palliative medical treatment. The will of the patient should not be ignored to prevent palliative medical treatment from becoming a duty that limits the individual's autonomy. If the decision to end one's own life is taken freely and in full knowledge of all relevant circumstances, then it is a decision that rejects existing alternatives, and it may also refuse palliative care treatment.[140]

Some of the complainants, who are emergency[141] or palliative care physicians[142], expressed their concern about the risks of criminal liability in the scope of their work. At their work, doctors are repeatedly confronted with suicide wishes from patients. Although their work is characterised by palliative medical therapies and suicide prevention, according to the complainants, palliative medicine reaches its limits in individual cases where a patient's pain can no longer be eased. In such cases, they accept suicide assistance in principle. According to them, the complainants also argued that section 217 is imprecise since it does not ensure impunity either in restrictive physician-assisted suicide or in the case of palliative medical care when patients voluntarily stop taking food and fluids, which ultimately leads to death. The same risk of punishment also exists in the case of medication supply given to outpatients if a suicidal patient takes a lethal dose.[143]

In contrast, in their statements, representatives of German medical associations and various palliative care associations considered section 217 of the criminal code to be constitutional.[144] In their opinion, the scenarios intended to justify the guarantee of necessary assisted suicide services are be based on inadequate or insufficient palliative medical treatment. In particular, reference was made by these associations to the possibility of palliative sedation, which reduces the symptoms in cases that cannot be treated with other means in an ethically justifiable manner. Palliative seda-

---

vidual who wishes to commit suicide with others' help has the right to do so under the – constitutional – conditions of a future legal framework.

140 *Ibid.* n° 298, 299.

141 *Ibid.* n° 71 et seq.

142 *Ibid.* n° 75 et seq.

143 *Ibid.* n° 77.

144 *Ibid.* n° 142 et seq.

tion is to be regarded as a medical treatment measure, unlike the help to suicide provided by a doctor.[145]

Moreover, the chairs for palliative medicine representatives had already unanimously declared themselves against suicide assistance in 2014. They considered that assisted suicide was not a medical task meeting people's concerns about a dignified death. On the other hand, the Chairs were in favour of an intensive public debate on questions of illness, dying, death and the expansion of palliative medical care.[146]

IV. Prospects on assisted suicide and palliative care

The judgment clearly reveals that a large part of the medical profession and the German palliative care associations have reservations regarding assisted suicide. An interesting argument they put forward is the possibility of palliative sedation, which refers to the attenuation of the patient's consciousness with the intention of relieving symptoms and not of accelerating death. In this respect, there is a difference with active assisted suicide: it is not the sedation that should trigger death, but the disease itself.[147] However, the boundaries between palliative sedation and assisted suicide can become blurry:[148]: for instance, sedation can lead to an accelerated death contrary to the original intention, or sedation could not be used following the guidelines, or sedation could be used with the intention of causing death. Therefore, one could say that as soon as the patient loses consciousness, this loss of consciousness is similar to a "social death" for the patient themselves as well as for next-of-kin or related persons. The distinction between assisted suicide and palliative sedation may be less evident for them than for physicians or other third parties.[149]

---

145 *Ibid.*n° 159.

146 *Ibid.*n° 287.

147 *Müller-Busch*, Terminale Sedierung – Ausweg im Einzelfall, Mittelweg oder schiefe Ebene?, in: *Kettler, Simon, Anselm, Lipp, Duttge*, Selbstbestimmung am Lebensende, Göttingen 2005, 124, 135.

148 *Ibid.* n° 124, 127, 129, 132.

149 *Den Hartogh*, Het recht op inslapen – Richtlijn houdt onvoldoende rekenning met opvatting 'goodsterven' Medisch Contact, (61), 1463 -1465. Cited by *Cirak*, Sedierung am Lebensende auf der Intensivstation, Dissertation (PhD thesis), Würzburg 2018, 2. https://www.researchgate.net/publication/332631879_Sedierung_am_Lebensende_auf_der_Palliativstation

From a legal perspective, ambiguities regarding the boundaries between those situations were removed when section 217 was declared void. Palliative physicians should no longer have to worry that they might be liable to prosecution under this provision.[150] In this respect, increased use of medically indicated and correctly given palliative sedation in hopeless disease situations could be considered as a last therapeutic option more than before. Assisted business-like suicide could thus be avoided in those cases.

On the other hand, palliative physicians are now risking being increasingly confronted with the blatant desire for assisted suicide without any reference to palliative sedation. It would then be up to the attending physician to decide whether to comply with this wish or not. There is no obligation to do so, as the Federal Constitutional Court has expressly stated.[151] Furthermore, surveys have shown that the majority of doctors reject providing assisted suicide.[152] This is reinforced by the fact that in large parts of the Federal Republic of Germany, the laws and codes of conduct for physicians provide professional exclusions in case of physician-assisted suicide.[153] As far as these rules for professional conduct are maintained,[154] medical assistance by a physician personally known to the patient will remain mostly the exception even after the abolition of section 217. The person looking for suicide services will contact a physician who will fulfil their wish to die through a business-like operating association.[155]

With this decision, the Court clearly decided to give the human dignity of severely ill persons at the end of their lives a second legal pillar in addition to palliative care, i.e. the possibility of receiving business-like assistance in the event of suicide. This should enable all individuals to decide for themselves what meaning they want to give to their lives and how or when they want to end them. Life and death form an indivisible unit, and as such, death might be seen as a part of life. Therefore, living a life with dignity also includes dying with dignity. This ultimate expression of one's dignity must no longer be stopped by the obligation for terminally ill

150 However, according to section 216 of the criminal code (killing upon request), an offence may be considered if the doctor deliberately follows the patient's wish to receive sedation that inevitably leads to death.

151 BverfG, *op. cit.*, n° 342.

152 *Ibid.* n° 284–286.

153 *Ibid.* n° 20 *et seq.*

154 To create sufficient room for the individual's decisions, a coherent design of the professional rules of conduct applicable to doctors should be provided (*ibid.* n° 341).

155 *Ibid.* n° 297

and suffering persons to take their own life by travelling abroad, hoarding sleeping pills, starving to death or committing a violent suicide.[156] In this respect, the Federal Constitutional Court rightly told the legislator to put an end to a situation that is unsatisfactory *de facto* and *de jure* for the afflicted persons.

When drafting new legal rules on suicide services, legal dignity and self-determination of the individual at the end of their life should not be compromised by the legislator because of common good interests or of socio-political reasons, including reasons protecting third parties.[157]. Instead, the legal system must adopt a protective and humane approach for services in assisted suicide. This implies that the legislator sufficiently prevents people willing to die from being abused. The Federal Constitutional Court has actually listed deterrent examples from other countries where professionalised assisted suicide services have been authorised for years and where socially intolerable practices have been observed.[158] Therefore, the legislator should formulate the legal regulation of assisted suicide in such a way that persons looking for help are protected from psychological or economic pressure or even from being forced to commit suicide. Comprehensive information and counselling, with the involvement of qualified doctors, especially from the palliative care sector, psychologists and relatives or other people close to the patient, could be the right way to counteract abuse[159] – amongst other measures. In order to guarantee the neutrality of counselling, the assumption of costs would also have to be regulated by the legislator. It must be possible for the person affected by an illness to give informed consent, as in the case of consent to any medical treatment in free and enlightened decision-making.[160] The formation of the person's free will requires awareness of options to suicide, and in particular, the possibilities of palliative care should be discussed.

---

156 Cf. *Hufen*, Selbstbestimmtes Sterben – das verweigerte Grundrecht, NJW 2018, 1534.

157 This assessment of the Federal Constitutional Court (*op. cit.* n° 301 et seq.) meets the jurisdiction of the European Court of Human Rights to Art 8. (1) ECHR, cf. ECtHR, Pretty v. The United Kingdom, Judgment of 29 April 2002, n° 2346/02, §§ 64 and 65). The ECtHR also recognises that observing the right to self-determination of an individual does not impede the legislator from imposing restrictions on this right to protect others' lives (§§ 70 *et seq.*); cf. *Muckel*, Verfassungswidrigkeit des Verbots der geschäftsmäßigen Förderung der Selbsttötung, JA 2020, 473, 476.

158 BVerfG, *op. cit.* n° 257.

159 *Ibid.* n° 339

160 *Ibid.* n° 242.

V. Concluding summary

The HPCA, which was introduced in 2015, was a decisive step in establishing comprehensive palliative care in Germany and offering unprecedented help for terminally ill patients. For almost five years, it was the socially accepted counterpart of business-like assisted suicide, which had been a punishable offence since the HPCA came into force. This situation has changed decisively since the latest judgement of the Federal Constitutional Court. When the Court declared section 217 of the Criminal Code void – a section which prohibits the facilitation of suicide as a recurrent pursuit –, it created an alternative consisting of professional help for individuals suffering from an incurable illness, parallel to palliative care. Now, the legislator has to set the legal framework for suicide assistance. This legal framework needs to follow the specifications of the Court, and the constitutional requirements pointed out in the judgement.

The future will show how many afflicted persons ultimately decide in favour of palliative care or assisted suicide. The legal possibility that professional help can be sought when a person wants to take their own life may give comfort to some seriously ill patients in a hopeless situation. However, patients might actually not take advantage of it. In this respect, the legislator could expand and strengthen palliative care to curb desires to commit suicide in cases of illness. Concerning assisted suicide services, legal rules should guarantee independent counselling and prevent abuses in order to offer more opportunities for ensuring people a dignified death, a dignified death which should correspond to the personality, the conviction or the self-perception of each individual.

Bibliographie

Den Hartogh Govert, Het recht op inslapen – Richtlijn houdt onvoldoende rekenning met opvatting 'goodsterven' Medisch Contact, (61), 1463 -1465. Cited by *Cirak Marianne*, Sedierung am Lebensende auf der Intensivstation, Dissertation (PhD thesis), Würzburg 2018. https://www.researchgate.net/publication/332631879_Sedierung_am_Lebensende_auf_der_Palliativstation

Hufen Friedhelm, Selbstbestimmtes Sterben – das verweigerte Grundrecht, NJW 2018, 1534.

Maier Bernd Oliver/ Sitte Thomas in: *Thöns/Sitte*, Repetitorium Palliativmedizin, 3. ed., Berlin, 2015, 1–13.

Muckel Stefan, Verfassungswidrigkeit des Verbots der geschäftsmäßgen Förderung der Selbsttötung, JA 2020, 473, 476.

Peglow Kerstin, End of Life legislation under German Civil Law, in: *Rohlfing-Dijoux/ Hellmann*, Perspectives of law and culture on the end of life legislations in France, Germany, India, Italy and United Kingdom, Baden-Baden 2019, 187–196.

Müller-Busch Christof, Terminale Sedierung – Ausweg im Einzelfall, Mittelweg oder schiefe Ebene?, in: *Kettler, Simon, Anselm, Lipp, Duttge*, Selbstbestimmung am Lebensende, Göttingen 2005, 124 -135.

Sophie Garcelon, Ancien avocat, Consultante et Coach professionnel – Wingsanté, *Deep and continuous sedation until death – 2 February, 2016 French law strengthening the rights of patients at the end of life*

Summary

French laws relating to the end-of-life have recently evolved through two major texts adopted in 2005 and 2016. These texts strike a balance between accepting death without suffering (or with as little suffering as possible) and prohibiting active assistance in dying.

Nevertheless, they raise many issues worth looking further into. Some of these practical issues are discussed in this article.

Introduction

In a popular press article in December 2020[161], Dominique PON, Director of the Pasteur clinic in Toulouse, relayed an idea formulated to create a digital platform to "store throughout our lives what constitutes our digital memory". The idea is both to value each human life, to positively transmit and accept our own finitude. It's about making sense of the time we have left: "Thinking about transmission helps us stay alive."

This idea is original, humanistic and generous, although it raises many technical and ethical questions. It has the merit of bringing a positive outlook on human finitude and contributing to the acceptance of death. However, this acceptance remains difficult for the human being who, at the end of his/her life, becomes "a patient" as well as his entourage. The

161 « Mort numérique : Eternesia, le projet qui veut inscrire nos vies au patrimoine mondial de l'humanité », 20 Minutes, December 11, 2020.

question of the passing from life to death then arises for him/her, his/her relatives and the medical teams who provide care to him/her.

French "end of life" legislation meets the difficult frontier between accepting death when it becomes close and irremediable, respecting the patient's will to die, and forbidding active assistance to death.

This delicate balance also raises essential practical questions for the various actors involved. If a new legislative evolution is not in the pipe right now, indications as to the practical implementation of this text seem crucial.

I- French Law recent evolution on "end of life issues": accept death, avoid suffering while forbidding assistance to death

French legislation evolved through two major texts, passed in 2005 and 2016, both carried by the same Parliament member, Dr Leonetti, after whom they were called. The 2016 text, named the "Clayes-Leonetti Act" was also carried by Parliament member Clayes.

1- A first significant step: The 2005 Leonetti Act

For the first time in French Law, a text passed on 22 April, 2005[162] enabled the cessation of treatment in case of "unreasonable therapeutic obstinacy". This concept targets acts or treatment appearing to be useless, disproportionate or having no other effect than artificial survival.

The law's original purpose is to "let the patient die naturally", without any active intervention of the practitioner when death appears to be certain and close.

The doctor is expected to make all necessary efforts to ease the pain and respect the patient's dignity. Therefore, the 2005 law allows the use of drugs in order to limit patients' pain, should it risk abbreviating life[163].

The law based on respecting the patient's express will managed to find a middle way acceptable to both proponents of accompanying patients to their death and a more conservative part of the population, fiercely opposed to any kind of "assisted suicide".

---

162 Loi n°2005-370 du 22 avril 2005 portant sur le droit des malades en fin de vie.
163 Art. L 1110-5 CSP

The patient may refuse treatment and must make his/her decision in full awareness of the consequences. The legal rationale is based on the fact that all medical act or treatment relies on the patient's consent. As such, any patient making a decision should be conscious, informed and able to understand the risks of stopping said treatment.

The patient's will being a key issue; the medical staff is expected to provide exhaustive and clear information. The amount of information given and the length of time given to the patient to reach a decision must be clearly monitored and stated in the patient's medical file.

Should the patient be unconscious or unable to express his/her will, the practitioner is expected to initiate a collective decision-making process and search for the patient's will through end-of-life instructions and relatives' opinion.

The disposition aims to give patients the right to avoid suffering before dying: to ensure a certain comfort for the last moments, to « deeply sleep until death ». Nevertheless, in practice, the law resulted in days of suffering for certain patients, for whom pain relievers were ineffective.

A second bill was presented to and passed by Parliament in 2016.

2- Second step: The 2016 Clayes-Leonetti Act

After ten years of practical application of the Leonetti Act, of discussions about how to ease suffering before death, the CLAYES-LEONETTI Act[164], passed on 2 February, 2016, strengthens the basis laid by the previous act and creates new rights for patients reaching the end of life.

The Clayes-Leonetti Act upheld the 2005 law: upon patient's decision and collective decision-making process, medical acts or treatment might be suspended if they appear to be useless, disproportionate or having no other effect than artificial survival.

Article 2 of the new law went further, stating that artificial nutrition and hydration are considered as treatment and may be stopped in order to avoid unreasonable obstinacy[165]. Therefore, should the treatments be stopped, there should be no nutrition nor hydration without the patient's consent.

164 Loi n° 2016–87du 2 février 2016 créant de nouveaux droits en faveur des malades et des personnes en fin de vie

165 Article L1110–5–1 al 2 Code de la santé publique

Article 3 provides patients with the right to obtain "deep and continuous sedation", provoking alteration of consciousness until death, combined with the stop of treatments[166].

The French 2016 legislation confirms that any patient is entitled to refuse a treatment; the doctor has an obligation to respect the patient's will after providing complete and understandable information on one's choice consequences.

Following this idea, the 2016 act adds the possibility to start deep and continuous sedation until death following the cessation of treatment. This text provides a right to put patients into a coma while bringing an end to treatment[167].

French Health Authorities offers the following definition of sedation[168]: "Sedation is the search, by medicinal means, for a decrease in alertness that can go as far as loss of consciousness. It aims to diminish or eliminate the perception of a situation experienced as unbearable by the patient when all the available means adapted to this situation have been proposed and/or implemented without allowing the expected relief. Sedation can be applied intermittently, transiently or continuously.

Nonetheless, detractors of the law argue that letting a patient die from hunger and thirst is in no way exempt from cruelty.

3- The prohibition on assisted death

Technically, deep sedation is aimed to relieve pain and suffering before ineluctable and close death, as opposed to any kind of action leading to abbreviating life or accelerating death.

Any initiative leading to abbreviating life would be considered as active assistance for dying and punished. Euthanasia is still prohibited by French law: the penal code establishes prison sentences (up to 5 years of imprisonment) and fines (between 45 000 and 75 000 euros)[169].

However, boundaries are thin, and a certain part of the population considers the administration of palliative treatment aiming for deep and

166 Article L1110–5–2 Code de la santé publique

167 Art 1110–5 – 1 and 2 Code de la santé publique

168 Haute Autorité de Santé; "Comment mettre en oeuvre une sédation profonde et continue jusqu'au décès »; Rapport bibliographique; Février 2018; p.14

169 Art. 221–4, 3°, Art. 221 – 5 Code Pénal

continuous sedation with a side effect of faster death as *indirect euthanasia*[170] or a positive act accelerating the up-coming of death.

Nonetheless, the 2021 government has decided to maintain the text as it is, without further evolution,

4- No evolution to be led in 2021 as part of the Bioethics Law

End of life was discussed in Parliament in the context of a discussion on the Bioethical Law presented by the government, as some members of parliament deem that the current texts are no longer sufficient. Indeed, they consider bringing amendments into the debate, aiming to open the possibility of allowing suicide assistance. Their main argument relies on the fact that assistance to die is allowed in countries like Switzerland, Luxembourg or the Netherlands and should also be accepted in France.

Nevertheless, the government underlined that it would not suggest any amendment to the legislation in order to maintain the current balance.

While active assistance in dying is still ruled out, the emphasis is on a future palliative care plan. As it happens, patients' access to their rights poses the most significant difficulty.

In a press release dated June 25, 2021, the French National Consultative Ethics Committee (CCNE) sets up a working group on the end of life in order to reopen ethical debate in this field and to draw up an assessment.

In 2018, through the States General on bioethics, the same CCNE came to the conclusion that the 2016 law on the end of life does not have to be amended while stressing "the imperative need for it to be better known, better applied and accompanied by new means capable of leading to a real development of palliative care in our country ".

With this 2021 working group, the CCNE intends to reopen ethical reflection on the end of life, while positions continue to fuel the public debate on assisted suicide. The committee "will make its contribution by taking stock of the end-of-life situation in France both in terms of the appropriation and application of the current law and previous laws". The CCNE also intends to identify "the exceptional situations, such as slow growing neurovegetative diseases, with which the law is confronted".

170 Stephanie Rohlfing-Dijoux; "Leonetti Clayes Act" -The end of life legislation in France related to the risk of criminal liability of the medical practitioner; Mauritius Criminal Law Review; 2018; p.92

The debate is therefore still pending and it is possible that we will see evolution in the next few years.

II- At the crossing of legal principles and medical practice issues

The principles at the heart of legislation dealing with end-of-life urge medical practitioners to exercise utmost caution when implementing palliative care. In addition to showing great humanity towards patients and their families, several rules have to be respected.

1- Conditions for deep sedation and general principals implied

The 2005 and 2016 legislation place the patient at their core. They aim at offering the possibility of deep sedation if patients ask for it.

– The patient's condition

The 2016 law authorises deep and continues sedation until death in three cases[171]:

- The patient is suffering from an incurable illness in the terminal phase
- His/her life prognostic is engaged (hours or days)
- The patient experiences severe refractory symptoms that he/she considers unbearable

In the patient's situation, should the patient be unable to express his or her will, deep and continuous sedation occurs following a decision to limit or stop a life-maintaining treatment. The purpose of deep sedation is not to cause death or accelerate the onset of death but to ensure that the patient does not suffer.

– The patient's will

At the heart of the law is recognising the patient as an actor of his own health and his own end of life. The right to refuse a treatment given to the patient relies on the fact that he/she knows and understands the consequences.

Therefore, the question surrounding the patient's information is crucial: information on the consequences of withdrawing treatment should be clearly provided, time should be allowed for the patient to make up his/her mind. It is expected from the doctor that he/she has several discussions with the patient in order to ascertain the patient's will.

171 Art L1110–5 -2 Code de la Santé publique

Finally, the medical file should be completed with the provided information, discussions, reactions, final will (or hesitations).

Should the patient be unconscious and unable to provide his/her consent, his will should be determined through all possible means[172]. The patient may have given end-of-life instructions (« directives anticipées »- "advance directive"), mentioning the fact that he/she does not want to be kept alive artificially. These written and signed documents are legally binding on physicians[173]. The 2016 law compels physicians to follow end-of-life instructions. Under the former law, the doctor kept the final decision.

The « person of confidence » designated by the patient has a dominant position on all other non-medical opinions. If no « person of confidence » was designated, the doctor shall ask family members' advisory opinion.

2- Deep sedation meets practical constraints

No decision for deep and continuous sedation can be reached without a collegial procedure, whether or not the person can express his or her will; it must allow the physician to ensure that the patient's situation meets the conditions for using sedation provided by law. The law refers the definition of this procedure to the Code of Medical Ethics: article R. 4127–37–2-III provides for consultation with the members of the health care team present if it exists, and the collection of a reasoned opinion from at least one physician, called in a consultative capacity.

In its guide for health professionals[174], the French National Authority for Health establishes the following procedures :

- the team caring for the patient must have access to a palliative care team, including by telephone when the patient is at home or in a nursing home.
- The doctor in charge of the patient is responsible for the decision. It is up to him to write the prescription and accompany the nurse during the initiation of treatment; both must be available 24 hours a day.
- Relatives must be cared for before, during and after sedation.

172 Art.L 1111–11 CSP, Art. R.4127 – 37–2 al 1 CSP

173 Art L.1111 – 11 al.3 Code de la santé publique, amended by Art. 8 loi n°2016–87 du 2.02.2016

174 Haute Autorité de Santé; "Comment mettre en oeuvre une sédation profonde et continue jusqu'au décès »; Rapport bibliographique; Février 2018; p.14

- Therefore, the physician can rely on the nurses who will administer the treatment, the mobile palliative care team, the palliative care network or the nearest palliative care unit, and must take the advice of a colleague, called as a consultant. Information and discussion with loved ones are also essential. In all cases, the reason for the decision must be included in the patient's follow-up file in the transmission notebook.

Likewise, the wish to limit or stop treatment expressed in the advance directives or, failing this, the testimony of the trusted person or relatives of the wish expressed by the patient are recorded in the patient's file. The courts sanction the absence of a collegial procedure as well as the absence of motivation for the decision to implement deep sedation[175].

These fundamental principles are intended to protect the patient, his entourage and the doctor himself. For the physician, it is the respect of these key principles (research of the patient's will, collegiality, information of the relatives, traceability) that will allow him to defend himself in case of possible questioning.

However, in practice, while this system is perfectly understood by the professionals concerned, it poses concrete difficulties when the patient has chosen to stay at home. Indeed, deep and continuous sedation can be carried out in a healthcare establishment, but also at home or in a residential facility for dependent elderly people (Ehpad), even if a doctor in charge of the patient feels isolated on his or her territory.

In October 2019, a general practitioner from Normandy was tried for his use of deep sedation on his patients, using anesthetic products that the local pharmacy was unable to provide. It appeared that the doctor was obtaining the products from his wife, herself a anesthesiologist at the local hospital. This case revealed not only the irregularity of the drug obtaining process, but also the gap between legal principles and practical solutions outside of hospital infrastructures. It led to an outcry of support within the medical community. Nine hundred family doctors "acknowledged they had accompanied patients at the end of their lives to help them leave with dignity, with no pain, sometimes by violating the law »[176].

This high-profile case also highlighted the unequal treatment of patients treated at home, and those cared for in hospitals.

---

175 TA Pau, 10 janvier 2020, n°2000039; Revue Juridique Personnes et Famille, n°3, 1er mars 2020; Note de A. Boulanger « L'illégalité manifeste d'une décision médicale d'arrêt de traitements vitaux »

176 Fin de vie à domicile : le débat relancé – Le généraliste N°2895 – 17 janvier 2020

French law, therefore, seeks a delicate balance between several fundamental principles: respect for the patient's life and dignity, the patient's right to refuse care considered unreasonable obstinacy, the right not to suffer, the right to die at home.

Faced with patients' demand to end their lives at home, some doctors found themselves in difficulty obtaining products, gathering the team, finding the necessary support. The authorities seem to have taken the measure of these difficulties,

As part of its recommendations for good practice, the French National Authority for Health specifies: "it is necessary to adapt the regulations governing the prescription, dispensing and reimbursement of the drugs concerned by the health insurance system, in order to enable the effective implementation at home of this recommendation for good practice in the management of drugs in palliative and end-of-life situations.»[177]

Conclusion

If a delicate balance seems to have been struck by French law concerning end-of-life support, a real effort of organisation, training and reinforcement of human resources still remains to be made. And this with the dual objective of patient safety and legal security for healthcare professionals.

Bibliograhie

LEONETTI Act, passed on 22 April, 2005 relating to patients rights and end of life

CLAYES-LEONETTI Act, passed on 2 February, 2016 creating new rights for patients reaching the end of life

Décret of 3 August, 2016, modifying the medical deontology code, about collegial proceedings and deep and continuous sedation

Stéphanie Rohlfing-Dijoux; Leonetti Clayes Act – the end-of-life legislation in France related to the risk of a criminal liability of the medical practitioner; Mauritius Criminal Law Review; 2018, p.92

Le Généraliste; Fin de vie à domicile : le débat relancé; 17 janvier 2020; N°2895

Haute Autorité de Santé; Guide du parcours de soins : Comment mettre en œuvre une sédation profonde et continue maintenue jusqu'au décès?; 2018

177 Pratiques sédatives chez l'adulte pour le médecin généraliste – Recommandation de bonne pratique – Janvier 2020

Haute Autorité de Santé; Antalgie des douleurs rebelles et pratiques sédatives chez l'adulte : prise en charge médicamenteuse en situations palliatives jusqu'en fin de vie; Fiche outil 2; Pratiques sédatives chez l'adulte pour le médecin généraliste; Janvier 2020

CHAPTER III: Application of end of life rules to vulnerable persons

Angie Schneider, PhD Privatdozentin, Universität Potsdam, *End-of-life and terminal care for minors under German law*

A. Introduction

There is no specific statutory rule of end-of-life and terminal care for minors under German law. But questions of euthanasia and terminal care for minors can arise in the same way as for adults. Accidents or serious illnesses can put minors in a situation in which imminent death or the expectation of undue pain until death occurs can make euthanasia or terminal care a subject of discussion. Minors will not regularly have taken any precautions for such a life situation or thought about such decisions. Moreover, the age of minors and their limited life experience compared to adults must cast doubt on the ability to understand the consequences and implications of their decisions with regard to such measures.

In the absence of a specific statutory rule, measures concerning end-of-life and terminal care present themselves as the result of a balancing process. The solutions must essentially be found by weighing up three constitutionally protected interests, which may contradict each other in individual cases: The minors rights of self-determination and physical integrity, the parents right of parental custody and the states care obligation.

B. Right of self-determination

I. Statutory bases

In German law the right to individual self-determination is constitutionally protected as an aspect of the general right of personality and human dignity in Article 2 (1) with Article 1(1) of the German Constitution (*Grundgesetz*). The general right of personality includes a right to self-determined death as an expression of personal autonomy.[178] Spefications of the right of self-determination are the autonomy of patients and requirement of consent to medical measures. Patient autonomy can include decisions about letting one's own death take place.[179] The Federal Court of Justice (*Bundesgerichtshof*) also has recognised that it is a matter of human dignity to respect the right of self-determination exercised in a state of consent even if the person is no longer able to make decisions on his or her own responsibility.[180] This right is expressed in a living will according to § 1901a of the German Civil Code (*Bürgerliches Gesetzbuch*), which enables an adult who is able to give consent to specify in writing whether he consents to or prohibits specifiexaminations of his state of health, treatment or medical interventions not yet directly imminent at the time of determination. In creating § 1901a of the German Civil Code, the legislator assumed that the right of self-determination of a person included the right to endanger himself up to the point of self-abandonment and thus also to refuse life-prolonging measures irrespective of the medical indication for the treatment.[181]

At European level, comparable protection is achieved through Article 8 of the European Convention on Human Rights. Article 8 covers the protection of private life, which the European Court of Human Rights (ECHR) interprets broadly. The very essence of the Convention is respect for human dignity and human freedom.[182] In particular, the European Court of Human Rights emphasised: "In an era of growing medical sophistication combined with longer life expectancies, many people are concerned that they should not be forced to linger on in old age or in states of advanced physical or mental decrepitude which conflict with strongly held ideas of self and personal identity.".[183] The European Court of Human Rights considers that the concept of the autonomy of a person

178 Federal Constitutional Court (*Bundesverfassungsgericht*) 26.2.2020 – 2 BvR 2347/15 a.o., NJW 2020, p. 905 (907).

179 Federal Constitutional Court 28.5.1993 – 2 BvF 2/90, 2 BvF 4/92, 2 BvF 5/92, NJW 1993, p. 1751; Federal Court of Justice 3.7.2019 – 5 StR 393/18, NJW 2019, p. 3089 (3091).

180 Federal Court of Justice 17.3.2003 – XII ZB 2/03, NJW 2003, p. 1588; Federal Court of Justice 3.7.2019 – 5 StR 393/18, NJW 2019, p. 3089 (3091).

181 BT-Drs. 16/8442, p. 8.

182 ECHR 29.4.2002 – 2346/02, NJW 2002, p. 2851 (2853) [Pretty / United Kingdom].

183 ECHR 29.4.2002 – 2346/02, NJW 2002, p. 2851 (2853) [Pretty / United Kingdom]; ECHR 20.1.2011 – 31322/07, NJW 2011, p. 3773 (3774) [Haas / Switzerland]; ECHR 19.7.2012 – 497/09, NJW 2013, p. 2953 (2955) [Koch / Germany].

is an important principle[184] and, in interpreting the guarantees of Article 8 of the European Convention on Human Rights: "An individual's right to decide in which way and at which time life should end, provided that he or she was in a position freely to form her own will and to act accordingly, was one of the aspects of the right to respect for private life within the meaning of Article 8 of the Convention.".[185]

II. Minors

These principles also apply to minors. It belongs to the right of self-determination that minors have to decide themselves on the implementation of all medical measures. The term of medical matters also includes measures of end-of-life and terminal care. However, the prerequisite for an effective decision on the implementation of euthanasia and terminal care is that minors are able to make such56) a decision on their own responsibility.

1. Ability to consent

It is therefore necessary an ability to consent. The ability to consent is not an ability that only belongs to adults. Because of its personal character, the ability to consent does not depend on legal capacity to contract, but on the natural ability to understand and to control. It means an ability to understand the nature, significance, impacts and risks of medical measures and to orientate its will accordingly.[186]

The ability to give consent must be assessed on a case-by-case basis. In particular, there is no fixed age limit and it is not decisive whether the minor is capable of contracting.[187] The age of the minor, his mental

184 ECHR 29.4.2002 – 2346/02, NJW 2002, p. 2851 (2853) [Pretty / United Kingdom].

185 ECHR 20.1.2011 – 31322/07, NJW 2011, p. 3773 (3774) [Haas / Switzerland]; ECHR 19.7.2012 – 497/09, NJW 2013, p. 2953 (2955) [Koch / Germany].

186 Federal Court of Justice 5.12.1958 – VI ZR 266/57, NJW 1959, p. 811; Federal Court of Justice 16.11.1971 – VI ZR 76/70, NJW 1972, p. 335 (337); Laufs/Katzenmeier/Lipp-*Katzenmeier*, Arztrecht, 7th ed. 2015, Kap. V m.n. 52; *Lipp*, Freiheit und Fürsorge, 2000, pp. 84 ff.; MüKo-*Huber*, Münchener Kommentar zum Bürgerlichen Gesetzbuch, 8th ed. 2020, § 1626 BGB p. 40.

187 Laufs/Katzenmeier/Lipp-*Katzenmeier*, Arztrecht, 7th ed. 2015, Kap. V m.n. 51 f.; Laufs/Kern/Rehborn-*Kern*, Handbuch des Arztrechts, 5th ed. 2019, § 65 m.n. 3.

development, the severity of the illness and the intervention, as well as the urgency of the case, are important clues in the decision whether a minor is able to form its own will.[188]

2. Absence of ability to consent

Problems will occur with the absence of ability to consent. Minors, in particular younger minors are not or not yet able to give their consent.[189] The same applies if minors are currently or permanently unable to form their own will (in case of unconsciousness, coma, strong influence of medication). The absence of the possibility of forming its own free will in the last examples can affect adults and minors. With adults, the decision on medical measures is regularly delegated to a custodian. In the case of minors, the power of decision obliged their legal representatives. These are usually the parents (§§ 1626 (1), 1627, 1629 (1) of the German Civil Code).

III. Parental custody

1. Preliminary remarks

Parental custody is also constitutionally protected. According to Article 6 (2) of the German Constituion, care and upbringing of children is the natural right of parents and a duty primarily incumbent upon them.

The constitutionally protected educational right of the parents is concretized and developed in § 1626 of the German Civil Code: The parents have the duty and the right to care for the minor child (parental custody). The parental custody includes the care for the person of the child (care for the person of the child). In the care and upbringing of the child, the parents take account of the growing ability and the growing need of the child for independent responsible action. They discuss questions of parental custody with the child to the extent that, in accordance with the stage of development of the child, it is advisable, and they seek agreement.

---

188 Laufs/Kern/Rehborn-*Kern*, Handbuch des Arztrechts, 5th ed. 2019, § 65 m.n. 3; MüKo-*Huber*, Münchener Kommentar zum Bürgerlichen Gesetzbuch, 8th ed. 2020, § 1626 BGB m.n. 42.

189 Laufs/Katzenmeier/Lipp-*Katzenmeier*, Arztrecht, 7th ed. 2015, Kap. V m.n. 52.

2. Medical and similar measures

Parental rights and parental custody are interpreted widely. It is recognised that parents have the right to decide on medical measures, they are also responsible for decisions on the termination of life-sustaining measures,[190] if the minors do not have the ability to understand. Only if minors have the ability to consent, will they get power to consent.[191] It is regularly assumed that medical measures for minors who have not yet reached the age of 14 require the additional consent of their parents.[192]

The need for additional parental consent is also required for serious interventions.[193] The same will apply to measures such as euthanasia and terminal care. These measures are also covered by parental custody. Parents are basically responsible for decisions about maintenance of life-sustaining measures and termination of life-sustaining measures. The Court of Appeal (*Oberlandesgericht*, in the following: *OLG*) Hamm concretised in a decision in 2007: "In the case of minors, parents have the right to give or to refuse consent to medical treatment for the minor. But parents have also to consider the minors own wishes with their growing mature.".[194]

IV. State care obligation

The last aspect leads to the limits of parental custody. The decision of the OLG Hamm has already established that parents have to consider the minors own wishes. However, the limits of parental custody also apply if the minors are unable to consent in medical or other measures. So parents do not have an unlimited right of disposal over the health of their children who are themselves unable of giving consent. The parents' right of decision with regard to medical measures for their child exists only within the limits of the child's well-being.[195]

---

190 Palandt-*Götz*, Bürgerliches Gesetzbuch, 79th ed. 2020, § 1626 BGB m.n. 15; *Spickhoff* FamRZ 2007, p. 2046 (2048).

191 Laufs/Katzenmeier/Lipp-*Katzenmeier*, Arztrecht, 7th ed. 2015, Kap. V m.n. 52.

192 Laufs/Katzenmeier/Lipp-*Katzenmeier*, Arztrecht, 7th ed. 2015, Kap. V m.n. 52.

193 Federal Court of Justice 28.6.1988 – VI ZR 288/87, NJW 1988, p. 2946; OLG Hamm 16.7.1998 – 15 W 274/98, NJW 1998, p. 3424 (3425); *Lipp*, Freiheit und Fürsorge, 2000, pp. 33 f.

194 OLG Hamm 24.5.2007 – 1 UF 78/07, FamRZ 2007, p. 2098 (2099).

195 MüKo-*Huber*, Münchener Kommentar zum Bürgerlichen Gesetzbuch, 8th ed. 2020, § 1626 BGB m.n. 45.

If parents do not take enough account of the best interests of the child in their decisions, the state must ensure that the child is protected. The state care obligation ist laid down in Article 6 (2) of the German Constitution: The care and upbringing of children is the natural right of parents and a duty primarily incumbent upon them. But the state shall watch over them in the performance of this duty. And especially the protection of minors may require a limitation of parental custody, because an uncontrolled decision-making power of the parents may be detrimental to the children.

C. Rights of minors

I. Compliance

The minors rights of self-determination and physical integrity can therefor be influenced by the parental custody and the states care obligation.

Of cours there are situations in which the rights of minors do not need protection because their rights are not at risk. This is the case if the minor is able to give consent and / or the opinions of parents and minors consist. The legislator also assumes or at least hopes that minors and parents will in many cases reach a mutually agreed decision. This finds its expression in § 1626 of the German Civil Code: Parents discuss questions of parental custody with the child to the extent that, in accordance with the stage of development of the child, it is advisable, and they seek agreement.

II. Conflicts

But now there are other situations. For example the minors absence of ability to consent or conflicting opinions of parents and minors. And in these cases there is the question: How can the rights of self-determination and physical integrity of minors beeing realised?

1. Living will

a. Applicableness

The protection of minors could be implemented by means of a living will. This presupposes the applicableness of the rules on living wills. § 1901a (1) of the German Civil Code states: "If a person of full age who is able to consent has determined in writing, for the event of his becoming unable to consent, whether he consents to or prohibits specific tests of his state of health, treatment or medical interventions not yet directly immanent at the time of determination (living will)", this will must be expressed and enforced. § 1901a of the German Cicil Code restricts the living will to the definitions of persons of full age. This is criticised as inconsistent or even unconstitutional, since according to an almost uncontested view, minors can also be capable of giving consent, and leads to a refusal of self-determination in the form of living will to a minor who is capable of giving consent and who can intellectually and voluntarily grasp the opportunities and risks of a concrete potential intervention.[196] Nevertheless, it must be assumed that § 1901a of the German Civil Code is not applicable to minors. At most, it may be considered that a living will issued by a minor in compliance with the requirements of § 1901a of the German Civil Code becomes effective upon reaching the age of majority, if it is evident that the now adult wishes to adhere to his declaration.[197] Of course, that does not change the general inapplicability of § 1901a of the German Civil Code.

b. Consequences

This means: § 1901a of the German Civil Code and legal consequences of this rule are not applicable. Furthermore parents' decisions about medical measures do not require the approval of the court (§ 1904 of the German Civil Code). § 1904 BGB states: "The consent of the custodian to an examination of the state of health of the person under custodianship, to therapeutic treatment or to an operation is subject to the approval of the custodianship court if the justified danger exists that the person under custodianship will die or will suffer serious injury to his health that lasts for a long period by reason of the measure. Without the approval, the measure may be carried out only if delay entails danger." Both § 1901a

196 S. *Müller* DNotZ 2010, p. 169 (182); *Lange* ZEV 2009, p. 537 (539); *Spickhoff* FamRZ 2009, p. 1949 (1951); *Sternberg-Lieben/Reichmann* NJW 2012, p. 257; zum Problem auch *Rieger* FamRZ 2010, p. 1601 (1603).

197 MüKo-A. *Schneider*, Münchener Kommentar zum Bürgerlichen Gesetzbuch, 8th ed. 2020, § 1901a BGB m.n. 10; different BeckOGKBGB/*Diener* m.n. 31; *Jürgens/Loer* m.n. 5; restrictively Jurgeleit/*Kieß*, m.n. 14.

of the German Civil Code as well as § 1904 of the German Civil Code, which regulate the relationship between the custodian and the person under custodianship, are neither directly nor analogously applicable to the relationship between parents and minors. The duties of the custodian in § 1901a of the German Civil Code are an expression of its general obligation to respect the wishes of the person under custodianship. In the relationship between parents and their children, on the other hand, it must be observed that the parents – protected by Article 6 (2) of the German Constituion – can assert their own values up to the objective limit of the welfare of the child.[198] Likewise, § 1626 of the German Civil Code does not oblige the parents of a minor to act as his or her legal representative against their own convictions to the same extent as the custodian as the legal representative of the person under custodianship.[199] Accordingly, in the case of minors, there is a tension between the right of care and parental custody (and, if applicable, the subsidiary state duty of care) which does not arise in the custodianship law and which is contrary to the legal similarity as a prerequisite for an analogy with the rules of legal custodianship. In any case, an analogy further presupposes the existence of a legal loophole that is contrary to plan, which justifies the intention of the legislator expressed in the law to be valid even where the legislator has omitted an express provision.[200] When creating § 1904 of the German Civil Code, however, the legislator was aware that these problems could not only affect adults but also minors, and nevertheless limited the terms of § 1904 of the German Civil Code to adults.[201] A judicial consent to the termination of life-sustaining measures in application of § 1904 BGB is therefore not possible.[202] In this sense, the OLG Brandenburg, for example, established in a case in which a child was only viable after an accident with the aid of artificial respiration and artificial nutrition, that a family court authorisation for the consent of the parents to terminate these life-supporting measures could not be granted because there is no

198 OLG Hamm 24.5.2007 – 1 UF 78/07, FamRZ 2007, p. 2098 (2099).

199 OLG Hamm 24.5.2007 – 1 UF 78/07, FamRZ 2007, p. 2098 (2099); *Rieger* FamRZ 2010, p. 1601 (1603).

200 OLG Hamm 24.5.2007 – 1 UF 78/07, FamRZ 2007, p. 2089 (2099); *Rieger* FamRZ 2010, p. 1601 (1603).

201 BT-Drucks. 11/4528, pp. 71 f.; OLG Brandenburg 17.2.2000 – 10 UF 45/99, FamRZ 2000, p. 1033 (1034).

202 OLG Hamm 24.5.2007 – 1 UF 78/07, FamRZ 2007, p. 2089 (2099); OLG Brandenburg 17.2.2000 – 10 UF 45/99, FamRZ 2000, p. 1033; *Spickhoff* FamRZ 2007, p. 2047; *Rieger* FamRZ 2010, p. 1601 (1603).

statutory basis.[203] At least, the only thing left for parents is the following: For their own legal safety, parents must bring about an "artificial dissent" with the youth welfare office in order to at least indirectly bring about a court decision on the termination of life-sustaining measures.[204]

In the absence of applicability of §§ 1901a, 1904 of the German Civil Code, it must therefore be stated that a living will means no protection of the minors rights of self-determination and physical integrity. On the other hand, there is no statutory basis in this context which would make the decision of parents subject to judicial authorisation. Such a legal basis is required, however, since only this enables the state to take measures in the area of parental custody protected by the German Constitution. The parental right in Article 6 (2) of the German Constitution ensures parents a right of defence against state intervention and permits measures of the state only in the context of Article 6 (2) oft he German Constitution.[205]

2. Court measures in the case of endangerment of the best interests of the child

a. Endangerment of the interests of the child

Protection of the rights of minors can be achieved by restricting parental custody. The German Constitution determines the parents' right and duty of education on the one hand and that the state shall watch over them in the performance of this duty on the other. The state watch exercises the family court by examining the best interests of the child (§ 1666 of the German Civil Code).

According to this, § 1666 (1) and (3) German Civil Code applies: “Where the physical, mental or psychological best interests of the child or its property are endangered and the parents do not wish or are not able to avert the danger, the family court must take the measures necessary to avert the danger. The court measures include in particular: part or complete removal of parental custody.“

---

203 OLG Brandenburg 17.7.2000 – 10 UF 45/99, FamRZ 2000, pp. 133 f..

204 MüKo-A. *Schneider*, Münchener Kommentar zum Strafgesetzbuch, 3th ed. 2017, preliminary § 211 m.n. 153; *Spickhoff* FamRZ 2007, 2046 (2048).

205 Federal Constitutional Court 29.7.1964 – 1 BvL 20/63, 1 BvL 31/66, 1 BvL 5/67, BVerfGE 24, p. 119 (138 f.); Federal Constitutional Court 24.3.1981 – 1 BvR 1516/78, 1 BvR 984/80, 1 BvR 1337/80, NJW 1981, p. 1201; OLG Brandenburg 17.2.2000 – 10 UF 45/99, FamRZ 2000, pp. 1033 f.

This rule is part of the states care obligation. The states care obligation restricts the constitutionally protected parental custody in order to safe the constitutionally protected rights of minors.

b. Removal of parental custody

A decision of the OLG Hamm may give an example, how state duty obligation may affect parental custody and the rights of self-determination and physical integrity of minors.

The decision was based on the following facts: In 2007 a three-year-old child suffered a cardiac respiratory arrest of more than 30 minutes during a diagnostic procedure. The lack of oxygen caused a severe brain damage. The child suffers from spastic attacks which cannot be sufficiently controlled with tablets. It is suspected that it suffers pain during the attacks. The child is fed via a transnasal gastric tube and is almost incapable of human communication. The damage to the brain is irreversible. The parents have decided to take their child home and stop nutrition and fluids under palliative medical care by a specialist, which should ultimately lead to the death of the child. The court stated: Abuse of parental custody may also occur in cases where parents are convinced that they acted for the benefit of the child concerned. The decision of parents to let their irreversibly brain-damaged child die as a result of the interruption of nutrition can represent an exceeding of the discretionary scope granted to them in Article 6 of the German Constitution. Since the presumed will of a three-year-old child cannot be determined, criteria which correspond to general values must be used.

Such criterias may be the hopelessness of the medical prognosis, the existing preservation of essential vital functions such as respiration, heartbeat and circulation or the protection of human life as a priority in cases of doubt.

As a result, the court deciced in this case to the removal of part of the parental custody, namely the removal of the right of residence and the right to health care, and the appointment of a supplementary curator to decide on the question of further life-sustaining medical measures.

So the parents had no longer the power to decide about medical and end-of-life measures.

D. Summary and outlook

It can therefore be concluded that only in the case of minors who have almost reached a special age they have an ability to understand the nature, significance, impacts and risks of medical measures, in particular of end-of-life and terminal care. In all other cases decisions on end-of-life and terminal care are the responsibility of the parents. The growing ability of minors to self-determination may conflict with parental custody. A living will means no solution because § 1901a of the German Civil Code is only applicable to persons of full age. If the parents' decision is not compatible with the best interests of the minor the partial removal of parental custody and the appointment of a supplementary curator is possible to protect the minors rights. In this cases, courts seem to give priority to the principle of "in dubio pro vita" so as not to allow irreversible measures which could result in the death of the minor.[206] The Federal Court of Justice statet in 2019: “Human life is a legal good of the highest order and absolutely worth preserving.“.[207] Although we must not forget that the Federal Constitutional Court has established the high value of the right of self-determination in 2020: “The right to die in a self-determined manner includes the freedom to take one's own life. The individual's decision to put an end to his life in accordance with his understanding of quality of life and the meaning of his own existence is to be respected in the starting point as an act of autonomous self-determination by state and society. The freedom to take one's own life shall include the freedom to seek help from third parties for this purpose and to seek help where it is offered.“.[208] However, such a broad understanding can only be transferred to minors if they have the ability to act in a self-determined manner.

206 Federal Constitutional Court 6.6.2007 – 1 BvQ 18/07, FamRZ 2007, p. 2046; *Spickhoff* FamRZ 2007, p. 2046 (2048).

207 Federal Court of Justice 2.4.2019 – VI ZR 13/18, FamRZ 2019, 999.

208 Federal Constitutional Court 26.2.2020 – 2 BvR 2347/15 a.o., NJW 2020, pp. 905 (907 f.).

Stephanie Rohlfing-Dijoux, Professor University Paris Nanterre, *The application of end-of life legislation to minors : A Comparative approach between French, German and English Law*

Abstract

The application of end-of-life legislation raises specific issues when dealing with a minor patient. The parents' role in decision-making in the triangular relationship between patient, parents and medical team is defined differently depending on the legal systems examined here. The case of divorced or separated parents aggravates the problem. The involvement of the child himself, depending on his age and degree of maturity, in the decision-making process is also not homogeneous from one legal system to another. The contribution will look at French law in the first part and try to point out the differences between German and English law by analysing practical cases in the three countries. At the end, proposals will be made as to how a solution can be found that respects the role of each and especially the interests of the child. In the event of a conflict between the people involved in this difficult decision, mediation seems to be an option.

L'application de la législation de fin de vie aux mineurs : Une approche comparative entre les droits français, allemand et anglais.

L'application de la législation de fin-de-vie soulève des questions spécifiques lorsqu'il s'agit d'un patient mineur. Le rôle des parents dans la prise de décision dans la relation triangulaire entre patient, parents et équipe médicale est défini d'une manière différente selon les systèmes de droit examinés ici. Le cas de parents divorcés ou séparés aggrave le problème. L'implication de l'enfant lui-même, selon son âge et degré de maturité, dans la prise de décision n'est pas non plus homogène d'un système de droit à un autre. La contribution examinera d'abord le droit français dans une première partie et essaye de pointer les différences avec les droits allemand et anglais par le biais de l'analyse de cas pratiques dans les trois pays. A la fin, des propositions comment une solution qui respecte le rôle de chacun et surtout l'intérêt de l'enfant, peut être trouvé, seront formulées. En cas de conflit entre les personnes participant à cette décision difficile, le recours à la médiation semble être une piste.

The French end-of-life legislation is mainly concentrated in the Claeys-Léonetti Act of 2 February 2016, a redraft of the former Léonetti Act of 2005. The fundamental principle of this legislation is to allow ill people to have an end-of-life with dignity and be accompanied at the last moments of their lives. One of the most important sides of the reform is strengthening the patient's rights and autonomy. Suppose an adult is not able to express his will because of an alteration of his consciousness due to his illness. In this case, the medical team will search for his will using his advances directives and questioning his person of confidence, who will act as a witness of the patient's will. The living will of a patient is even binding for the physicians. The new legislation aims to guarantee the respect of the will of the patient in all circumstances. It is a part of the fundamental right of self-determination of each human being including the right to dispose of one's body and life. This right is protected by several national and international legislation, such as Article 1 of the European Convention of Human Rights and the European Charta of Fundamental Rights. However, it clashes with the principle of absolute protection of life, a core point in our constitutions.

With the new French Act, the legislator shifted away from a paternalistic approach to an approach where the patient gets full respect and his will and autonomy is at the core of the legislation[209]. The patient becomes the central actor of the law and may refuse medical treatment, ask for sedation if other remedies are not effective enough to appease their pain, and have a right to be fully informed of their state of health to ensure to make reasonable decisions.

The law of the end-of-life is full of contradictions. The state has a constitutional obligation to protect every life of human beings. On the other hand, every person has the right to refuse medical care, to refuse therapeutical obstinacy and has even a right to suicide[210]. How can these two conflicting rights and obligations be reconciled? The starting point would have to be the formation of wills. Is the choice to die really definitely expressed? Is the person in a situation where he is able to express his will regarding this fundamental decision? This is questionable in the case of mentally ill people and emergency situations in which one can make no considered decision. What about the will of minors? Can a child decide about his life and body only from the completed 18 years of life or from individual understanding? Is the child in the same way as an adult bearer of fundamental rights? The declaration of children rights of the United

---

209 Stephanie Rohlfing-Dijoux/Benoît Renger, *The strengthening of the rights of Patients by the reform of the « Claeys-Leonetti Act »* in France and the Liability of Medical Doctors, in Rohlfing-Dijoux/Luther/Prasannanshu Interactions between Culture and Law in India and Europe, p.141 (143).

210 Michael Eichberger, *Judgment of the Federal Constitutional Court of 26 February 2020 on the Criminalisation of Assisted Suicide Services*, p.16 (in this book).

Nations of 20 November 1959 provides special protection and special care for children[211].

This study will focus on whether this reasonable decision can be made by a minor child, if the child can fully understand the stakes and issues of the decision. It also targets the parental situations and tries to find out the best form of participation of the parents in the decision making for the best interests of parents and the child.

The same problems occur in several countries. This paper examines these questions by reference to the jurisprudence of the last years in France and in Germany and England/Wales.

I. The particular situation of minors in France

Minor children with a severe and incurable illness at the end of their life are in a particular situation where they need special protection. They aren't fully authorised to decide by themselves in an autonomic way.

> Nevertheless, minors are protected by special legislation according to them fundamental rights on an international level. The International Convention on the Rights of the Child, adopted by the General Assembly of the United Nations on 20 November 1989 stipulates in its Art 12 § 1 "*States Parties shall assure to the child who is capable of forming his or her own views the right to express those views freely in all matters affecting the child, the views of the child being given due weight in accordance with the age and maturity of the child.*" The European Convention on bioethics (Orviedo Convention) of 4 April 1997 specifies in its Art 6 § 2 « *Where, according to law, a minor does not have the capacity to consent to an intervention, the intervention may only be carried out with the authorisation of his or her representative or an authority or a person or body provided for by law.*
> *The opinion of the minor shall be taken into consideration as an increasingly determining factor in proportion to his or her age and degree of maturity.* »

The European Convention on Bioethics prevails over national laws. It influences the European Court of Human Rights' rulings and a number of national rulings. However, on the other hand, all member states have

211 Nathalie Lelièvre, *Adolescent et soins, vers une autonomie de la volonté?* Droit et douleur, 2005, p.247.

still not ratified this convention. Germany and the United Kingdom, for example, refused to sign or ratify it. France ratified it on 13 December 2011 for its application from 1 April 2012.

Nonetheless, the new French end-of-life legislation does neither contain special provisions for minors nor an interdiction to his application to children. So, it has to be applied in the same way as for adults but should be combined with the dispositions for minors in family law and minor protection law. The end-of-life rules for children are at the crossroad between family law, medical law and ethics.

In French Civil law, a minor is considered a person legally incompetent and incapable of acting, such as in English or German law. His legal representers are his parents. This incapacity lasts from birth to the age of 18 without any nuance regarding the age of the child and his growing maturity. But the legislator should take into account the different states of development of a child in the legislation concerning the patient's rights.

In French law, neither in German law, the civil law capacity (majority) and the health majority of a minor are synchronous. The law doesn't operate any distinction in our countries. In other countries, such as Quebec, health majority is fixed at the early age of 14[212].

Hence, only the parents or a legal guardian are competent to decide regarding the health of minors according to the scope of parental rights and the best interests of the child (Art. 371–1 Civil Code). Nevertheless, they have to associate the minor to the decision *"according to his age and degree of maturity"*[213]. Indeed, the minor's consent is not necessary, and their opinion should be sought but is only one factor to be taken into account, among others. However, in the report of an evaluation of the Act of 2 February 2016 relative on end-of-life, the French Inspection of Social Affairs (IGAS) recommended according to adolescents the possibility to draw advanced directives and to design a person of confidence from the age of 15[214].

Conflicts may arise if a minor patient and his parents disagree for the biological testament of the minor or if the parents do not align with the decision of the medical team and both can't find consent for the medical

212 Nathalie Lelièvre, *Adolescent et soins, vers une autonomie de la volonté?* Droit et douleur, 2005, p.247.

213 Art. 375–1 Code civil « Les parents associent l'enfant aux décisions qui le concernent, selon son âge et son dégrée de maturité ».

214 Rapport du 11 juin 2018 sur l'Évaluation de l'application de la loi du 2 février 2016 sur la fin de vie (IGAS) p. 83, n°443.

decision concerning the child. The same situation occurs if both parents don't agree in case of divorced parents.

The right of custody and the parental authority remains in French law shared by the two parents even in case of separation or divorce[215]. For medical decisions regarding everyday life, one parent is supposed to represent the other. Only for fundamental interventions posing a risk to a child, the consent of both parents is required. If the parents or one parent refuse to consent to vital medical treatment, "*the medical team can refer the case to the public prosecutor's office to initiate the educational assistance measures that will enable him/her to receive the necessary care*" *(Art. 28 of the Bylaw of 14 January 1974)*. In case of emergency, the doctor can intervene without the parental consent after noticing the opposition of the parents (Art L. 1111–4 § 9 French Health Code[216])[217]. The same article states that the minor's consent has to be looked for if he/she is able to express his will (§ 7). Even if their consent is not binding, their will should be taken into account, particularly if the medical treatment is severe. The minor has to be heard by the medical team and informed about his state of health, the necessary treatments, the risks and cure prospects[218]. Of course, the implication of the minor has to be adapted accordingly to their age. Particularly, if the minor is closed to the majority's age, his involvement has to be intensive, and the physicians have to try to get the consent of the minor. Even if the minor is not allowed to refuse care to which their parents have given their consent, ethically and for the care's success, it is essential to get the adolescent's adherence. One can conclude that the child's age is an essential parameter for the application of the rules on the consent for medical treatments.

However, if the medical decision concerns the withdrawal of life-sustaining treatments, the usual rules aren't applicable. The provisions of the Clays-Léonetti Act are primary. The specific dispositions for minors are situated in the by-law of the new Act. Article R. 4127–37–2 III. French Health Code precise that "*when the decision of limitation or withdrawal of treatments concerns a minor or a person of full age under legal guardianship, the physician has to search for the opinion of the owner of the right of custody or*

215 Loi du 4 mars 2002 (Act of 4 March 2002).

216 Modifié par Ordonnance n° 2020–232 du 11 mars 2020 – art. 2.

217 Nathalie Lelièvre, *Adolescent et soins, vers une autonomie de la volonté?* Droit et douleur, 2005, p.249.

218 Nathalie Lelièvre, *Adolescent et soins, vers une autonomie de la volonté?* Droit et douleur, 2005, p.250.

the legal guardian, except in situations of emergency, where the consultation of these persons is impossible." According to the wording of the law, it is only a question of the parents' opinion, the consent is in no way sought, and the opinion is not binding. It is a medical decision made exclusively by physicians and never by the family. This was confirmed in the landmark case "Lambert" by the French Council of State[219].

Hence, one can find a contradiction between the conditions to make medical decisions for regular health care for minors and decisions impacting end-of-life situation and the withdrawal of life-sustaining treatments.

1. The importance of age in the decision making

In the case of newborn babies and neonatal reanimation, the problem is different from young adolescents' situation due to the total dependence of a baby on their parents. It is possible to distinguish the following three categories of minor children: nurslings, children and adolescents. Their difference is due to their different degree of maturity and consequently their capacity to explain their willingness[220].

2. End-of-life in newborn cases – who is entitled to make the decision?

In a French case, very mediatised, where an extremely preterm born baby (after five months and a half of pregnancy) was placed in a neonatal intensive care unit in the hospital of Poitier[221]. The parents were against a reanimation of the newborn and expressed their opinion through several social media and press releases. The child represents a brain injury due to very significant prematurity, which indicates the risk of future disability of the child. In the case of disagreement between the parents and the physicians, the parents' consent is not necessary. The only criteria for the medical decision are the interests of the child. The opinion of the parents is only consultative.

---

219 Conseil d'Etat, 14 February 2014, n°.375081, *Lambert*; Conseil d'Etat, 24 June2014, n°.375081, *Lambert*.

220 Rapport du 11 juin 2018 sur l'Évaluation de l'application de la loi du 2 février 2016 sur la fin de vie (IGAS) p. 83, n°443.

221 O. Noizet-Yverneau, C. Daubin, K. Bréhaux, R. Robert, *Arrêter la réanimation chez l'enfant « grand prématuré » : qui décide?* in Ethique et santé (2016), p.38.

Thus, the decisional conflict between the parents and the medical team became the subject of societal public discussions. One can see the same mediatisation on social media in the case of Alfie Evans in England[222].

In specific paediatric situations, the physician always must consult the owners of the right of custody. Even if the parents' opinion is only consultative, it is very complicated for the medical team to decide against the parents' opinion. And in this case, parents used social media to put pressure on the physician's decision making. In the sense that parents are against their child's resuscitation, it is even more difficult for doctors to go against this opinion. If the child has significant late damage that is associated with a considerable handicap, the parents and the family must bear this burden in the long term[223]. This, at least, speaks in favour of giving the parents' opinion a significant place.

As a newborn cannot participate in a decision on his or her life, only parents and the medical team are involved in the decision finding. The decision between death and a possible lifelong severe-handicap or long suffering without hope for the child's cure is a real dilemma. The medical team faces ethical quandaries that are impossible for the parents to settle. Often emotionally vulnerable parents, are not capable of deciding in the child's objective interests. A final decision of the medical team (including physicians, other caregivers and psychologists) in a collective procedure has more objectivity and can weigh up all aspects. Furthermore, the fact that the parents can't make the decision could help fight against their feeling of guilt and contribute to mourning in case of the child's death[224]. On the other hand, a medical decision does not guarantee that the parents' views on life and religion will be taken into account in the decision. This can lead to a problem of acceptance of the medical team's decision by the parents, who have to fully bear the consequences of the decision.

This difficulty is even more pronounced in the case of divorced parents who disagree on the decision for their child. For this case it is particularly important that the final decision owns to the medical team and not the family.

---

222 Kartina A. Choong, *Charlie Gard and Alfie Evans: Their Medico-Legal Journeys*, in Medical Futility in Paediatrics: Interdisciplinary and International Perspectives, p.2 (13).

223 O. Noizet-Yverneau, C. Daubin, K. Bréhaux, R. Robert, *Arrêter la réanimation chez l'enfant « grand prématuré » : qui décide?* in Ethique et santé (2016), p.38.

224 Ibidem nr.15, p.39.

Nevertheless, in practice, the parents' opinion turns out to be very important because it seems to be most difficult for the medical team to decide against the will of the parents. The unconditional respect of the collective decision-making is essential in these cases to give the family an important role and consider their extreme distress[225]. The particular situation due to the child's age and the decision's irreversibility has been considered from case to case as well by the French State Council (Conseil d'Etat) as by the ECtHR[226].

The report of the Commission of social affairs in France in 2015[227] considers that the opinion of the owners of the parental authority is more than a simple testimony and corresponds to the expression of the person of confidence without according the value of a consent[228]. However, the particular legislation for end-of-life situations veers away from the traditional role devolved to parental authority by Civil Law.

3. End-of-life of adolescents – the case of a parent-child conflict?

A teenager of an age where he has the natural ability to understand the consequences of an intervention[229] and therefore to consent has the power of self-determination over his body, and can, among other things, choose interventions on his body in all areas, from the banalest (such as holes in earlobes, piercings, or tattoos), to any medical treatment and ultimately also life. However, he can only exercise this right with parental permission.

If there is a dispute between the parents and the child related to an important health decision for the child, the parents' decision prevails to the extent that it is following the interests of the child. However, if the decision concerns the end of the minor's life, neither the parents nor the adolescent are decision-makers. It is a medical decision that takes into account the opinion of both, but only in a consultative manner.

225 Stephanie Rohlfing-Dijoux, *The Application of End-of-life Legislation to Minors in France,* in Medical Futility in Paediatrics : Interdisciplinary and International Perspectives, p.250 (257).

226 ECtHR, judgment no. 46043/14, 5th June 2015, nr.423.

227 Rapport de la commission des affaires sociales du 17 avril 2015.

228 Stephanie Rohlfing-Dijoux, *The Application of End-of-life Legislation to Minors in France,* in Medical Futility in Paediatrics : Interdisciplinary and International Perspectives, p.250 (257).

229 Angie Schneider, *End-of-life and terminal care for minors under German law,* in this book p.55 (56).

II. Aspects of comparative law

1. England and Wales

In recent years, there have been several cases in England and Wales involving end-of-life decisions for minor patients, involving conflicts in the triangular situation between the medical team, the parents and the minor patient, feeding the ethical and legal discussion issues in these compassionate cases. The different cases are turning around the question of the limitation of parental rights and the concept of the best interests of the child.

One of these patients was Charlie Gard, a small boy of 11-month age, contracted a genetic illness and died in July 2017 after a legal battle between his parents and the hospital around the decision to maintain the child artificially in life. The parents wanted to undergo Charlie a nucleoside therapy, whereas the hospital believed that withdrawal of artificial ventilation and providing of only palliative care was in the best interests of the child[230]. After hearing the medical team and other medical experts, the High Court ruled that continued medical treatment with nucleoside therapy would have no curative effect on the child and would only prolong his suffering.[231] In this case, the High Court held that parental rights might be limited by superior control by the court so that decisions regarding the child's medical treatment are in their best interests. The Court of Appeal upheld the decision of the Hight Court[232]. The parents lodged an appeal, but the Supreme Court declined the permission to appeal[233]. Nevertheless, the parents took the case to the European Court of Human Rights (ECtHR), which declared the application inadmissible[234].

Another patient was Ashya King afflicted with cancer. A 5 years old boy was "kidnapped" by his parents from the hospital in August 2014 and brought to Prague to permit him a treatment of proton, that had

---

230 Kartina A. Choong, *Charlie Gard and Alfie Evans: Their Medico-Legal Journeys*, in Medical Futility in Paediatrics: Interdisciplinary and International Perspectives, p.2 (4).

231 *Great Ormond Street Hospital v Yates, Gard & Gard* [2017] EWHC 972 (Fam), para. 93.

232 *Great Ormond Street Hospital & Gard* [2017] EWCA Civ 410.

233 *In the matter of Charlie Gard* (Supreme Court, 8th June 2017).

234 *Gard & Others v United Kingdom*, ECtHR, application no. 39793/17, 27th June 2017.

been refused for him in Great Britain[235]. The child is currently 12 years old and has been declared cured. In the *King* decision, the High Court emphasises the fundamental role of the parents and underlines that the parental authority can only be removed if the threshold of a 'significant harm' is exceeded[236].

In the case of Alfie Evans, a little boy of 23-month age, the parents' opinion was also against the medical decision to withdraw life-sustaining measures. Therefore, a long and hard legal battle with important media coverage was conducted by the parents until his death, overcome on 28 April 2018. The High Court, the Court of Appeal[237] and the Supreme Court[238] each ruled against the parents and in favour of the medical team. The parents take·the case to the European Court of Human Rights (ECtHR). But three judges of the ECtHR held that the parents' application was inadmissible because no violation of human rights was apparent?[239]

The parents sought support abroad, especially in Italy and Poland, and wanted to have the child transferred to a specialised hospital in Rome. The hospital in Liverpool did not agree to Alfie's transfer as they saw a high risk of the child dying during the journey. The parents used social media to show widespread solidarity among the population to put pressure on the hospital. They argued that their custody rights gave them the right to decide on their son's whereabouts. This right was denied to them by the British courts because the parents' decision was not in the best interests of the child. In England and Wales, the Children's Act 1989 states that the state must intervene if a child is harmed. This means that the rights of parents custody are not absolute and that a court can intervene at the hospital's request if it considers that the parents' decisions are not in following the best interests and welfare of the child. If a public institution, such as a public hospital, disagrees with the parents' decision, it must refer the case to the court to withdraw parental custody. Doctors cannot act directly against the parents' decision, such as in France in cases of medical futility where the medical team decide to withdraw life sustaining measures.

In all these cases, it can be seen that the best interests (BI) of the child and the child's welfare are paramount notions that guide the decisions in

---

235 *Ashya King*, High Court [2014] EWHC 2964 (Fam).

236 Ibidem, nr.27, para.31

237 In the matter of *Alfie Evans*, Court of Appeal on 6 March 2018, Re E (A Child) [2018] EWCA Civ 550.

238 Alfie Evans, Supreme Court on 20th March 2018.

239 ECtHR *Evans v United Kingdom* (application no. 14238/18) 23th April 2018.

England and Wales[240]. Unfortunately, the BI is not an absolute value. As an ethical concept, it is also influenced by cultural and religious considerations and may be interpreted differently way by courts, the medical team and parents. The contentious nature of "medical futility cases" results from the fact that both sides claim to act in the best interests of the child. Both sides think to act in the best interests of the child, and their behaviour is sustained by good faith. The ethical principle of beneficence prohibits the maintenance of life-sustaining measures if they should be considered as medical futility. But generally, all parties are persuaded they are acting in the BI of the child. They all have good arguments without any chance of agreeing. Therefore, the role of the courts is significant, and they have an enormous scope for discretion and interpretation, which doesn't help for the predictability and certainty of decisions[241].

All these cases have the common difficulty that one can trace a conflict between parents and the medical team around law and ethical concepts like medical futility, best interests and welfare of the child and significant harm. The interpretation and application of these principles are subject to the discretion of the courts. The different cases reveal the varied ways in which "best interests" can be interpreted. The difficulty here is that often the application of the concepts is based on medical facts that courts can only control to a limited extent. That is also the reason for the contrasting court decisions.

2. The solution of German Law

In German law, there is a fundamental priority of the parents' right of custody regarding every health decision for the child. No exception is made for end-of-life situations of a minor.

In a situation where the parents wished to end the artificial life-support treatment of their 4-year-old daughter in Germany and let her die in peace against the advice of the doctors, a German court clarified the conditions for withdrawal of parental authority in cases of dispute between parents

---

240 William Segrim, *Best interests : The « Gold Standard » or a « Gold Plating »? Should significant harm be a threshold criterion in paediatric cases?*, in Medical Futility in Paediatrics: Interdisciplinary and International Perspectives, p.51 (52).

241 Sarah Sargent, *Charlie's Law : Clarifying the legal standard to be used in medical decision-making for children*, in Medical Futility in Paediatrics: Interdisciplinary and International Perspectives, p.78 (88).

and the medical team over decisions on the end of the child's life. After five months of treatment, the parents wanted to take their child home, where she was to die under medical supervision by not receiving any other nutrition or fluids. The local first instance court (Amtsgericht) decided to withdraw parental custody and parental right of residence in the context of health care and appointed a legal guardian. On appeal by the parents, the Higher Regional Court (Oberlandesgericht)[242] overturned the decision and discontinued the proceedings for the parental custody withdrawal, as there was no abuse of custody. The legal guardian has applied for a temporary injunction at the Federal Constitutional Court (BVerfG) to suspend the decision of the Higher Regional Court until a decision has been made on her constitutional complaint[243]. The BVerfG granted the application. When the decision was communicated to the parents, the child had already died.

The conditions for withdrawal of parental authority are stipulated in paragraph 1666 German Civil Code (BGB): It is only possible in the event of abuse of parental authority and only if the parents' decision to stop artificial life-supporting treatments (in the case evoked, hydration and artificial feeding) is contrary to the child's welfare. Paragraph 1666 BGB allows parents some leeway in their decisions. Courts can only control the parents' decision to a limited extent regarding the comprehensibility of the justification and sufficient consideration of the child's fundamental right to life to avoid abuse. The medical team have to accept the parents' decision up to the limit of misuse of the parental authority (§ 1666 BGB)[244]. That is why there are few court decisions in this area.

For adolescents, the key concept in German Law is the right to auto-determination, linked to the child's natural ability to understand. Corresponding to the § 1626 II BGB, parents have to associate adolescents in decision-making concerning body and health interventions according to their concrete capacity for understanding.

Nevertheless, adolescents' right to auto-determination does not include decisions relative to the withdrawal of life-sustaining measures and mea-

242 Beschluss des OLG Hamm 24.05.2007 – 1 UF 78/07; Angie Schneider, *End-of-life and terminal care for minors under German law,* in this book p.55 (58).

243 BVerfG, Beschluss vom 6.6.2007 – 1 BvQ 18/07.

244 Annegret Lorenz, *Das Selbstbestimmungsrecht des einsichtsfähigen Minderjährigen-bei Eingriffen in die körperliche Intergrität*, NZFamR 2017, p.782 (783).

sures related to assisted dying of minors in German law. Hence, minors are not allowed to draft binding advanced directives (§ 1901 a BGB)[245].

With younger children, the parents decide for their child. In the case of very young children, a "presumed will of the child" can hardly be used because the very young child could not yet form such a will due to a lack of existing values. This means that, within certain limits, the parents' choice or "general values" must be taken into account.

In cases where the parents' decision of does not match with the best interests of the child, a legal guardian may be appointed by the court to represent the interests of the child. In the case described above, the court decided that the parents' decision was not contrary to the child's interests because the medical expertise showed no conscious communication with the child could be established. Only the child's reflexes could remain.

Recommendations

One possibility to defuse the conflict between the minor's parents and the medical profession could be the use of mediation[246]. The English courts have also made this proposal in the cases set out below[247]. The report of the French inspection for social affairs (Inspection Générale des Affaires Sociales – IGAS) called for the use of mediation in all cases of medical futility on minors in the future[248]. The opportunity of introducing recourse to mediation in the event of disagreement, particularly between parents and the medical team, is indisputable but raises some questions. Could the mediation be compulsory if consent is not found in the collective procedures? Can mandatory parental participation in mediation be introduced without destroying the negotiations' chances of success? Mediation could become systematic and mandatory, but the problem is to go along with sanctions if a minor's parents refuse to participate in such a mediation procedure.

245 Detlev Sternberg-Lieben/ Philipp C. Reichmann, *Die gesetzliche Regelung der Patientenverfügung und das medizinische Selbstbestimmungsrecht Minderjähriger*, NJW 2012, 257 (258)

246 Jo Samanta, *The vexed question of best interests in decisions relating to infants and medical futility*, in Medical Futility in Paediatrics: Interdisciplinary and International Perspectives p.27, 43.

247 *Great Ormond Street v Yates, Gard & Gard* [2017] EWHC Civ 410, per Justice Francis at para. 130.

248 Rapport du 11 juin 2018 sur l'Évaluation de l'application de la loi du 2 février 2016 sur la fin de vie (IGAS) p. 73, recommandation n°22.

The mediation could be used in the same way also in the case of a parent-child conflict.

Conclusion

Even if there are some differences between French, German and English law, the adopted solution is generally similar. The role given to parents must be fundamental. Decision-maker or not, the parents must be closely involved in the decision. The way to do this may differ from one system to another. The English and German courts solution takes into account the role of parental authority granted by law. There is no conflict of provisions between the rules of parental authority and the specific rules of end-of-life legislation in these countries. However, French law only grants a consultative role to parents, so that they do not have to bear the burden of this decision. That's why here, the standard rules for the right of custody are not appliable for these sensitive end-of-life situations. In this system the role of the doctor is paramount. He does not decide on his own, but after a collective procedure involving all the people who have direct contact with the patient. The decision is above all a medical decision. The attending physician can and must decide as a last resort, possibly against the parents' advice and without judicial authorisation.

In England and Wales, the concept of the 'best interests' of the child is of paramount importance in the case law and is used to displace the parental rights for child's care. Parental rights give parents decision-making power over decisions concerning the health of their children, including end-of-life decisions. Only in extreme situations where the parental decision is not compatible with the best interests of the child, custody can be withdrawn by the courts.

Only in French law, the right of custody of parents is displaced for end-of-life decisions. This way of resolving the conflict between the standard provisions on parental authority and the Public Health Code's regulatory provisions favouring the latter in France seems questionable. A clarifying intervention by the French legislator would be desirable and seems necessary to avoid further litigation. It is doubtful whether the parents' opinion should be given a more important place in the decision-making process in France.

All examined countries take more or less account of the children's age for their participation in decision making. With regard to adolescents' specific situation, it can be seen that German law, both in case law and in legislative provisions, takes most account of their ability to participate in decisions directly affecting them. The key concept for the exercise of rights by adolescents is the "natural ability to understand". There is no absolute age barrier, but it has to be decided individually from case to case. Nevertheless, their legal situation can be improved by according them a right to draft up their living will, what is till now reserved to adults of full age.

Bibliography:

Cases:

Bundesverfassungsgericht (Germany), Judgement of 6 June 2007, no. 1 BvQ 18/07

Conseil d'Etat (France) 14 February 2014, no. 375081, *aff. Lambert*

Conseil d'Etat (France) 24 June 2014, no. 375081, *aff. Lambert*

ECtHR, Judgement of 27 June 2017, no. 39793/17, *Gard et al v. United Kingdom*, ECLI:CE:ECHR:2017:0627DEC003979317

ECtHR, Judgment of 5 June 2015, no. 46043/14, Lambert et al v. France [GC], ECLI:CE:ECHR:2015:0605JUD004604314

ECtHR, Judgement of 23 April 2018, no. 14238/18, *Evans v United Kingdom*

England and Wales Court of Appeal (EWCA) Civ 550, Supreme Court, 8 June 2017, *In the matter of Charlie Gard*

England and Wales Court of Appeal (EWCA) Re E (A Child) [2018], 6 March 2018, *Alfie Evans*

England and Wales Court of Appeal (EWCA) Civ 410, [2017], 23 May 2017, *Great Ormond Street Hospital & Gard*

England and Wales High Court (EWHC) nr. 2964 (Fam) [2014], *Ashya King*

England and Wales High Court (EWHC) 972 (Fam), para. 93, [2017], 11 April 2017, *Great Ormond Street Hospital v Yates, Gard & Gard*

England and Wales Supreme Court, 20 March 2018, *Alf*

ie Evans

OLG Hamm (Germany), judgement of 24 May 2007, no. 1 UF 78/07

Bibliography:

Choong, Kartina A., Charlie Gard and Alfie Evans: Their Medico-Legal Journeys, in Medical Futility in Paediatrics: Interdisciplinary and International Perspectives, Trivent 2019, p.2

Commission des affaires sociales of 17 April 2015, Report

Eichberger, Michael, Judgment of the Federal Constitutional Court of 26 February 2020 on the Criminalisation of Assisted Suicide Services, p. 16

Inspection Générale des Affaires Sociales (IGAS), Report of 11 June 2018 *"sur l'Évaluation de l'application de la loi du 2 février 2016 sur la fin de vie"*, p. 83, n°443

Law, Richard MW/Choong, Kartina A, *Covid-19: Refracting decision making through the prism of resource allocation*, in Medico-Legal Journal 2020, p.1

Lelièvre, Nathalie, *Adolescent et soins, vers une autonomie de la volonté?* Droit et douleur, 2005, p.247 s.

Lorenz, Annegret, *Das Selbstbestimmungsrecht des einsichtsfähigen Minderjährigen bei Eingriffen in die körperliche Integrität*, NZFamR 2017, p.782 (783)

Noizet-Yverneau/ Daubin, C./Bréhaux K./Robert R., Arrêter la réanimation chez l'enfant « grand prématuré » : qui décide? in Ethique et santé (2016), p.39

Rohlfing-Dijoux, Stephanie, The Application of End-of-life Legislation to Minors in France, in Medical Futility in Paediatrics: Interdisciplinary and International Perspectives, Trivent 2019, p.250 (257)

Rohlfing-Dijoux, Stephanie/Renger, Benoît, The strengthening of the rights of Patients by the reform of the « Claeys-Leonetti Act » in France and the Liability of Medical Doctors, in Rohlfing-Dijoux/Luther/Prasannanshu Interactions between Culture and Law in India and Europe, p.141 (143)

Schneider, Angie, End-of-life and terminal care for minors under German Law, p.55

Sargent Sarah, Charlie's Law : Clarifying the legal standard to be used in medical decision-making for children, in Medical Futility in Paediatrics: Interdisciplinary and International Perspectives, Trivent 2019, p.78 (88)

Sternberg-Lieben, Detlev/Reichmann, Philipp C., Die gesetzliche Regelung der Patientenverfügung und das medizinische Selbstbestimmungsrecht Minderjähriger, NJW 2012, 257 (258)

Seagrim, William, Best interests: The « Gold Standard » or a « Gold Plating »? Should significant harm be a threshold criterion in paediatric cases?, in Medical Futility in Paediatrics: Interdisciplinary and International Perspectives, Trivent 2019, p.51

Kartina A. Choong, Associate Professor University of Central Lancashire, UK, *Re M (Declaration of Death of Child) [2020]: "No Best Interests to Consider"?*

Abstract

When Midrar Namiq was diagnosed brain stem dead at the age of two weeks old, Manchester University NHS Foundation Trust applied for a declaration that it would be lawful to make arrangements for his mechanical ventilation to be

switched off. This declaration, which was granted by the High Court, was upheld by the Court of Appeal. Although the child's parents had protested against the withdrawal of ventilatory support on the basis of their religious beliefs, this point was sidelined by the courts. Rather, they viewed their task solely as one to identify whether the child is brain stem dead, hence clinically (and legally) dead, in accordance with the protocol and criteria established by the Academy of Medical Royal Colleges and the Royal College of Paediatrics and Child Health. This frame of reference has led to the conclusion that no consideration of best interests was necessary, as the concept is only relevant for patients who are still alive but who are incompetent on grounds of mental incapacity and/or age. This paper contends that had the parents' religious objections been taken into proper account, best interests is potentially a pertinent consideration in this case. Although the outcome may still be the same, it would be reached through a different legal route.

A. Introduction

The case of Midrar Namiq came before the English Courts in early 2020. Compared to several other cases relating to the withdrawal of mechanical ventilation from infants in recent times,[249] the media coverage of his parents' fight against the medical team's decision to switch off his ventilation was generally low-key. While this may well have been the case because it was eclipsed by more attention-grabbing news like Brexit and the novel coronavirus, it should not escape notice that there is often a sharp contrast in media interest and public sympathy when it comes to parental opposition to the withdrawal of ventilation relating to infants whose brain stems are alive, as opposed to those who are diagnosed as brain stem dead. The former requires the judiciary to engage the best interests test no matter how profoundly brain damaged the child is.[250] This could, nevertheless, lead to a declaration that it would be lawful to withdraw the ventilation where its continuation was deemed to be medically futile.[251] Members of the public have not, of late, been slow to express their discontentment

249 The most notable of which were Charlie Gard and Alfie Evans.

250 See e.g. *Great Ormond Street Hospital v Yates, Gard & Gard* [2017] EWHC 972 (Fam); *Alder Hey Children's NHS Foundation Trust v Evans, James & Evans* [2018] EWHC 308 (Fam); and *Kings College Hospital NHS Foundation Trust v Thomas, Haastrup & Haastrup* [2018] EWHC 127 (Fam).

251 *Ibid.*

when their assessment of the child's best interests did not align with those of the judiciary and the medical profession.[252] In the meantime, as stated by the courts in Midrar Namiq's case, "there are no best interests to consider"[253] for brain stem dead patients, as such individuals are considered clinically and legally dead. The test is only necessary for patients who are still alive but are incompetent on grounds of mental incapacity and/or age.[254] The public too, through the noticeable absence of the impassioned reaction which usually accompanies a declaration that it is lawful to withdraw ventilation in a so-called "medical futility" case, seems to have accepted the notion that brain stem death equates the death of the person. Hence as the ventilation is to be removed from one who is already pronounced clinically dead, it does not seem to provoke as much ethico-legal reflections and objections when compared to its removal from patients whose brain stems were still alive no matter how severely brain-damaged they otherwise were.

However, had the parents' religious beliefs been given due recognition, the fact that Midrar was still, as his father highlighted, "showing signs of life"[255] (particularly respiration and heartbeat) albeit with ventilatory support, could give rise to the contention that he was still alive from an Islamic perspective. The matter could then be approached from the angle of "medical futility", warranting a best interests assessment.

B. Midrar Namiq: Dead or Alive?

Midrar Namiq was born at St Mary's Hospital in Manchester on 18 September 2019. His mother's membranes had ruptured on the way to hospital, and the umbilical cord prolapsed. This cut off the oxygen supply to his brain for a significant period. Successfully intubated at birth where a slow heartbeat was detected, he was transferred to the hospital's Neonatal Intensive Care Unit (NICU) and placed on a ventilator. On 1 and 2

---

252 N. Triggle, 'Charlie Gard: A Case That Changed Everything?', BBC News, 29 July 2017; J. Thomas, 'Police Confirm Alfie Evans Protest Was Peaceful After Emotional Night Outside Alder Hey Hospital', Liverpool Echo, 13 April 2018.

253 *Manchester University NHS Foundation Trust v Namiq, Ali & Namiq* [2020] EWHC 5 (Fam), *per* Lieven J. at paragraph 32. This was subsequently confirmed by the Court of Appeal – see *Re M (Declaration of Death of Child)* [2020] EWCA Civ 164 at paragraph 96.

254 *Re M (Declaration of Death of Child)*, *ibid.*, paragraph 24.

255 Anonymous, 'Life-support Case Doctors "Do Not Need Naming" ', BBC News, 17 February 2020.

October 2019, DNC (death by neurological criteria) tests were carried out and these confirmed that his brain stem was dead. A third DNC test was conducted on 4 November 2019 and this too showed that his brain stem was dead. This was followed by an MRI scan on 5 November 2019 which demonstrated "catastrophic appearances with internal brain liquefaction including brain stem supportive for brain stem test. Complete effacement of intracranial CSF [cerebral spinal fluid] spaces including ventricles and cisterns".[256] Following these findings, the hospital proposed to switch the ventilator off. When his parents protested on the basis of their Islamic religious beliefs, Manchester University NHS Foundation Trust (which runs the hospital) made an application to the High Court on 26 November 2019. It sought for declarations that (a) Midrar did not have the requisite capacity to make decisions concerning his medical treatment; and (b) it was lawful for the hospital to withdraw his mechanical ventilation.

I. Death by Neurological Criteria

The case was heard by Mrs Justice Lieven who framed her task as identifying whether Midrar was dead, according to the DNC tests set out by the Academy of Medical Royal Colleges and the Royal College of Paediatrics and Child Health.[257] Death is defined by these professional bodies as the "irreversible loss of the capacity for consciousness, combined with irreversible loss of the capacity to breathe".[258] Since the irreversible cessation of brain stem function will produce this clinical state, brain stem death is said to be equivalent to the death of the individual.[259] Satisfied that doctors had followed the prescribed protocols and that Midrar had met the relevant criteria for the diagnosis of brain stem death, Mrs Justice Lieven clarified that there were no best interests to consider as Midrar had "irreversibly lost whatever one might define as life".[260] The following declarations were made on 28 January 2020: that (a) Midrar had

---

256 *Re M (Declaration of Death of Child)*, paragraph 17.

257 *Manchester University NHS Foundation Trust v Namiq, Ali & Namiq*, paragraph 4.

258 Academy of Medical Royal Colleges, 'A Code of Practice for the Diagnosis and Confirmation of Death' (2008), p. 11; Royal College of Paediatrics and Child Health, 'The Diagnosis of Death by Neurological Criteria in Infants Less than Two Months Old' (2015), p. 8.

259 *Ibid.*

260 *Manchester University NHS Foundation Trust v Namiq, Ali & Namiq*, paragraph 32.

no capacity to make decisions concerning his medical treatment namely the administration of mechanical ventilation; and (b) it was lawful for the hospital to make arrangements for the ventilation to be withdrawn.

Midrar's parents immediately applied to appeal against the decision to allow the withdrawal of the mechanical ventilation. The application for permission to appeal was heard by Sir Andrew McFarlane, Lord Justice Patten and Lady Justice King in the Court of Appeal. They unanimously agreed that Mrs Justice Lieven was correct in identifying that the issue which called for determination was whether Midrar was dead, in accordance with the DNC tests as set out by the two afore-mentioned professional bodies, and if satisfied that these were met, to declare that it would be lawful for the ventilator to be removed.[261] They also agreed that once it was satisfied on the balance of probabilities that the guidances issued by the Academy of Medical Royal Colleges and the Royal College of Paediatrics and Child Health have been properly applied, it is unnecessary to engage in a best interests analysis.[262] Neither would this exercise be appropriate as "the child is already dead"[263] and "where a person is dead, the question of best interests is, tragically no longer relevant".[264] The Court of Appeal therefore upheld the declaration made by the High Court and refused permission to appeal. It nevertheless suggested and prescribed a clearer form of words to be used by High Court judges in the future. First, that such a declaration should expressly declare that the patient has died at a particular time and date, before granting permission and declaring that it is lawful for mechanical ventilation and other medical interventions to be withdrawn. Second, that the purpose of such a declaration should also be identified as one which is to allow the person who has died "dignity in death".[265]

Within days of the Court of Appeal's judgement, Midrar was disconnected from his ventilator.[266]

261 *Re M (Declaration of Death of Child)*, paragraph 23.

262 *Ibid.*, paragraph 96.

263 *Ibid.*

264 *Ibid.*, paragraph 24.

265 *Ibid.*, paragraph 60. This is in line with, and in approval of, the formulation used by Mr Justice Hayden in *Re A (A Child)* [2015] EWHC 443 (Fam).

266 Anonymous, 'Midrar Ali: Baby's Ventilator Disconnected After Court Ruling', BBC News, 26 February 2020.

II. Death from a Religious Perspective

The parents had voiced their objection to the proposal to withdraw the ventilation on the basis of their religious beliefs, arguing that Midrar was still alive.[267] However, how Islam defines death was not a matter which received attention in the judgments. Both the High Court and the Court of Appeal were, as highlighted, resolute that their task was to identify whether Midrar was dead in accordance with the protocols and criteria established by the medical profession. It was emphasised that it was not open to them to "contemplate a different test"[268] since brain stem death has been established as the legal definition of death by the House of Lords, the predecessor of the Supreme Court, in the 1993 case of *Airedale NHS Trust v Bland*.[269] This is notwithstanding the fact that, although the religious concept of sanctity of life was mentioned in the judgment,[270] how death is defined from a religious perspective was not an issue that directly came up in the case. The House of Lords was not therefore presented with the opportunity to explore this matter then. In fact, such contestations seemed to have come before the English courts only in the last 5 years. But when they came, this was in quick succession. From *Re A (A Child)* in 2015, to *Oxford University NHS Trust v AB (A Minor), CD & EF*[271] in 2019 and now *Re M (Declaration of Death in Child)* in 2020. All three concerned objections raised by the parents of children whose ventilator and life-sustaining medical treatment were about to be terminated by the medical team upon a diagnosis of brain stem death. Like Midrar's case, in *Re A (A Child)* this was on the basis of the family's Islamic faith, and in *Oxford University NHS Trust v AB (A Minor), CD & EF*, their Christian faith. Just as in Midrar's case, the courts took the view that once brain stem death had occurred, the ventilated child was dead for clinical and legal purposes, and no best interests assessments were necessary.

---

267 In fact, his father, who is a biomedical scientist, went as far as to assert that Midrar was not brain stem dead – see *Manchester University NHS Foundation Trust v Namiq, Ali & Namiq*, paragraph 51. On appeal, the parents also asked the court to take into consideration the wider approach used in jurisdictions which diagnose death by reference to the whole-brain. This issue will be analysed elsewhere.

268 *Re M (Declaration of Death of Child)*, paragraph 91.

269 [1993] AC 789 *per* Lord Keith at 856 and Lord Goff at 863.

270 *Ibid.*, *per* Lord Hoffman at 826.

271 [2019] EWHC 3516 (Fam).

Had Midrar's parents' religious objection been given sufficient consideration, Islamic scholars and leaders could be invited to testify that some within the religion still do not accept that brain stem death equates the death of a person.[272] Rather, death is demarcated by the departure of the soul,[273] and it is the presence or absence of respiration and heartbeat which signify whether the soul still inhabits or has left the body. Thus as long as a brain stem dead person is still breathing and maintain a heartbeat, even if only through the support of a mechanical ventilator, he is still considered alive.[274] Had this worldview been given recognition in the courts, a best interests analysis would be called for, as Midrar was still breathing and his heart was still beating, hence alive, when and after he was pronounced brain stem dead.

C. Recommendations and Conclusion

Although neurological death has developed firm roots in England and Wales, the idea that brain stem death equates the death of the person is not always shared by religious communities which relate death with the departure of the soul from the body. Not only is the presence or absence of the soul usually associated with the corresponding presence or absence of breathing and heartbeat, there also does not seem to be any indications in religious scriptures that the brain is the exclusive residence of the soul.[275] Thus when the courts came to the conclusion that Midrar Namiq had no best interests to consider, the fact that this was derived from the finding that he was already dead on account of having been diagnosed as brain stem dead meant that a different conclusion could be reached on this matter if the courts had recognised the parents' religious viewpoint.

---

272 See e.g. A. Bedir & S. Aksoy, 'Brain Death Revisited: It Is Not "Complete Death" According to Islamic Sources' (2011) 37 *Journal of Medical Ethics* 290; M.Y. Rady & J.L. Verheijde, 'A Response to the Legitimacy of Brain Death in Islam' (2016) 55 *Journal of Religion and Health* 1198; H. Chamsi-Pasha & M.A. Albar, 'Do Not Resuscitate, Brain Death, and Organ Transplantation: Islamic Perspective' (2017) 7(2) *Avicenna Journal of Medicine* 35; A.C. Miller, et. al., 'Brain Death and Islam: The Interface of Religion, Culture, History, Law, and Modern Medicine' (2014) 146(4) *Chest* 1092.

273 Quran, Surah al-Zumar, verse 42.

274 A. Bedir & S. Aksoy, op.cit., passim.

275 J.L. Verheijde & M. Potts, 'Commentary on the Concept of Brain Death Within the Catholic Bioethical Framework' (2010) 16(3) *Christian Bioethics* 246 at 253.

However, even if a best interests assessment had been conducted in this case, it is unlikely that a different outcome would be reached. Apart from the diagnosis of brain stem death, a significant proportion of Midrar's brain had, as observed above, turned to liquid. All these point to a potential finding that the continuation of ventilation would be futile (from a secular medico-legal perspective), following which it would be in Midrar's best interests to have it withdrawn. This, in a sense, demonstrates the limitations of the court as a venue for facilitating faith-based dissensions on neurological death. At most, this legal route could serve as an acknowledgement that the idea that brain stem death equates the death of the person, is not universally accepted. And that there are competing, yet no less viable nor less deeply held, ways of perceiving when life ends. That Midrar's case is the third which have been brought before the courts on this issue in the last 5 years, signifies the depth of its dissenters' conviction. It also signifies that the case may not be the last to make its way to the courtroom.

It is ultimately Parliament which is best placed to safeguard the interests of faith communities on this matter. A fundamental step in this direction would be by facilitating the reasonable accommodation of religious objections to neurological death via legislation. For this, the legislative framework adopted in New Jersey would be instructive. According to its Declaration of Death Act 1991, if a declaration of death by neurological criteria would violate the religious beliefs of the patient, "death shall be declared, and the time of death fixed, solely upon the diagnosis of cardio-respiratory criteria".[276] This is on account of the fact that this traditionally well-accepted method is more sympathetic to faith communities' emphasis on the cessation of breathing and heartbeat when determining death. Further, the Act prohibits any healthcare practitioner or provider or other authorities from denying funding for the continuation of life-support to those patients until such time that their hearts would stop beating naturally, which is usually within days or weeks after neurological death occurred.[277] It is only at that point when the cardiopulmonary criteria for death are met, that the patient would be pronounced legally dead.[278]

If a similar model is implemented in England and Wales, it would obviate the need to go to court for disputes relating to religious objection.

---

276 Section 5.

277 Section 7.

278 T. Pope, ' Brain Death and the Law: Hard Cases and Legal Challenges' (2018) *Hastings Center Report* S46 at S48.

In bestowing a religious exemption from brain stem death and placing a corresponding duty on hospitals and medical personnel to allow and facilitate an alternative definition of death, it could spare family members additional pain and distress at a time when they are already struggling emotionally.[279] It would allow them to be reconciled with their impending loss on terms they can accept, without the threat of a unilateral withdrawal of life support looming in the background.[280] This would also lessen friction and angst between them and the medical team at a time when therapeutic alliance should be strong rather than diluted.[281] Such a law also anticipates an endpoint, be this a natural one as described above or when accommodation extends beyond what would be considered "reasonable".[282] It could therefore: serve as a practical and compassionate compromise in conflicts relating to brain stem death,[283] and empowers faith communities in a meaningful way.[284]

Bibliography

Academy of Medical Royal Colleges, 'A Code of Practice for the Diagnosis and Confirmation of Death' (2008).

Airedale NHS Trust v Bland [1993] AC 789.

Alder Hey Children's NHS Foundation Trust v Evans, James & Evans [2018] EWHC 308 (Fam).

Anonymous, 'Life-support Case Doctors "Do Not Need Naming" ', BBC News, 17 February 2020.

Anonymous, 'Midrar Ali: Baby's Ventilator Disconnected After Court Ruling', BBC News, 26 February 2020.

Bedir, A. & Aksoy, S., 'Brain Death Revisited: It Is Not "Complete Death" According to Islamic Sources' (2011) 37 *Journal of Medical Ethics* 290.

---

279 L.S.M. Johnson, 'The Case for Reasonable Accommodation of Conscientious Objections to Declarations of Brain Death' (2016) *Bioethical Inquiry* 105 at 112.

280 *Ibid.*, p. 113.

281 A. Lewis, et. al., 'Prolonging Support After Brain Death: When Families Ask for More' (2016) 24 *Neurocritical Care* 481 at 485.

282 M.L. Smith & A.L. Flamm, 'Accommodating Religious Beliefs in the ICU: A Narrative Account of a Disputed Death' (2011) 1(1) *Narrative Enquiry in Bioethics* 55 at 63.

283 L.S.M. Johnson, *op.cit.*, pp. 113–114.

284 R.S. Olick, 'Brain Death, Religious Freedom, and Public Policy: New Jersey's Landmark Legislative Initiative' (1991) 1(4) *Kennedy Institute of Ethics Journal* 275 at 278.

Chamsi-Pasha, H. & Albar, M.A., 'Do Not Resuscitate, Brain Death, and Organ Transplantation: Islamic Perspective' (2017) 7(2) *Avicenna Journal of Medicine* 35.

Great Ormond Street Hospital v Yates, Gard & Gard [2017] EWHC 972 (Fam).

Johnson, L.S.M., 'The Case for Reasonable Accommodation of Conscientious Objections to Declarations of Brain Death' (2016) *Bioethical Inquiry* 105.

Kings College Hospital NHS Foundation Trust v Thomas, Haastrup & Haastrup [2018] EWHC 127 (Fam).

Lewis, A., et. al., 'Prolonging Support After Brain Death: When Families Ask for More' (2016) 24 *Neurocritical Care* 481.

Manchester University NHS Foundation Trust v Namiq, Ali & Namiq [2020] EWHC 5 (Fam).

Miller, A.C., et. al., 'Brain Death and Islam: The Interface of Religion, Culture, History, Law, and Modern Medicine' (2014) 146(4) *Chest* 1092.

Olick, R. S., 'Brain Death, Religious Freedom, and Public Policy: New Jersey's Landmark Legislative Initiative' (1991) 1(4) *Kennedy Institute of Ethics Journal* 275.

Pope, T., 'Brain Death and the Law: Hard Cases and Legal Challenges' (2018) *Hastings Center Report* S46.

Quran, Surah al-Zumar, verse 42.

Rady, M.Y. & Verheijde, J.L., 'A Response to the Legitimacy of Brain Death in Islam' (2016) 55 *Journal of Religion and Health* 1198.

Re A (A Child) [2015] EWHC 443 (Fam).

Re M (Declaration of Death of Child) [2020] EWCA Civ 164.

Royal College of Paediatrics and Child Health, 'The Diagnosis of Death by Neurological Criteria in Infants Less Than Two Months Old' (2015).

Smith, M.L. & Flamm, A.L., 'Accommodating Religious Beliefs in the ICU: A Narrative Account of a Disputed Death' (2011) 1(1) *Narrative Enquiry in Bioethics* 55.

Thomas, J., 'Police Confirm Alfie Evans Protest Was Peaceful After Emotional Night Outside Alder Hey Hospital', Liverpool Echo, 13 April 2018.

Triggle, N., 'Charlie Gard: A Case That Changed Everything?', BBC News, 29 July 2017.

Verheijde, J.L. & Potts, M., 'Commentary on the Concept of Brain Death Within the Catholic Bioethical Framework' (2010) 16(3) *Christian Bioethics* 246.

CHAPTER IV: Clarifying the bounderies between assisted suicide and other forms of ending one's own life

Volker Lipp, Professor Dr. Dr. h. c., Georg-August-University Göttingen, Germany: *« Euthanasia » – A Comparative Legal Perspective*

Abstract (English/German)

This article shows that there is a clear tendency within human rights jurisprudence towards a right to die with dignity covering assisted suicide, and a growing number of countries allowing assisted suicide under certain conditions which, however, vary considerably. In contrast, terminating life upon request has been legalized only by few countries, and only once a court has brought this within the scope of a human right to die. It is therefore necessary to avoid the broad and notoriously vague term of "euthanasia" and to distinguish between assisted suicide and terminating life upon request.

Wie dieser Beitrag zeigt, erkennt die Rechtsprechung zunehmend ein Menschenrecht auf einen würdevollen Tod an, und eine wachsende Zahl von Ländern lassen den assistierten Suizid unter bestimmten Bedingungen zu, die freilich sehr unterschiedlich ausgestaltet sind. Demgegenüber erlauben nur wenige Staaten die Tötung auf Verlangen, und diese ist bisher nur einmal von einem Gericht in den Schutzbereich des Menschenrechts auf einen selbstbestimmten Tod einbezogen worden. Es ist deshalb geboten, den notorisch vagen Begriff „Euthanasie" zu vermeiden und stattdessen zwischen assistiertem Suizid und Tötung auf Verlangen zu unterscheiden.

A. Introduction

The etymology of euthanasia is "good death"[285]. Human beings have always wished not only to have a good life but also to have a good death. In modern times this has also become a medical issue. Due to numerous factors, including rising living-standards, lifestyle improvements and, most importantly, advances in healthcare and medicine, people today

---

285 Originally coming from Greek, eu~, good, and thánatos, death.

live longer than ever before. One side effect of rising living expectancy and medical progress, however, is that, in some cases, not just the general situation of a person but her or his current medical condition can become unbearable, bringing about the wish to die ultimately.

This article tries to give a brief comparative overview of the current law related to euthanasia, more specifically to terminating life and assisted suicide in selected countries. Attention will also be given to the European Convention of Human Rights and the case law of the European Court of Human Rights.

B. “Euthanasia” and other concepts

Euthanasia is ambiguous as a concept. There is no generally accepted definition, due to various perspectives from which the topic can be approached, namely ethics, (international) human rights, and legal systems. In order to avoid confusion, I will not use “euthanasia” for the purposes of this article, but rather differentiate various forms of end-of-life decisions.

In this article, the term “terminating life” will be used instead of “(active) euthanasia” to describe the intentional killing of another person in order to relieve the latter’s suffering. Depending on the role of consent, “upon request” or “voluntary” will denote cases where somebody kills a person who wants to be killed, “non-voluntary” where a person is put to death without consent including cases where the consent has been unobtainable due to a person’s medical condition (e.g. unconsciousness), and “involuntary” where a person’s life has been ended against her or his will.

The term “assisted suicide” refers to the intentional killing of oneself (suicide) with the assistance of another person. Unlike in the cases of terminating life upon request, the person intending to end her or his life carries out the action her- or himself. A physician-assisted suicide, consequently, refers to a suicide with the assistance of a physician.

From both, “terminating life” as well as assisted suicide, I distinguish cases of “letting die”. This means cases where life-sustaining medical treatment of a patient is limited, terminated or withheld because it is medically inappropriate (“futile”) or because the patient does not, or does no longer, accept this treatment. Albeit these cases sometimes are called “passive euthanasia” I also do not use this term since those cases are about applying medical treatment, or withholding it, whereas the medical context is irrelevant in cases of euthanasia as defined above. I will therefore touch upon "letting die" only in the context of human rights, and with the aim to distinguish these cases from "euthanasia" covered in this article.

C. Terminating life and assisted suicide from the perspective of human rights

The European Convention of Human Rights (hereafter "the Convention") expressly guarantees the right to life in its Article 2, at the top of the catalogue of human rights enshrining "one of the basic values of the democratic societies making up the Council of Europe"[286]. The Member States are accordingly obliged to protect every human life and implement a general ban on killing.[287] In the context of terminating life and assisted suicide it might be asked whether there is an opposite right – namely, the right to die, which could be deduced from the Convention; and if not, whether terminating life and/or assisted suicide violate the right to life and should therefore be banned. Both questions have been addressed by the European Court of Human Rights (thereafter "ECHR") in its case law with respect to assisted suicide and letting die. So far, there have been no cases involving terminating life upon request.

I. Assisted suicide

The ECHR clarified the question of whether the right to die can be derived from the right to life (Article 2 of the Convention) in *Pretty v. United Kingdom*[288]. The applicant was dying of an incurable degenerative disease and wished that her husband would help her to commit suicide as she was unable to do so herself. Since assisting suicide was a crime in English law, she requested that her husband be guaranteed freedom from prosecution if he helped her, which was refused. The ECHR held that the right to life of Article 2 cannot, without distortion of language, be interpreted as conferring also the diametrically opposite right – namely, the right to die.[289]

286 ECHR, Judgement of 27 September 1995, no. 18984/91, *McCann et al v. United Kingdom* [GC], ECLI:CE:ECHR:1995:0927JUD001898491, § 147.

287 *Grabenwarter*, European Convention on Human Rights. Commentary, 1st ed., Munich 2014, Art. 2 no. 16.

288 ECHR, Judgement of 29 April 2002, no. 2346/02, *Pretty v. United Kingdom*, ECLI:CE:ECHR:2002:0429JUD000234602.

289 Ibid., § 39.

However, it did not exclude that issues concerning the end of life could be protected by other provisions of the Convention, and concluded that the right to decide the manner of one's own death constitutes an element of private life which is protected by Article 8 of the Convention.[290]

In the second on the (up to now) rather short list of cases regarding assisted suicide, the ECHR elaborated on the right to decide upon one's own death as an aspect of "private life" protected by Article 8 of the Convention. In the case *Haas v. Switzerland*[291] the applicant had been suffering from serious bipolar affective disorder for years which, as he claimed, hindered his ability to live in a dignified manner. Swiss law allowed to obtain a lethal drug for the purpose of committing suicide. However, the applicant did not meet the conditions for access to such a drug. The ECHR stated that an "individual's right to decide by what means and at what point his or her life will end, provided he or she is capable of freely reaching a decision on this question and acting in consequence, is one of the aspects of the right to respect for private life within the meaning of Article 8 of the Convention"[292]. It then was assessing whether there was a "positive obligation" under Article 8 for the State to ensure access to a substance enabling suicide.[293] The ECHR was sympathetic towards such an obligation but did not, in the end, decide that point. Even assuming that, on the one side, States have a positive obligation to take measures to facilitate suicide in dignity, the right to life obliges them on the other side to put in place a procedure capable of ensuring that a person's decision to end life did in fact reflect the subject's free will and protect them from hasty decisions and abuse.[294] The ECHR noted that a vast majority of Member States appeared to attach more weight to the protection of life than to the right of an individual to end it and only few allowed, under certain conditions, physicians to assist in a suicide or to terminate life upon request.[295] Member States therefore are granted a wide margin of appreciation in such matters.[296] As the Swiss authorities had examined the

290 Ibid., § 67; ECHR, Guide on Article 8 of the Convention on Human Rights "31 August 2020", § 124, available at https://www.echr.coe.int/documents/guide_art_8_eng.pdf, access on 15.02.2021.

291 ECHR, Judgement of 20 January 2011, no. 31322/07, *Haas v. Switzerland*, ECLI:CE:ECHR:2011:0120JUD003132207.

292 Ibid., § 51.

293 Ibid., § 53.

294 Ibid., §§ 56 – 61.

295 Ibid., § 55.

296 Ibid., § 58.

application on the merits, the applicant's right to choose the time and manner of his death was not merely theoretical or illusory and, therefore, Article 8 of the Convention had not been not violated.[297]

In the case *Koch v. Germany*[298] the German Federal Institute for Drugs and Medical Devices (Bundesinstitut für Arzneimittel und Medizinprodukte – BfArM) had rejected a request by a husband and his wife regarding authorisation to obtain a lethal dose of a drug that would have enabled the wife to commit suicide in Germany. As a consequence, the applicant accompanied his wife to Switzerland, where she legally acquired such a drug and committed suicide. The German courts dismissed the husband's appeal against the Federal Institute's decision because he could neither claim that his own rights were violated, nor could he rely on the rights of his wife now deceased. The husband then applied to the ECHR arguing that the refusal of the German courts to examine his complaint on the merits violated his own rights under Article 8 of the Convention. The ECHR decided that the husband, in this particular case, had in fact been directly affected in his own right under Article 8, and that the Federal Institute as well as the courts should have examined the merits of his claim.[299] As this had not been the case, and there were no grounds to justify this under Article 8 (2) of the Convention, the ECHR held that this procedural aspect of Article 8 had been violated.[300] It did not, however, rule on the wife's rights under Article 8.[301]

Another case from Switzerland also concerned the access to a drug to commit suicide.[302] The applicant in this case was not suffering from any terminal disease. She nevertheless wished to end her life by taking a lethal dose of sodium pentobarbital but did not manage to acquire the necessary prescription from a physician. Subsequently, she requested the lethal dose of medication from the Swiss Health Board yet unsuccessfully. All appeals had been dismissed. The main issue in this case was "whether the State had failed to provide sufficient guidelines defining if and, in the case of the affirmative, under which circumstances medical practitioners were authorised to issue a medical prescription to a person in the applicant's

297 Ibid., §§ 60, 61.

298 ECHR, Judgement of 19 July 2012, no. 497/09, *Koch v. Germany,* ECLI:CE:ECHR:2012:0719JUD000049709.

299 Ibid., §§ 43 – 54.

300 Ibid., §§ 65 – 72.

301 Ibid., §§ 73 – 84.

302 ECHR, Judgement of 14 May 2013, no. 67810/10, *Gross v. Switzerland,* ECLI:CE:ECHR:2013:0514JUD006781010.

condition"[303]. The Chamber of the ECHR concluded that "Swiss law, while providing the possibility of obtaining a lethal dose of sodium pentobarbital by medical prescription, [did] not provide sufficient guidelines ensuring clarity regarding the extent of this right"[304]. There had accordingly been a violation of Article 8 of the Convention. If it had become final, this decision would have overruled the decision in the earlier case of *Haas v. Switzerland*. However, after Switzerland having requested the case to be referred to the Grand Chamber, the applicant finally committed suicide and deliberately took steps beforehand to hide this from the ECHR. The Grand Chamber therefore set aside the Chamber's decision and declared the application inadmissible, pursuant to Article 35 (3) lit. a) of the Convention.[305] Nevertheless, the case remains informative, showing the tendency of the Court regarding the issue of assisted suicide.

II. Terminating Life upon Request and Letting die

So far, there have been no cases involving terminating life upon request. In the field of letting die most complaints were declared inadmissible. Well known even to lay audiences is the case *Gard and others v. United Kingdom*[306], concerning the withdrawal of life-sustaining treatment from an infant against the wishes of the child's parents. Currently a case from Belgium[307] is pending before the Court.

Only the case of *Lambert and others v. France*[308] has been decided on the merits. The applicants argued that withdrawing of life-sustaining treatment, the legality of which had been confirmed by the French Conseil d'État, would be contrary to the State's obligations under Article 2 of the Convention. The ECHR found that there was no consensus among the Member States of the Council of Europe regarding permitting the withdrawal of artificial life-sustaining treatment, but the majority of Mem-

303 Ibid., § 63.

304 Ibid., § 67.

305 ECHR, Judgement of 30 September 2014, no. 67810/10, *Gross v. Switzerland* [GC], ECLI:CE:ECHR:2014:0930JUD006781010.

306 ECHR, Judgement of 27 June 2017, no. 39793/17, *Gard et al v. United Kingdom*, ECLI:CE:ECHR:2017:0627DEC003979317.

307 *Mortier v. Belgium*, no. 78017/17.

308 ECHR, Judgement of 5 June 2015, no. 46043/14, *Lambert et al v. France* [GC], ECLI:CE:ECHR:2015:0605JUD004604314.

bers allowed it.[309] While the respective regulatory settings varied, there was a consensus as to the crucial importance of the patient's wishes in the decision-making process as well as to the necessity of putting in place procedures to ensure that a patient's consent was expressed or its existence verified.[310] In this context, the ECHR emphasized that the States must be afforded a margin of appreciation, not just on whether to permit the withdrawal of artificial life-sustaining treatment and the detailed arrangements governing such withdrawal, but also as regards the means of striking a balance between the protection of a patient's right to life and the protection of the right to the respect of private life and personal autonomy. According to the Court, this margin of appreciation, however, is not unlimited, and it reserves the power to review whether the State has complied with its obligations under Article 2 of the Convention.[311]

D. Some Civil Law Countries in Continental Europe

I. The Netherlands

The Netherlands was a pioneer in legalising terminating life upon request and physician-assisted suicide.[312] In April, 2001, the Dutch legislator enacted the Termination of Life on Request and Assisted Suicide Act[313] (hereafter "the Assisted Suicide Act"), which came into force a year later.

Both terminating life upon request and assisted suicide remain criminal offences according to the Dutch Criminal Code [Section 293 (1) and Section 294 (2) first sentence][314]. Section 293 (2) of the Dutch Criminal Code states, however, that if terminating life upon request is carried out by a physician acting in accordance with the criteria of due care embodied in

309 Ibid., § 72.

310 Ibid., § 74.

311 Ibid., § 144 et seq.

312 For more information to the historical development and regulatory settings before the enactment of the Assisted Suicide Act see *Keown*, Euthanasia in the Netherlands: sliding down the slippery slope?, in: *Keown* (ed.), Euthanasia Examined, ethical, clinical and legal perspective, Cambridge 2010, p. 261 et seq.; *Otlowski*, Voluntary Euthanasia and the Common Law, Oxford 1997, p. 392; *Khorrami*, Die „Euthanasie – Gesetze" im Vergleich, Medizinrecht (MedR) 2003, 19 (21).

313 Available at https://wetten.overheid.nl/BWBR0012410/2020-03-19, access on 15.02.2021.

314 Available at www.legislationline.org, access on 15.02.2021.

it in Section 2 of the Euthanasia Act[323] as terminating somebody's life upon request. Section 3 of the Euthanasia Act specifies the conditions of impunity of the physician.

The patient must be in a futile situation, enduring constant and unbearable physical and psychological suffering as a result of a serious and incurable pathological condition that cannot be alleviated. Whereas in the beginning, the patient requesting death had to be an adult or emancipated minor, since 2014 also minors of any age can make such a request.[324] The physician has to make sure that the patient is conscious at the moment of making the request which implies that the decision is made voluntarily, deliberately and stable, with the absence of external pressure. The physician has the duty to provide comprehensive information to the patient and ensure that terminating her or his life corresponds with the patient's free will and represents the only remaining solution. As in the Netherlands, a second independent and qualified physician must assess the patient's condition, but there is no obligatory psychiatric evaluation in Belgium, too.

In Belgium the patient can also make a request by a written advance directive (Section 4 of the Euthanasia Act). Such a request can be carried out when three following conditions are met: First, the person must be suffering from an accidental or pathological disease which is serious and incurable; second, the patient must be unconscious, which excludes patients with dementia, for example; and third, the patient's situation must be irreversible according to the current state of scientific knowledge. These requirements have to be assessed by a physician. Until recently, the law required such a statement to be dated not earlier than five years prior to the person's inability to express her or his own will. In 2020, however, the law was changed in favour of unlimited validity since this requirement was regarded a "useless administrative restriction".[325]

The 2020 amendment also addressed the fact that some hospitals were using the so-called *clauses de conscience collective* to prohibit their physicians

---

323 Available at www.ejustice.just.fgov.be, access on 15.02.2021.

324 Loi du 28 février 2014 modifiant la loi du 28 mai 2002 relative à l'euthanasie, en vue d'étendre l'euthanasie aux mineurs, no. 2014009093, available at http://www.ejustice.just.fgov.be, access on 15.02.2021.

325 *Chambre des représentants de Belgique*, Proposition de loi modifiant la loi du 28 mai 2002 relative à l'euthanasie, en ce qui concerne la suppression de la durée de validité de la déclaration anticipée, no. 1830/001, available at https://leif.be, access on 15.02.2021.

from carrying out terminating of life upon request.[326] The Euthanasia Act now states that no written or unwritten clause may prevent a physician from terminating a patient's life under the law.[327]

Physicians are free to decide whether or not they will carry out terminating of life upon request (Section 14 of the Euthanasia Act). However, in case of a refusal, they are obliged to fulfil certain obligations, depending on the reasons for the refusal. If the physician refuses because of her or his conscience, he or she must inform the patient or a designated trusted person, specifying the reasons and referring the patient or trusted person to another physician. If refusing for medical reasons, the physician is obliged to inform the patient or trusted person in due time, stating reasons. The medical reason shall be recorded in the patient's medical file.

III. Luxembourg

In Luxembourg, a physician may terminate life upon request and assist with a suicide under conditions defined in Section 2 of the Euthanasia and Assisted Suicide Act of 2009[328] (thereafter "the Act"). In both cases, the patient must be a conscious adult in a futile situation, enduring constant and unbearable physical and psychological suffering as a result of a serious and incurable pathological condition that cannot be alleviated. The request of a patient must be voluntary, deliberate and stable, with the absence of external pressure, and made in writing. The Act also allows to make the request for terminating one's life by an advance directive (Section 4 of the Act).

Despite the Luxembourgish Act showing considerable similarity to its Benelux counterparts, there are nevertheless a few differences. For example, only an adult[329] can request euthanasia or assisted suicide. Furthermore, Luxembourg regulated physician assisted suicide in the Act together with terminating life upon request notwithstanding the first being no criminal offence whereas the latter is. Finally, unlike the Netherlands

326 *Lossignol*, L'euthanasie et le détournement la clause de conscience, Revue medicale de Bruxelles (RevMedBrux) 2016, 384 (386).

327 For more background information see the Avis of the Conseil d'État from 29 January 2020, available at www.raadvst-consetat.be, access on 15.02.2021.

328 Available at http://legilux.public.lu, access on 15.02.2021.

329 Under Luxembourgish law, a person 18 years or older.

or Belgium (since 2020), an advance directive requesting assistance with suicide or terminating one's life has to be confirmed every five years.

IV. Switzerland

In Switzerland, on the one hand, terminating somebody else's life upon request is a crime under Section 114 of the Swiss Criminal Code[330] mitigating the sanctions of manslaughter (Section 113).[331] On the other hand, assisting somebody with her or his suicide is considered a crime only when carried out for selfish motives according to Section 115 of the Swiss Criminal Code. This provision dates back to 1942[332], and has no medical background. It was much later when organisations such as Dignitas or Exit began to use it as a statutory basis for organizing assisted suicide. "Selfish motives" cover all forms of personal advantage, of a material, ideal or affective nature.[333] This prohibits assisted suicide becoming commercialized. Fees which are charged by these organisations are accepted as long as they do not exceed their administrative expenses.[334]

While the person assisting a suicide does not *de jure* have to be a physician, the involvement of a physician is *de facto* necessary. In its decision of 2006[335], which was confirmed by the ECHR, the Federal Supreme Court (Bundesgericht) of Switzerland ruled that a lethal drug being used to commit suicide must be prescribed by a physician. This is supposed to prevent abuse. Furthermore, such a requirement should, on the basis of

---

330 Available at https://www.fedlex.admin.ch, access on 15.02.2021.

331 *Tag*, Strafrecht am Ende des Lebens – Sterbehilfe und Hilfe zum Suizid in der Schweiz, Zeitschrift für die gesamte Strafrechtswissenschaft (ZStW) 2016, 73 (75 et seq.).

332 *Schwarzenegger*, Selbstsüchtige Beweggründe bei der Verleitung und Beihilfe zum Selbstmord (Art. 115 StGB), in: *Petermann* (ed.): Sicherheitsfragen der Sterbehilfe, St. Gallen 2008, p. 100 et seq.; *Bartsch/Landilt/Ristic/Reisch/Ajdacic-Gross*, Assissted Suicide in Switzerland, Deutsches Ärzteblatt International (DtschÄrzteblInt) 2019, 545 (545); *Engi*, Die „Selbstsüchtigen Beweggründe" von Art. 115 StGB im Licht der Normenentstehungsgeschichte, Jusletter 2009, available at https://jusletter.weblaw.ch, access on 15.02.2021.

333 Bundesgericht, Judgement of 16 June 2010, no. 1C_438/2009, available at https://www.bger.ch, access on 15.02.2021.

334 *Schwarzenegger*, in: Basler Kommentar zum Strafrecht (BSK-StGB/JStGB), 4th ed., Basel 2018, Art. 115, no. 13 et seq.

335 Bundesgericht, Judgement of 3 November 2006, no. 2A.48/2006, available at https://www.bger.ch, access on 15.02.2021.

the physician's duty of care, protect a person against rash decisions and ensure that the decision corresponds with the subject's free will.

V. Germany

For historical reasons, the sensitive term "euthanasia" is not used in Germany.[336] It has been replaced by the term "*Sterbehilfe*" (assistance in dying) which is as unclear and ambiguous as "euthanasia" covering everything from terminating life (upon request) and assisted suicide until letting die.

Terminating somebody else's life upon request is a crime under Section 216 of the German Criminal Code[337] mitigating the sanctions of manslaughter (Section 212 German Criminal Code).

Up until 2015, the law did not expressly address the issue of assisted suicide, which was therefore considered to be legal in most cases, and has become legal again since the end of February 2020, provided the decision to commit suicide is a voluntary one. Between 2015 and 2020, however, assisting somebody to commit suicide with the intention to do so repeatedly was a crime under Section 217 of the German Criminal Code. Relatives and persons close to the person wishing to commit suicide were exempt from criminal liability. The legislator's main intention was to ban organisations providing assisted suicide services in Germany and to prevent assisted suicide from becoming normal.[338] In its ruling of 26 February 2020,[339] the German Federal Constitutional Court (Bundesverfassungsgericht – BVerfG – hereafter "the Constitutional Court") declared Section 217 of the Criminal Code to be unconstitutional and void. The Constitutional Court underlined that the State must respect an individual's decision to end life as an act of personal autonomy and self-determination.[340] The right to self-determined death also includes the right to receive assistance by others. As Section 217 of the Criminal Code effectively outlawed the chance

336 For an overview see *Hohendorf*, Der Tot als Erlösung vom Leiden: Geschichte und Ethik der Sterbehilfe seit dem Ende des 19. Jahrhunderts in Deutschland, Göttingen 2013.

337 Available at https://www.gesetze-im-internet.de, access on 15.02.2021.

338 Bundestag-Drucksache (BT-Drucks.) 18/5373, p. 8 et seq., available at https://dip21.bundestag.de, access on 15.02.2021.

339 Bundesverfassungsgericht, Judgement of 26 February 2020, no. 2 BvR 2347/15, ECLI:DE:BVerfG:2020:rs20200226.2bvr234715, available also in English at https://www.bundesverfassungsgericht.de, access on 15.02.2021.

340 Ibid., § 210.

to get help from others, namely physicians, it interfered with the right to self-determined death. After applying a comprehensive proportionality test, the Constitutional Court concluded that such interference was not justified and that the provision thus violated the Constitution.[341]

Consequently, the debate has now turned to other questions, namely if the legislator should regulate assisted suicide and specify the conditions of a "free will", "voluntary decision" etc., and the possibilities to obtain a drug to commit suicide.[342]

In 2017, the Federal Administrative Court decided a case[343] where a claimant wished to obtain a license for acquiring a lethal dose of a sodium pentobarbital to commit suicide. Under German law, sodium pentobarbital was a marketable and prescriptible drug. However, in order to obtain the amount necessary to commit suicide, a license from the Federal Institute for Drugs and Medical Devices (hereafter "the Institute") was necessary. The Federal Administrative Court acknowledged that the acquisition of a lethal dose of a drug for the purpose of committing suicide was contrary to the purpose of the act on narcotic drugs and therefore generally prohibited.[344] Yet such a general prohibition would interfere with the human right of patients to decide autonomously about their death as protected by the German Basic Law (Grundgesetz).[345] The Court concluded that the state has to grant access to a drug that enables the patient to commit suicide in a dignified and painless manner if the patient is severely and incurable ill and her or his situation is unbearable.[346] This

341 Ibid., § 219 et seq.

342 *Boehme-Neßler*, Das Grundrecht auf Suizid, Neue Zeitschrift für Verwaltungsrecht (NVwZ) 2020, 1012 et seq.; *Cording/Saß*, Die Freiverantwortlichkeit der Entscheidung für einen assistierten Suizid. Ein Diskussionsbeitrag aus forensisch-psychiatrischen Perspektive, Neue Juristische Wochenschrift (NJW) 2020, 2695 et seq.; *Berghäuser/Boer/Borasio/Hohendorf/Rixen/Spittler*, Brauchen wir eine Neuordnung der Sterbehilfe in Deutschland?, Medizinrecht (MedR) 2020, 207 et seq.

343 Bundesverwaltungsgericht, Judgement of 2 March 2017, no. 3 C 19.15, ECLI:DE:BVerwG:2017:020317U3C19.15.0, available in English at https://www.bverwg.de, access on 15.02.2021.

344 Ibid., § 18aa).

345 Ibid., § 22bb).

346 Ibid., § 31.

decision was both welcomed and criticised.[347] In practice, such a licence has not been granted yet, neither by the Institute nor by the courts.[348]

E. Some Common Law Countries: North America

I. The United States of America

In the U.S., the State of Oregon was the first to legislate on assisted suicide. Its Death with Dignity Act was based upon a citizens' initiative in 1994 and enacted three years later.[349] Since then, seven other US States and Washington D.C.[350] have enacted statutes enabling their residents to make use of assisted suicide. In addition, the Supreme Court of Montana held in *Baxter v. Montana*[351] that consent of a mentally competent, terminally ill patient hindered the prosecution of a physician who had assisted him in committing suicide. Nonetheless, the Court did not make a broader ruling which would acknowledge a right to assisted suicide as such.[352]

Assisted suicide frequently involves a physician prescribing a lethal dose of medication (called aid-in-dying medication) for self-administration. The request for such a medication must follow several requirements. First, a request is limited to residents of the respective State. Second, only an adult with the ability to make and communicate health care decisions can make such a request. Third, only a terminal disease may be taken into considera-

347 See e.g., *Deutscher Ethikrat*, Ad-hoc Empfehlung of 1 June 2017, available at www.ethikrat.org, also in English, access on 15.02.2021.

348 Bundesverfassungsgericht, Judgement of 20 May 2020, no. 1 BvL 2/20 ECLI:DE: BVerfG:2020:lk20200520. 1bvl000220; Bundesverwaltungsgericht, Judgement of 28 May 2019, no. 3 C 6.17, ECLI:DE:BVerwG:2019:280519U3C6.17.0; Verwaltungsgericht Köln, nos. 7 K 13803/17, 7 K 14642/17, 7 K 8560/18, Judgement of 24 November 2020, ECLI:DE:VGK:2019:1119.7K13803.17.00.

349 *Ganzini*, Legalized Physician Assisted Death in Oregon – Eighteen Years Experience, in: *Borasio/Jox/Taupitz/Wiesing* (eds.), Assistierter Suizid: Der Stand der Wissenschaft, Berlin/Heidelberg 2017, p. 7.

350 California, End of Life Option Act; Colorado, End of Life Options Act; District of Columbia, D.C. Death with Dignity Act; Hawai'I, Our Care, Our Choice Act; Maine, Death with Dignity Act; New Jersey, Aid in Dying for the Terminally Ill Act; Vermont, Patient Choice and Control at the End of Life Act; Washington, Death with Dignity Act. Full versions of the cited acts can be accessed at https://www.deathwithdignity.org, access on 15.02.2021.

351 Supreme Court of Montana, Judgement of 31 December 2009 – *Baxter v. Montana*, available at https://law.justia.com, access on 15.02.2021.

352 *Pollock*, Criminal Law, 10th ed., Waltham 2013, p. 187.

tion as grounds for the prescription (in some States in combination with a particular life-expectancy, e.g. in Colorado, a maximum of 6 months according to Section 25–48–102 of the End of Life Options Act). However, the patient does not have to face an intolerable suffering in order to make such a request.

Depending on the State, special rules governing the formal requirements must be respected. For example, in Washington a valid request must be made via a certain form, then dated, signed and witnessed by at least two individuals (Section 70.245030 of the Death with Dignity Act), whereas Colorado requires two oral requests, separated by at least fifteen days, and a valid written request to attending physician (Section 25–48–104 of the End of Life Options Act).

II. Canada

In Canada, terminating life upon request and assisting with a suicide are, as a rule, both criminal offences. After the Supreme Court of Canada had held in 2015 that the general prohibition of a physician-assisted death unjustifiably infringes the Canadian Charter of Rights and Freedoms,[353] the Criminal Code was amended. Now Section 241.1. of the Canadian Criminal Code[354] allows and regulates "medical assistance in dying" meaning both, physician assisted suicide and terminating life by a physician upon request.

Canadian law makes a great effort to specify the requirements for a request for medical assistance in dying. First, the person must be eligible for health services funded by a (provincial) government in Canada. Second, the person must be suffering from a grievous and irremediable medical condition. Third the person must be at least 18 years old and capable of making decisions regarding her or his health. The request must be made voluntarily, without any external pressure, and after having been informed of the means available to relieve suffering, including palliative care. The request must be made in writing in the presence of two witnesses, after the

---

353 Supreme Court of Canada, Judgement of 2 June 2015 – *Carter v. Canada* (Attorney General), available at https://scc-csc.lexum.com, access on 15.02.2021. For more information see *Martin,* Assisted Suicide and the European Convention on Human Rights: A Critical Analysis of the Case Law, Trinity College Law Review 2018, 244 (252).

354 Available at https://laws-lois.justice.gc.ca/eng/acts/c-46/page-53.html#h-119931, access on 15.02.2021.

patient has been informed by a physician that their medical condition is indeed grievous and irremediable. The patient must be informed that it is possible to withdraw the request at any time. There is also a waiting period of at least ten days between the request and the act of assisted dying.

Notable about the Canadian regulation is the obligation of the physician prescribing the substance for the purposes of medical assistance in dying to inform the pharmacist dispensing the substance for which purse it is intended. There is no obligation on the part of the dispenser, or any other person, to provide or assist in providing medical assistance in dying.

F. Conclusion

While there is a human right to life under European as well as under international human rights instruments, no human right to die has been acknowledged up to now, neither on the European nor on the international level, by such an instrument. However, some courts acknowledged such a right to die on the national level, and there is a clear tendency within the case-law of the European Court of Human Rights towards such a right under Article 8 of the European Convention on Human Rights albeit the Court grants thc Member States a wide margin of appreciation.

Based on their general approach to the question of end-of-life decisions, countries can be divided roughly into three groups. The first and largest group bans all forms of assisted suicide and terminating life upon request (e.g. Czech Republic, Slovakia and Poland). In the second group which has been growing, terminating life upon request is banned but assisted suicide including physician-assisted suicide is legal under certain conditions (e.g. Switzerland, Germany, Austria [from 1 January 2022][355], and some States in the US). In the third and smallest group, physician-assisted suicide and terminating life upon request are legal under certain conditions (the Benelux countries and Canada).

Nonetheless, even within these groups national laws show significant differences with respect to the method of regulation and the individual requirements. Some legislators have chosen the way of special laws (e.g.

355 The Austrian Constitutional Court (Verfassungsgerichtshof – VfGH) declared the prohibition of any form of assisted suicide without exception to be unconstitutional and void from 1 January 2022 onwards, see judgement of 11 December 2020, no. GH 139/19, available at https://www.vfgh.gv.at/rechtsprechung/Ausgewaehlte_Entscheidungen.de.html, also in English, access on 15.2.2021.

Luxembourg, Belgium [with respect to terminating of life upon request]), others have amended their criminal code (e.g. the Netherlands, Switzerland), or rely on their general law with no explicit regulation (e.g. Germany [for the time being], Belgium [with respect to assisted suicide]). Considering the individual requirements, legal regimes differ substantively regarding the person making such a request and the possibility of advance directives. Only in Belgium and the Netherlands can such a request be made by a minor, most legislations require the applicant to be an adult. While in some countries the applicant has to suffer from an incurable and fatal illness (e.g. Belgium or Luxembourg), other countries do not limit the request to specific situations (e.g. the Netherlands or Germany [for assisted suicide]). In the US and Canada, applicants must reside in the respective states, the background of which is to avoid "suicide tourism", whereas in Europe it is possible to seek such an assistance abroad. Last, an advance directive requesting assistance with one's suicide or terminating one's life is expressly acknowledged only in the Benelux countries.

This brief overview shows that there is no great divide between Civil and Common law countries but a common tendency towards allowing and regulating assisted suicide. This tendency is, inter alia, backed by, if not based upon, a growing body of jurisprudence acknowledging a human right to die with dignity including the right to commit suicide with the help of others. Yet there are significant differences between the countries allowing assisted suicide regarding the requirements, both material and procedural.

In contrast, terminating life upon request has been legalized only by the Benelux countries and Canada. All other countries regard this to be a form of killing and, consequently, strictly ban it by criminal law. These positions are mirrored on the level of human rights. Human rights jurisprudence has not extended the human right to die with dignity to terminating life upon request with the Canadian Supreme Court being the notable exception.

Bearing in mind these fundamental differences as well as the variety of regulatory approaches it is absolutely necessary for analytical reasons as well as for the public debate to avoid the broad and notoriously vague term of "euthanasia" and to distinguish between assisted suicide and terminating life upon request.

Bibliography :

Cases:

Bundesgericht (Switzerland), Judgement of 16 June 2010, no. 1C_438/2009

Bundesgericht (Switzerland), Judgement of 3 November 2006, no. 2A.48/2006

Bundesverfassungsgericht (Germany), Judgement of 20 May 2020, no. 1 BvL 2/20 ECLI:DE:BVerfG:2020:lk20200520.1bvl000220

Bundesverfassungsgericht (Germany), Judgement of 26 February 2020, no. 2 BvR 2347/15, ECLI:DE:BVerfG:2020:rs20200226.2bvr2347

Bundesverwaltungsgericht (Germany), Judgement of 2 March 2017, no. 3 C 19.15, ECLI:DE:BVerwG:2017:020317U3C19.15.0

Bundesverwaltungsgericht (Germany), Judgement of 28 May 2019, no. 3 C 6.17, ECLI:DE:BVerwG:2019:280519U3C6.17.0

Conseil d'État (Belgium), Avis from 20 June 2001, no. 31.441/AV-AG

Conseil d'État (Belgium), Avis from 29 January 2020, no. 66.816/AG

ECHR, Judgement of 14 May 2013, no. 67810/10, *Gross v. Switzerland*, ECLI:CE:ECHR:2013:0514JUD006781010

ECHR, Judgement of 19 July 2012, no. 497/09, *Koch v. Germany*, ECLI:CE:ECHR:2012:0719JUD000049709

ECHR, Judgement of 20 January 2011, no. 31322/07, *Haas v. Switzerland*, ECLI:CE:ECHR:2011:0120JUD003132207

ECHR, Judgement of 27 June 2017, no. 39793/17, *Gard et al v. United Kingdom*, ECLI:CE:ECHR:2017:0627DEC003979317

ECHR, Judgement of 27 September 1995, no. 18984/91, *McCann et al v. United Kingdom* [GC], ECLI:CE:ECHR:1995:0927JUD001898491

ECHR, Judgement of 29 April 2002, no. 2346/02, *Pretty v. United Kingdom*, ECLI:CE:ECHR:2002:0429JUD000234602

ECHR, Judgement of 30 September 2014, no. 67810/10, *Gross v. Switzerland* [GC], ECLI:CE:ECHR:2014:0930JUD006781010

ECHR, Judgement of 5 June 2015, no. 46043/14, *Lambert et al v. France* [GC], ECLI:CE:ECHR:2015:0605JUD004604314

Hoge Raad (Netherlands), Judgement of 21 April 2020, no. 19/05015, ECLI:NL:HR:2020:713

Supreme Court of Canada, Judgement of 2 June 2015 – *Carter v. Canada* (Attorney General)

Supreme Court of Montana (United States of America), Judgement of 31 December 2009 -*Baxter v. Montana*

Verfassungsgerichtshof (Austria), Judgement of 11 December 2020, no. GH 139/19

Verwaltungsgericht Köln (Germany), Judgement of 24 November 2020, nos. 7 K 13803/17, 7 K 14642/17, 7 K 8560/18, ECLI:DE:VGK:2019:1119.7K13803.17.00

Bibliography:

Bartsch, Christine/Landilt, Karin/Ristic, Anita/Reisch, Thomas/Ajdacic-Gross, Vladeta, Assissted Suicide in Switzerland, Deutsches Ärzteblatt International (DtschÄrztebIInt) 2019, p. 545 – 552

Basler Kommentar zum Strafrecht (BSK-StGB/JStGB), Niggli, Marcel Alexander/ Wiprächtiger, Hans (eds.), 4th ed., Basel 2018

Berghäuser, Gloria/Boer, Theo A./Borasio, Gian Domenico/Hohendorf, Gerrit/Rixen, Stephan/Spittler, Johan F., Brauchen wir eine Neuordnung der Sterbehilfe in Deutschland?, Medizinrecht (MedR) 2020, p. 207 – 2011

Boehme-Neßler, Volker, Das Grundrecht auf Suizid, Neue Zeitschrift für Verwaltungsrecht (NVwZ) 2020, p. 1012 – 1015

Bood, Alex/Griffiths, John/Weyers, Heleen, Euthanasia and Law in the Netherlands, Amsterdam 1998

Commission fédérale de contrôle et d'évaluation de l'euthanasie, Huitième rapport aux Chambres législatives année 2016 – 2017, https://organesdeconcertation.sante.belgique.be/sites/default/files/documents/8_rapport-euthanasie_2016-2017-fr.pdf (access on 15.02.2021)

Cording, Clemens/Saß, Henning, Die Freiverantwortlichkeit der Entscheidung für einen assistierten Suizid. Ein Diskussionsbeitrag aus forensisch-psychiatrischen Perspektive, Neue Juristische Wochenschrift (NJW) 2020, p. 2695 – 2697

Deutscher Ethikrat, Suizidprävention statt Suizidunterstützung. Erinnerung an eine Forderung des Deutschen Ethikrates anlässlich einer Entscheidung des Bundesverwaltungsgerichts. Ad-hoc Empfehlung of 1 June 2017, https://www.ethikrat.org/mitteilungen/2017/ethikrat-verneint-anspruch-auf-staatliche-unterstuetzung-bei-suizid/ (access on 15.02.2021)

ECHR, Guide on Article 8 of the Convention on Human Rights, last update on 31 August 2020, https://www.echr.coe.int/documents/guide_art_8_eng.pdf (access on 15.02.2021)

Engi, Lorenz, Die „Selbstsüchtigen Beweggründe" von Art. 115 StGB im Licht der Normenentstehungsgeschichte, Jusletter 2009, https://jusletter.weblaw.ch/jusissues/2009/520/_7373.html__ONCE&login=false#sectionc56b149c-baf1-40a2-a313-bb53d138f1b2 (access on 15.02.2021)

Ganzini, Linda, Legalized Physician Assisted Death in Oregon – Eighteen Years' Experience, in: Borasio, Gian Domenico/Jox, Ralf J./Taupitz, Jochen/Wiesing, Urban (eds.), Assistierter Suizid: Der Stand der Wissenschaft, Berlin/Heidelberg 2017, p. 7 – 20

Gavela, Kallia, Ärztlich assistierter Suizid und organisierte Sterbehilfe, Berlin/Heidelberg 2013

Grabenwarter, Christoph, European Convention on Human Rights. Commentary, 1st ed., Munich 2014

Hohendorf, Gerrit, Der Tot als Erlösung vom Leiden: Geschichte und Ethik der Sterbehilfe seit dem Ende des 19. Jahrhunderts in Deutschland, Göttingen 2013

Keown, John, Euthanasia in the Netherlands: sliding down the slippery slope?, in: Keown, John (ed.), Euthanasia Examined, ethical, clinical and legal perspective, Cambridge 2010, p. 261 – 296

Khorrami, Katharina, Die „Euthanasie – Gesetze" im Vergleich, Medizinrecht (MedR) 2003, p. 19 – 25

Lossignol, Dominique, L'euthanasie et le détournement la clause de conscience, Revue medicale de Bruxelles (Rev Med Brux) 2016, p. 384 – 389

Martin, Stevie S., Assisted Suicide and the European Convention on Human Rights: A Critical Analysis of the Case Law, Trinity College Law Review 2018, p. 244 – 275

Nys, Herman, A discussion of the Legal Rules on Euthanasia in Belgium Briefly Compared with the Rules in Luxembourg and the Netherlands, in: Jones, David Albert/Gastmans, Chris/MacKellar, Calum (eds.), Euthanasia and Assisted Suicide. Lessons from Belgium, Cambridge 2017, p. 5 – 6

Nys, Herman, Physician assisted suicide in Belgian Law, European Journal of Health Law 2005, p. 39 – 41

Otlowski, Margaret, Voluntary Euthanasia and the Common Law, Oxford 1997

Pollock, Joycelyn M., Criminal Law, 10th ed., Waltham 2013

Schwarzenegger, Christian, Selbstsüchtige Beweggründe bei der Verleitung und Beihilfe zum Selbstmord (Art. 115 StGB), in: Petermann, Frank Th. (ed.): Sicherheitsfragen der Sterbehilfe, St. Gallen 2008, p. 81 – 124

Tag, Brigitte, Strafrecht am Ende des Lebens – Sterbehilfe und Hilfe zum Suizid in der Schweiz, Zeitschrift für die gesamte Strafrechtswissenschaft (ZStW) 2016, p. 73 – 88

Weyers, Heleen, Euthanasie: Het proces van rechtsverandering, Amsterdam 2004

Uwe Hellmann, Professor Universität Potsdam, *The strengthening of patient autonomy in the case of medically assisted suicide by the 5th Criminal Senate of the BGH*[356]

Stärkung der Patientenautonomie bei dem ärztlich assistierten Suizid durch den 5. Strafsenat des BGH

Am 3. Juli 2019 verkündete der 5. Strafsenat des Bundesgerichtshofs zwei Urteile, die mit erfreulicher Klarheit die Patientenautonomie im Zusammenhang mit einem ärztlich assistierten Suizid stärken. Die Entscheidungen betreffen unterschiedliche ärztliche Tätigkeiten und der Strafsenat wollte offensichtlich die Gelegenheit nutzen, größere Rechtssicherheit für alle Ärzte zu schaffen,

356 Translation by Janek Downes.

die einen Menschen, der seinem Leben ein Ende setzen will, begleiten. Es ist kein Zufall, dass die beiden Urteile am selben Tag verkündet wurden, sondern die Entscheidungsgründe nehmen an einigen Stellen aufeinander Bezug. Im Folgenden werden die Entscheidungen, wie es in den dazu ergangenen Stellungnahmen ebenfalls zumeist geschieht, als „Hamburger-Fall" und „Berliner Fall" bezeichnet. Das Urteil des Bundesverfassungsgerichts vom 26. Februar 2020 zur Verfassungswidrigkeit des Straftatbestandes der geschäftsmäßigen Förderung der Selbsttötung (§ 217 StGB) ist für unser Thema zwar nicht unmittelbar relevant. Die eindeutige Feststellung, dass das allgemeine Persönlichkeitsrecht (Art. 2 Abs. 1 in Verbindung mit Art. 1 Abs. 1 Grundgesetz) das Recht gewährleistet, selbstbestimmt die Entscheidung zu treffen, sein Leben eigenhändig bewusst und gewollt zu beenden, unterstützt aber die tragenden Erwägungen der beiden BGH-Urteile.

On 3 July 2019, the 5th Criminal Senate of the BGH[357] *announced two rulings which, with gratifying clarity, strengthen patient autonomy in connection with medically assisted suicide. The decisions concern different medical activities and the Criminal Senate obviously wanted to take the opportunity to create greater legal certainty for all doctors who accompany a person who wants to end his life. It is not a mere coincidence that both rulings were announced on the same day, for the judgements refer to each other at several points. In the following, the decisions are referred to as the "Hamburg Case" and the "Berlin Case", as it is custom in the academic discussion. Even though the ruling of the Federal Constitutional Court of 26 February 2020*[358] *on the unconstitutionality of the offence of promoting suicide in an organized manner (§ 217 StGB) is not directly relevant to our topic, the clear statement that the right of personality (Article 2 (1) in conjunction with Article 1 (1) of the Grundgesetz, the German Constitution) guarantees the right to make a self-determined decision to end one's life deliberately and intentionally by one's own hand, supports the fundamental considerations of the BGH rulings.*

357 The BGH is the German Federal Court.

358 BVerfG 2 BvR 2347/15, 2 BvR 651/16, 2 BvR 1593/16, 2 BvR 2354/16, 2 BvR 2527/16 – 26. Februar 2020 = HRRS 2020 Nr. 190.

A. The Hamburg Case[359]

I. The case decided by the Regional Court of Hamburg at first instance was based on the following – abbreviated – facts:

The two women, 81 and 85 of age, who were willing to commit suicide, have lived in a flat together and ran their households largely independently. Their quality of life was limited due to several illnesses; however, these illnesses were not life-threatening. In 2010 they had set up a patient decree. As their health decreased, the women feared that they were physically and mentally overstrained with the other's care. After obtaining the relevant information, they finally refused to move to a nursing home or to hire a home care worker. They decided to depart from life together. Therefore, for a fee of 1000 euros, the women decided to join a death society, which demanded a report on the mental capacity of the women. This report was produced by the accused doctor. From a psychiatric point of view, he certified that both women had an unrestricted mental ability and from a medical-psychiatric point of view, he saw no objections to their request for suicide assistance. The accused initially refused the request of the two women to accompany them personally during their suicide, but later agreed to do so. As the accused arrived in the women's flat on the 10 November 2012, they gave account on their preparations concerning their suicide. As part of their preparation, they had signed a form in which they expressed their wish to end their lives in peace and dignity, and had drawn up a declaration in which – also with reference to their living wills – they forbade any person to take rescue measures if they were unable to act. They paid the doctor's fee of 1,100 euros and gave the doctor another 2,000 euros, to donate to a children's hospice; he donated the money as it was agreed. The doctor and the women then discussed the details of taking the medication. He promised the women that he would stay with them until their hearts stopped. He helped preparing the fatal drugs, but the intake of the mixture was carried out independently by the woman. Shortly after the woman fell asleep. The chance of rescue was only little. Survival would only have been possible with severe brain damage. The defendant refrained from calling an emergency doctor and other rescue efforts. After an hour both women were dead.

---

359 BGH 5 StR 132/18 – 3. Juli 2019 (LG Hamburg) = HRRS 2019 Nr. 1052.

II. The guiding principle for publication in the official compendium of decisions is:

> *"In consideration of the growing importance of the self-determination of the individual – also in decisions about his or her life –, in cases of self-inflicted suicide the doctor who knows the circumstances cannot be obliged to act against the will of the suicide with criminal consequences."*

III. The Senate first repeats irrefutable principles of German criminal law.

1. Since § 216 StGB threatens the killing on demand with punishment, the active killing of another human being is and remains punishable, even if the person expressly and seriously wishes his killing. On the other hand, aiding and abetting a suicide that was intended and carried out on one's own responsibility is unpunished, as this does not constitute a criminal offence. In order to distinguish the active killing of another person from assisted suicide, it is decisive who last controls the event leading to death:

> *"If the person wishing to die takes the death-bringing action himself, while retaining the free decision on his fate, he kills himself, albeit with outside help."*

2. This principle does not apply, however, if the suicidal person has not made his suicide decision on his own responsibility due to a lack of knowledge or responsibility. In particular, the minority of the suicide or deficiencies due to illness or intoxication, but also the evocation of the decision by coercion, threat or deception are considered. If the decision to commit suicide is based on a mere depressive mood of the moment, which is not supported by inner firmness and determination, one's own responsibility also falls away. If it is missing, the participant in the suicide may be liable to prosecution for a crime of homicide committed in indirect perpetration. The perpetrator then uses the suicide as a – not responsible – tool against himself and in this way controls the fatal event. These principles are not new, but the Senate clarifies that minors in general and adults, whose decision to commit suicide results from a momentary mood, a mental disorder or externally generated circumstances, are protected through criminal law.

IV. The actual progress of the decision lies in the fact that the Senate still respects the suicide decision that was made in a state of full responsibility even if the suicide victim has lost control of the event through the onset of unconsciousness.

A homicide perpetrated by omission could be considered. In the case that was decided, criminal liability already failed because rescue efforts made by the doctor after the onset of unconsciousness would not have led to averting death with a probability close to certainty. However, the Senate also denies a guarantor position (§ 13 (1) StGB), i.e. the existence of special circumstances which would have obligated the doctor to take life-saving measures. Escorting someone through the process of dying does not create the obligation to save the suicidal person's life. The previous conduct of the doctor – the rendering of expert opinions on the mental ability, advisory activity on the day of death, assistance in the preparation of the lethal drug solution – was not in breach of duty, which means that obligation to rescue arose from these actions either.

The "Hamburg Case" consists of an unclear section, but the aforementioned ruling of the Federal Constitutional Court deprives the section of it's basis. The Senate stated that by introducing the criminal offence of organized encouragement of suicide (§ 217 StGB), the legislature had expressed that it considered actions such as that of the defendant "punishable and thus also contrary to duty". However, the actions taken by the accused could not be rated as contrary to duty, for the offence in § 217 StGB was not yet enacted when the event took place. This passage gives the impression that the Senate wanted to keep a "back door" open in order to possibly be able to accept a rescue obligation for future cases of organized euthanasia. After the Federal Constitutional Court found § 217 StGB unconstitutional and therefore void, this path is blocked.

V. The 5th Criminal Senate still does not consider patient autonomy in the context of criminal liability for failure to provide assistance (§ 323c StGB) with regard to the characteristic of the accident, but rather with regard to the reasonableness of the provision of assistance, which is missing if the person affected is "in a situation of conflict between the general duty to help and the duty to respect the right to self-determination guaranteed in the general right of personality". From a dogmatic point of view, this reasoning is impure, because a suicide which is voluntary is not a "sudden event"[360]. In terms of criminal policy this view is correct because it counteracts the perpetrator's protective assertion that he considered the suicide to be committed by free will and therefore acted without any criminal intent. In order to guarantee protection of life, in cases where the person committing suicide really does not want to die, it is necessary to consider an accident in principle, but to

360 E.g. *Neumann*, StV 2020, 126, 128 f.; *Sowada*, NStZ 2019, 670, 672.

disclaim the reasonableness of the provision of assistance if the potential offender finds himself in a situation of conflict[361].

B. Berlin Case[362]

I. The verdict in the Berlin Case is even more significant because the family doctor of the woman willing to die was accused. The following facts were at issue:

Since the age of sixteen, a 44 year old woman suffered from an irritable bowel syndrome that was not life-threatening but caused severe cramp-like pain and was not treatable. Since life seemed no longer worth living under these circumstances, she turned to the accused, her family doctor, on 8 February 2013 with the request to support her in her suicide. The defendant gave in to this request, knowing the long history of illness and suffering as well as the unsuccessful therapy attempts, because he was convinced that a doctor should not leave a patient, whom he had treated for years, alone even in such a situation. He gave his patient an unknown quantity of the drug Luminal. On 15 February 2013, the day of his last home visit, he met the women in despair and determined to commit suicide. The doctor assumed that she was legally competent. During this visit, the woman handed over her flat keys to the defendant and asked him to look after her at home after taking the drugs until the time of her death. The defendant and his patient were aware that death would be preceded by a comatose phase. On February 16, 2013, the woman, in her right mind and fully aware of the consequences, took a lethal amount of Luminal. She informed the accused about this and he arrived in the flat and found her in a state of coma. Feeling obliged to her wish of death, he did not take on life saving measures, but examined her pulse, her pupil reflexes and her breathing. He visited the flat for several times over the next days. The accused gave the women a dose of metoclopramide to prevent vomiting at least once. The defendant also injected her with Buscopan, an antispasmodic drug used in palliative care, to prevent unnecessary pain. During the last two visits the woman was already in a pre-final state. One day before the woman's death the doctor called external parties to inform them about the case. He told them that life saving measures were not wanted. On 19 February 2013, the defendant established the woman's death. If the

361 *Mitsch*, medstra 2019, 117, 119.
362 BGH 5 StR 393/18 – 3. Juli 2019 (LG Berlin) = HRRS 2019 Nr. 1059.

deceased could have been saved with immediate medical treatment after taking the Luminal could not be determined with certainty.

The guiding principle for publication in the official compendium of decisions is:

> *"The physician's position as guarantor for the life of his patient ends when he only accompanies the patient's suicide."*

II. As in the Hamburg judgement, the Senate denies active killing. The accused had provided the suicide victim with the lethal drugs, but she had exercised "dominion over the events leading to death". The administration of the muscle-relaxing drugs during the dying process was not causal for the death success, because the administration of the drugs neither accelerated the dying process nor initiated a new deadly causal process. The telephone conversations with third parties would not have prevented rescue efforts in a punishable manner because the addressees had not yet made any rescue efforts.

III. The main benefit of this ruling is that the Senate determines the limits of the physician's guarantor status according to the will of the suicide patient. The accused doctor was no longer responsible for the woman's life by taking over the medical treatment. This obligation had ended when the patient (more than once) expressed her wish to die and combined this with the request – accepted by the defendant – that he should care for her when she was in the process of dying after taking the tablets. According to the agreement, the doctor was obliged only to prevent the woman from suffering and pain during the process of dying. The Senate was not able to base its decision on the ruling of the Federal Constitutional Court, for it had not yet existed, but also bases its ruling on the fact that (patient) autonomy includes the decision on one's own death and that in cases of self-inflicted suicide the doctor who knows the circumstances of the suicide is not obliged to act against the will of the dying person. By accepting the termination of the guarantors position, the "Berlin Case" differs from the previous leading decision on that topic, the so called "Wittig Case", in which the 3rd Criminal Senate had accepted a guarantors position of the family doctor for the life of the patient at the time of the suicide[363]. The 3rd Criminal Senate justified its view by stating that a doctor may not generally bow to the suicide's death wish[364] and, at any rate, in the

363 BGHSt 32, 367, 377.
364 BGHSt 32, 367, 371 ff., 380.

event of the suicide's unconsciousness, may not be guided solely by the will of the suicide declared prior to the occurrence of unconsciousness, but must make a decision on his own responsibility concerning a – possibly – successful intervention[365]. As a result, the 3rd Criminal Senate also stated for the impunity of the doctor, but justified the ruling with the doctor's conflict of conscience between the duty to rescue the person and the respect for the right of self-determination of the suicide. The 5th Criminal Senate also rejects a guarantor position from previous dangerous actions because of the procurement of the lethal drugs, citing the importance of the person's responsibility in connection with the desire to die. In only relating to the suicide's right of autonomy to concretise the obligation to take on life saving actions, the 5th Criminal Senate does not – differing from the considerations of the 3rd Criminal Senate – find itself in a moral conflict. The conclusion of the 5th Criminal Senate that the doctor did not need to take any measures to save the suicide's life is imprecise, however, because he was not allowed to take such measures at all due to his lost right of treatment[366].

IV. Criminal liability for failure to provide assistance (§ 323c StGB) fails – as in the Hamburg case – because it is unreasonable to provide assistance contrary to the expressed will of the suicide.

C. Conclusion

The two rulings of the 5th Criminal Senate – in conjunction with the decision of the Federal Constitutional Court – should provide doctors with a high degree of security against punishment in the event of self-inflicted suicide. Consequently, the right of self-determination of the suicide would also have to limit other guarantees, such as those of spouses[367].

365 BGHSt 32, 367, 378.
366 Applicable *Hillenkamp*, JZ 2019, 1053, 1056.
367 E.g. *Brechtken/Leifeld*, medstra 2019, 339, 344.

Géraldine Demme, MCF, Paris Nanterre University, *Assisted Dying under Swiss Law*

As a general principle, active euthanasia is prohibited in Switzerland. However, although the Swiss Penal Code makes killing on demand a punishable offence, suicide assistance is not punishable as long as it is not committed for "selfish reasons". Since the 1980s, suicide assistance organizations have been developing in Switzerland. Their activities – as long as they are not designed for profit – remain unpunished. After a brief look at the Swiss legal system, this article deals with the regulations and approach of the two best known euthanasia organizations in Switzerland, Dignitas and Exit, as well as with the role of the medical profession in this context.

Die aktive Sterbehilfe ist in der Schweiz verboten. § 114 des Schweizerischen Strafgesetzbuches stellt die Tötung auf Verlangen unter Strafe. Die Suizidbeihilfe ist hingegen nicht strafbar, solange sie nicht aus selbstsüchtigen Beweggründen begangen wird, § 115 des Schweizerischen Strafgesetzbuches. Seit den achtziger Jahren haben sich in der Schweiz Suizidhilfeorganisationen herausgebildet, deren Tätigkeit – solange sie nicht auf Profit ausgelegt ist – straflos bleibt. Nach einem kurzen Blick auf die Schweizerische Rechtsordnung, beschäftigt sich dieser Beitrag mit dem Satzungsrecht und der Herangehensweise der beiden bekanntesten Schweizerischen Sterbehilfeorganisationen, Dignitas und Exit, sowie mit der Rolle, die der Ärzteschaft in diesem Zusammenhang zukommt.

A. The Swiss Legal Framework for Assisted Dying

Killing another person constitutes a crime in Switzerland, punishable as manslaughter (Article 111 of the Swiss Criminal Code) with imprisonment of not less than five years or – if the motive, objective or method is particularly depraved – as murder (Article 112 of the Swiss Criminal Code) with imprisonment for life.

If the perpetrator is induced to kill at the genuine and insistent request of the victim (Article 114 of the Swiss Criminal Code), the killing is punishable by imprisonment for up to three years or a fine. Art. 114 of the Swiss Criminal Code states: "*Any person who for commendable motives, and in particular out of compassion for the victim, kills a person at that person's own genuine and insistent request is liable to imprisonment for up to three years or a fine.*"

Article 111 of the Swiss Criminal Code expressly treats the killing of a person as a punishable crime. If this article were to be applied literally, even suicide committed autonomously would be punishable. However, since the general opinion is that it is not the intention of article 111 to punish a person who has unsuccessfully tried to commit suicide for attempted manslaughter[368], a teleological interpretation is applied. Article 111 of the Swiss Criminal Code is restricted to the killing of another person. This means that the act of suicide is not a criminal offence.

Since suicide is not liable to prosecution, it follows that assisting with such an act cannot be a criminal offence either[369]. The Swiss legislator punishes only cases where a person has incited or assisted suicide for selfish motives, Article 115 provides a special criminal liability[370]. Article 115 of the Swiss Criminal Code states: "*Any person who for selfish motives incites or assists another to commit or attempt to commit suicide is, if that other person thereafter commits or attempts to commit suicide, liable to imprisonment for up to five years or a fine.*" The first prerequisite is that suicide has either been committed or at least attempted by a person under his own control and responsibility.

The two alternatives foreseen in Article 115 of the Swiss Criminal Code are that the decision to commit suicide was intentionally brought about (then incitement) or facilitated (then assistance) by the perpetrator. In both cases, the subjective element is that the perpetrator must have acted out of "selfish motives" in addition to the common element of intent (contingency intent is sufficient). This is the case when the perpetrator pursues a personal advantage that does not necessarily have to be of a material nature, for example greed, but also vengeance, hatred or malice. Complete indifference, however, is not enough[371].

Under Swiss law, a person assisting with suicide who acts without selfish motives will not be punished even if he or she fails to initiate any emergency measures after the suicide victim loses consciousness. At the time of the adoption of Article 115 in 1937, this wording was intended to avoid punishing the aiding of "honor suicides" – for example, when a friend brought a pistol into the cell of an officer on remand for a common crime so that he could judge himself – and not thought for sick people who want to shorten their life. The way in which the law has been formulated,

368 *Basler Kommentar*, Strafrecht I Art. 1–136 StGB, 2019, Art. 115, ref. 1, p. 2538.

369 *Ibid.*

370 So it is a *sui generis* offence in Switzerland. Cf. J. Hurtado Pozo, *Droit pénal, Partie spéciale*, Schulthess, Zürich: 2009, ref. 220, p. 69.

371 For more details about „selfish reasons": M. SCHUBARTH, „Assistierter Suizid – Außergewöhnlicher Todesfall?", in: *Sterbehilfe im Fokus der Gesetzgebung*, Frank Petermann, St. Gallen, 2010, p. 257.

however, has enabled organizations to develop an organized practice of assisted suicide in Switzerland.

Indeed, as far as assisted suicide organisations are concerned, it is generally assumed that the charges levied as admission fees and membership fees for their services do not justify selfish motives within the meaning of article 115. Irrespective of any differentiation required in individual cases, it is a fact that the activities of assisted suicide organisations in Switzerland will not be punished, unless they intend to generate a profit. However, the law does not set out any requirement as to the medical condition in which the person seeking suicide assistance should be.

This is the reason why the assisted dying reality in Switzerland is primarily shaped by the regulations of assisted dying organisations and the guidelines of the Swiss Academy of Medical Sciences (SAMS or SAMW).

B. The Practice of the Swiss Assisted Dying Organizations

The two most known assisted dying organisations in Switzerland are Exit and Dignitas.

Exit, created in 1982, offers suicide assistance solely to persons of the age of legal majority with either permanent residence in Switzerland or Swiss citizenship.

The association offers suicide assistance to patients suffering from incurable disease, intolerable suffering or disabling age related polypathologies. The most common diseases suffered by those wishing to commit suicide are terminal cancer, followed by age polymorbidity. Exit (Geneva and Basel) accompanied about 7.266 suicides from 2001 to 2018. The average age of people who were assisted in their suicide was 78 years[372].

Exit states that it has approximatively 130.000 members. It requires an annual fee of 45 Swiss Francs or 1.100 Swiss Francs for lifetime membership. Costs for suicide assistance may be added, between 1.100 and 3.700 Swiss Francs, depending on the length of the membership[373].

Dignitas, founded in 1998, offers suicide assistance irrespective of nationality or residence in Switzerland.

According to statistics published by Dignitas, this association count 9.822 members[374]. Dignitas accompanied 3.027 cases of suicide from its

372 https://exit.ch/verein/jahresberichte/jahresbericht-2018/
373 https://portal.exit.ch/register.
374 In 2019.

foundation in 1998 up to 2019. Most of the people wishing to commit suicide came from Germany (43.67 %), 12.32 % from France and only 6.18 % from Switzerland[375], which explains the frequently used word of "suicide tourism".

Dignitas charges a one-off fee of 200 Swiss Francs in addition to the minimum annual fee of 80 Swiss Francs. Persons wishing to pursue assisted suicide have to pay in addition at least 7.500 Swiss Francs[376].

What is the procedure for an accompanied suicide[377]? The person wishing to die must provide a current letter of diagnosis from their attending doctor and a certification of his or her capacity. A person from the assisted dying association visits the member who wants to die. During these visits, alternative options to suicide are discussed. If the member affirmatively expresses his or her wish to die, the prescription for the death remedy will be issued, either by the treating doctor of the person wishing to die or by a consultant doctor of the organization. The assisted dying organization then redeems the prescription at the pharmacy in the name of the patient with his power of attorney. On the date and within the conditions set by the person who wants to die (at home, in rooms provided...), in the presence of witnesses, the accompanying person delivers the lethal drug that the person who wants to die has to take himself. This is usually Pentobarbital Sodium which is drunk with water. Death usually occurs a short time thereafter through a combination of breathing and cardiac arrest. As this is an unnatural death, the competent authorities must be notified after death has occurred. If the inquiry shows the absence of selfish motives, these are open and shut cases.

C. The Role of the Swiss Medical Profession

The lethal drug used by these well-known assisted dying organizations is Pentobarbital Sodium. It is subject to the prescription requirement (Articles 24 and 26 Therapeutic Products Act (*Heilmittelgesetz*) and Articles 9 and 10, 1st paragraph Narcotics Act (*Betäubungsmittelgesetz*)).

---

375 http://www.dignitas.ch/images/stories/pdf/statistik-ftb-jahr-wohnsitz-1998-2019.pdf.

376 http://www.dignitas.ch/images/stories/pdf/informations-broschuere-dignitas-f.pdf, p. 13.

377 Cf. Exit, *Selbstbestimmung im Leben und im Sterben* (*information booklet*), p. 20, 21, available in German at: https://exit.1kcloud.com/ep15e6764e64899b/#20.

The prescription requirement of Pentobarbital Sodium was subject to a decision of the Suisse Federal Court in 2006[378]: A man who considered his life no longer worthy of human dignity due to an illness that was difficult to treat (he suffered from a severe bipolar affective disorder) joined Dignitas after two failed suicide attempts. But no medical prescription of Pentobarbital Sodium could be made available for him. He was of the opinion that, as a person with capacity, he had a right to this lethal drug in order to be able to end his own life without risk and pain. However, the Federal Court of Justice did not grant his request.

According to the ruling, the right to self-determination and the right to one's own death don't include the right to obtain suicide assistance. The State has primarily the duty to protect life. This does not mean that the State will go against an expressly wish of a person who wants to end his life, but it doesn't mean either that the State have an obligation to provide lethal drugs to assisted dying organization or to those people who wish to die.

For the implementation of the freedom to decide on the termination of one's own life, an unconditional release of Pentobarbital Sodium is not necessary. The judges ruled that the fact that possible alternatives to suicide are more risky or more painful is not enough to legitimize the prescription-free dispensing of Pentobarbital Sodium for the purpose of suicide. The prescription-only dispensing of Pentobarbital Sodium is intended to protect the health and safety of the population, to prevent criminal offences and to combat the risk of abuse in order to maintain public order[379]. A substance, the ingestion of which is intended to lead to death, cannot be given by the chemist alone and in ignorance of the circumstances. It requires a prior medical prescription also in the interest of the patient. The medication requires a diagnosis, indication and an informative discussion taken in accordance with the duties of the medical profession. Also the examination of the patient's capacity, the medical documents and the assessment of whether all possible treatment measures have been taken or have remained without result can ultimately only be carried out by a physician.

The judgement made clear that the assisted suicide with Pentobarbital Sodium requires always the assistance of a physician.

In this context, the revision of the medical-ethical guidelines of the Swiss Academy of Medical Sciences (SAMS or SAMW) is important. They

378 BGE 133 I 58.
379 BGE 133 I 58, p. 70.

were revised in 2018. According to these guidelines, assisted suicide is "*not a medical action to which patients could claim to be entitled*" but the guidelines also make clear that "*assisted suicide is a legally permissible activity*"[380].

In addition to the legal requirement that the final action in the process leading to death must always be performed by the patient, these guidelines approve physician-assisted suicides if the following conditions are met[381]:

> *The patient has capacity in relation to assisted suicide. It must be documented that incapacity has been carefully excluded by the physician. If a mental disorder, dementia or another condition frequently associated with lack of capacity is present, capacity must have been assessed by an appropriate specialist.*
> *The patient's desire is well-considered* (he doesn't act out of affect), *not due to external pressure and enduring* (i.e. constant). *If there is evidence of a problematic relationship of dependency* (for example in the form of a problematic care situation or problematic financial situation), *careful consideration must have been given to its possible influence on the desire for suicide.*
> *The symptoms of disease and/or functional impairments are a source of intolerable suffering for the patient.*
> *Medically indicated treatment options and other types of assistance and support have been sought and have proved ineffective or are rejected as unacceptable by the patient, who has capacity in this regard.*
> *The patient's desire not to continue living in this situation of intolerable suffering is comprehensible for the physician on the basis of the previous history and repeated discussions, and the physician finds it justifiable to perform assisted suicide in this particular case.*

If these conditions are fulfilled, physicians can perform assisted suicide in line with the guidelines.

What is striking is that the medical-ethical guidelines of the Academy do not make any minimum requirement regarding the state of illness or the probable natural time of death of the person who is willing to die. They merely link to the element of intolerable suffering. This is a major change compared with the previous guidelines, who only admitted assisted

380 Swiss Academy of Medical Sciences, *Management of Dying and Death, Medical Ethical Guidelines*, Bern: SAMW, 2018, p. 22.

381 *Ibid.*, p. 23.

suicide where the end of life was near[382]. But "intolerable suffering" is a subjective term, not objectively measurable or quantifiable. This may in principle include for example fragile or depressive young people or elderly people who are tired of life, even without any medical indication.

It is interesting to note that the Swiss Medical Association (FMH), which usually automatically adds the Academy's guidelines to the Code of Medical Ethics, has refused to incorporate them because of the vagueness and vastness of their terms[383].

Conclusion

The key is to find the right balance between, on the one hand, the option to put an end to unbearable suffering, and, on the other hand, ensuring that such option does not lead to a trivialization of assisted suicide. The failure to reach such balance is likely to lead to certain risks, especially in western societies increasingly characterized by individualism and the isolation of elderly people. We must always bear in mind that the issue at hand is broader than the termination of an individual's life. It carries consequences on the development of our society as a whole.

Selected bibliographic references

F. Petermann, *Sterbehilfe im Fokus der Gesetzgebung*, Zürich: Schulthess, 2010, 384 p.

C. Rehmann-Sutter, A. Bondolfi, J. Fischer, M. Leuthold (Hrsg.), *Beihilfe zum Suizid in der Schweiz. Beiträge aus Ethik, Recht und Medizin*, Frankfurt: Peter Lang, 2006, 376 p.

C. Schwarzenegger, I. Makoto (Hrsg.), *Autonomie am Lebensende – Kultur und Recht. Die aktuelle Diskussion in der Schweiz und in Japan*, Zürich: Dike Verlag, 2018, 159 p.

Swiss Academy of Medical Sciences, *Management of Dying and Death, Medical Ethical Guidelines*, Bern: SAMW, 2018, 35 p.

P. Venetz, *Suizidhilfeorganisationen und Strafrecht*, Zürich: Schulthess, 2008, 351 p.

382 Cf. Swiss Academy of Medical Sciences, *End-of-life care, Medical Ethical Guidelines*, Basel: SAMW, 2004, revised in 2013, p. 4.

383 N. STAFFORD, "Swiss doctors object to new suicide guidance", BMJ, 2018, 361.

CHAPTER V: Comparative law perspectives on end-of-life legislation: England – India – Japan

Dr. Richard Wai Ming Law, Consultant Physician in Acute Medicine, Department of Urgent Care, Tameside & Glossop NHS Foundation Trust, Ashton-under-Lyne, UK, *End-of-Life Care in the UK from a Resource Allocation Perspective*

A. Introduction

End-of-Life care is an area of intensive research for health planning and policy. Discourses on how best end-of-care care is delivered remain important discussions for all healthcare policy makers globally.[384] Patients approaching towards their terminal stage of life may at some point have engaged with the healthcare system to receive necessary critical care, cancer-related treatments, or formal institutionalised care. Some individuals that are approaching the last year of life, may have benefitted from resource-intensive treatments prior to death; whilst for others this may not necessarily hold true and for this cohort of patients, earlier palliative care interventions may have been more appropriate.[385] Though various observational research have demonstrated that significant amounts of medical resources are utilised for the care of patients who may be approaching end of life,[386] there remains a paucity of evidence as to the impact and extent how healthcare decisions in relation to resource allocation, rationing, and prioritisation affects healthcare delivery to this specific cohort of patients.[387]

With continuing advances made in medicine, and in particular life-sustaining care, such treatments require substantial medical resources to re-

---

384 M. Wright, J. Wood, T. Lynch, D. Clark, "Mapping Levels of Palliative Care Development: A Global View" *Journal of Pain and Symptom Management* 35:5 (2008) p469–485.

385 S. Karnik, A. Kanekar, "Ethical Issues Surrounding End-of-Life Care: A Narrative Review" *Healthcare* 4 (2016) p24

386 S. Wouters, J. van Exel, R. Baker, W. Brouwer, "Priority to End of Life Treatments? Views of the Public in the Netherlands" *Value in Health* 20:1 (2017) p107–117

387 M. A. Baily, "Futility, Autonomy, and Cost in End-of-Life Care" *The Journal of Law, Medicine & Ethics* 39 (2011) p172–182.

alise. Access to these treatments may be affected by decisions made by healthcare planners whom are continually conscious of the likely costs needed to secure availability in a manner that is comprehensive, fair, and based on clinical needs of patients.[388] Moreover, with the imperative that medical resources ought to be best utilised with maximal benefit, priority is often afforded to patients who are judged to benefit the most and quickly from resource-intense forms of care.[389] Therefore, individuals deemed to be approaching end of life would potentially benefit more if medical resources were invested into their palliative care rather than on treatments that may be medically futile.[390]

With an ageing population and increasing number of individuals with complex combinations of chronic illnesses, the population demographic of the UK is comparatively similar to any developed country with universal medical coverage.[391] Furthermore, as people are living longer; the expectation is to live longer irrespective to the likely quality of life. Therefore, patients may present to the healthcare system with clinical problems that may be difficult to manage and expensive to treat.[392] With the majority of the UK healthcare expenditure reserved for care of older adults,[393] decisions on how these resources are allocated significantly impacts on healthcare delivery.[394]

This paper explores the impact that resource allocation and healthcare prioritisation exerts on the provision of end-of-life care for patients engag-

---

388 L. A. Guindo, M. Wagner, R. Baltussen, D. Rindress, J. van Til, P. Kind, M. M. Goetghebeur, "From efficacy to equity: Literature review of decision criteria for resource allocation and healthcare decision making" *Cost Eff Resour Alloc* 10 (2012)

389 C. Mannelli, "Whose life to save? Scarce resources allocation in the COVID-19 outbreak" *Journal of Medical Ethics* 46 (2020) p364–366.

390 D. Youens, R. Moorin, "The Impact of Community-Based Palliative Care on Utilization and Cost of Acute Care Hospital Services in the Last Year of Life" *Journal of Palliative Medicine* 20:7 (2017) p736–744.

391 R. Robertson, *How does the NHS compare internationally? Big election questions*. The Kings Fund 2017 https://www.kingsfund.org.uk/publications/articles/big-election-questions-nhs-international-comparisons (accessed August 14, 2020)

392 S. M. McPhail, "Multimorbidity in Chronic Disease: Impact on Health Care Resources and Costs" *Risk Management and Healthcare Policy* 9 (2016) p143–156

393 D. Howdon, N. Rice. "Health Care Expenditures, Age, Proximity to Death and Morbidity: Implications for an Ageing Population" *Journal of Health Economics* 57 (2018) p60–74.

394 I. Rodriguez Santana, M. Aragón, N. Rice, A. R. Mason, "Trends in and drivers of healthcare expenditure in the English NHS: a retrospective analysis" *Health Econ Rev* 10 (2020)

ing with the UK healthcare system from an ethical-legal perspective. This is presented in several sections with each addressing an area relating to resource-intensive treatments in a resource-finite healthcare setting. A general background on how resources are distributed throughout the National Health Service (NHS) is presented with a focus on how this would affect end-of-life decision making. This is followed with a discussion on how resource allocation impacts on end-of-life care. Finally, English case law in relation to resource allocation is reviewed. This paper will conclude that although end-of-life care is rather under-resourced in the NHS, promulgating its utility may be effective in reducing patients from undergoing treatments that are clinically inappropriate or medically futile. Early palliative care interventions for patients at the end of life may be conducive to a productive allocation of NHS resources.

B. Resource Allocation in the NHS

In the UK, the health of the population and the provision of healthcare is considered to be a collective social responsibility rather than an individual luxury.[395] The wholly tax-payer funded NHS provides a comprehensive and universal medical cover to the general public that is free at the point of use and based on clinical need. Since its creation in 1948, the NHS promotes its primary objectives which include nationwide financing of healthcare services, control of healthcare distribution, appropriate service planning, and coordination of its delivery.[396] The annual budget allocated to the NHS by the UK government for the financial year 2019/20 was in excess of £134 billion.[397] Though the NHS enjoys year-on-year increases in funding, financial pressures created by significant overspending within the NHS has been observed over the recent decades.[398] Financial sustainability of the NHS is paramount and allocative decisions determines how the NHS strategically utilises its budget to provide universal medical coverage.

---

395 D. B. Resnik, "Responsibility for health: personal, social, and environmental" *Journal of Medical Ethics* 33 (2007) p444–445

396 F. Mosley and S. Lockwood, "Prioritizing Clinical Care in the Cash-Strapped NHS" *Surgery* 36:9 (2018) p491–496.

397 NHS Providers, *On the Day Briefing: March 2020 Budget*. London: NHS Providers https://nhsproviders.org/media/689303/nhs-providers-briefing-march-2020-budget.pdf (accessed August 14, 2020)

398 National Audit Office, *NHS Financial Sustainability* (London: NAO, 2019)

Hence, resource allocation, healthcare rationing, and priority setting are no strangers to the NHS.[399]

The size of the NHS budget is determined by various factors determined at the national (*macro*) level and the local (*micro*) level.[400] The UK central government decides on how much money should be allocated to the NHS at each of the four devolved nations of the UK.[401] The NHS in each of the respective nations, then appropriate funding to local Clinical Commissioning Groups (CCG). Decisions made within these groups, which are accountable to the Secretary of State for Health and Social Care, ultimately affects patient access of all clinical treatments within each locality. Such decisions are informed by local demographic data, patient clinical outcomes, and previous budgetary spending.[402] In addition, these factors may also contribute to observable regional differences in healthcare across the country and variations in healthcare delivery between individual hospitals. In England, CCGs control approximately 60 % of the total NHS budget and is primarily used to finance most hospital-based healthcare.[403]

Analytical studies have demonstrated that complex care for older adults commands a significant proportion of the total NHS budget dedicated to hospital based care.[404] Unfortunately, emergency hospital settings are not designed to provide long-term care for patients with chronic and complex

399 R. W. M. Law, K. A. Choong, "Covid-19: Refracting decision-making through the prism of resource allocation" *The Medico-Legal Journal* 88:2 (2020) p97–101

400 M. Igoumenidis, P. Kiekkas, E. Papastavrou, "The gap between macroeconomic and microeconomic health resources allocation decisions: The case of nurses" *Nursing Philosophy* 21:1 (2020); A. Herlitz, "Committing to Priorities: Incompleteness in Macro-Level Health Care Allocation and Its Implications" *Journal of Medicine and Philosophy* 43 (2018) p724–745

401 UK Parliament. *Funding and Commissioning Information* (London: UK Parliament, 2015)

402 NHS Commissioning Board. *Commissioning Policy: Ethical Framework for Priority Setting and Resource Allocation April 2013 Reference NHSCB/CP/01* (London: NHS Commissioning Board, 2013). https://www.england.nhs.uk/wp-content/uploads/2013/04/cp-01.pdf (accessed November 8, 2018).

403 National Health Service Act 2006. Under section 14R (as amended by the Health and Social Care Act 2012), each CCG is duty bound by legislation to provide medical care to the community it serves.

404 B. Gershlick, J. Kraindler, O. Idriss, A. Charlesworth, *Health and social care funding: Priorities for the new government* (London: The Health Foundation, 2019) https://www.health.org.uk/publications/long-reads/health-and-social-care-funding (accessed August 14, 2020)

care needs.[405] Dedicating finite resources to short term treatments on a *pro re nata* basis for individuals that actually require specialist chronic disease management raises questions about the just allocation of limited resources.[406] As patient demand continues to outstrip healthcare delivery, tensions may develop where patients compete with one another to access appropriate healthcare. Hence, clinicians are often faced with the ethical dilemma of having to prioritise which of their patients should proceed to receive treatment at high cost and in what patient order.[407] Resources are indefinitely limited and this can either affect the provision of treatment to all patients (*not enough resources for everyone*) or the provision of treatment to all patients at a particular point in time (*not all patient can be treated now*).[408] For the NHS to provide both emergency *and* long term care whilst at the same time be financially sound, discussions that involve resource allocation, rationing, and healthcare prioritisation are unavoidable.[409]

Although not felt by patients engaging with NHS care, all treatments will have a cost impact on the healthcare system. How much money is available and how it is appropriately invested in the various clinical services across the NHS contributes to the notion of finite resources. At the micro-allocation level, factors such as hospital bed capacity (*space*), clinical workforce (*people and time*), equipment and treatment (*commodity*), and organisational *planning* may all be constrained by limited resources.[410] Money may not necessarily be the resource that is in short supply, though it can be the common denominator that informs allocative decision-mak-

405 J. K. Harrison, K. E. Walesby, L. Hamilton, C. Armstrong, J. M. Starr, E. L. Reynish, *et al.* "Predicting discharge to institutional long-term care following acute hospitalisation: a systematic review and meta-analysis" *Age and Ageing* 46:4 (2017) p547–558

406 E. Persson, D. Andersson, L. Back, T. Davidson, E. Johannisson, G. Tinghög. "Discrepancy between Health Care Rationing at the Bedside and Policy Level" *Medical Decision Making* 38:7 (2018) p881–887

407 M. Magelssen, P. Nortvedt, J. H. Solbakk, "Rationing at the Bedside: Immoral or Unavoidable?" *Clinical Ethics* 11:4 (2016) p112–121

408 R. W. M. Law, "Resource-intense Treatments in a Resource-finite Environment" In: *Medical Futility in Paediatrics: Interdisciplinary and International Perspectives*, ed. K. A. Choong (Budapest: Trivent, 2019)

409 A. Charlesworth, K. Bloor. "70 years of NHS Funding: How do we Know How Much is Enough?" *British Medical Journal* 361 (2018): k2373.

410 V.B. Satkoske, D.A. Kappel & M.A. DeVita, "Disaster Ethics, Shifting Priorities in an Unstable and Dangerous Environment" *Critical Care Clinics* 35 (2019) p717–725.

ing. Therefore, maximising utility of resources and optimising healthcare delivery are integral to productive resource allocation.[411]

Healthcare resource allocation cannot be easily defined. The General Medical Council (GMC) professional guidance states that allocative decisions affecting patients' care should be: "…fair, based upon clinical need, and on likely effectiveness of treatments."[412] Furthermore, it also acknowledges that: "… treatment options available to patients may be affected by limits in resources."[413] Medical resource allocation constrains the ability of healthcare professionals to exercise "ideal" clinical practice whilst simultaneously be fair to all patients.[414] Hence, one approach to fair patient access to resource-intensive therapies is on a first-come first served basis.[415] Given that limited resources are incompatible with infinite availability of treatments, to provide unrestricted access to resource-expensive clinical treatments would be financially unsustainable for the NHS.

Though some patients may benefit from one particular expensive therapy more than others,[416] an important consideration may be afforded to the capacity of one individual to benefit quickly to that same treatment.[417] In circumstances such as incurable terminal cancer or advanced dementing illness, a delicate ethical balance ought to be struck between the quantity of life remaining and its likely quality. Proceeding with treatment at high cost for the purpose of simply prolonging life, may not necessarily be conducive to effective utilisation of finite medical resources.[418] However, these value judgements ought to be made against a backdrop that embraces the relevant ethical, legal, clinical, and socio-economic considerations.[419]

---

411 E. H. W. Kluge, "Resource Allocation in Healthcare: Implications of Models of Medicine as a Profession" *Medscape General Medicine* 9:1 (2007) p57

412 General Medical Council. *Leadership and Management for All Doctors* (Manchester: General Medical Council, 2012): para 85 (3).

413 Ibidem, para 84

414 G. Oei, "Explicit Versus Implicit Rationing: Let's Be Honest" *The American Journal of Bioethics* 16:7 (2016) p68–70

415 T. M. John, J. Millum, "First Come, First Served?" *Ethics* 130 (2020) p 179–207

416 M. Pruski, "Experience adjusted life years and critical medical allocations within the British context: which patient should live?" *Medicine, Health Care and Philosophy* 21:4 (2018) p 561–568

417 D. J. C. Wilkinson, E. Butcherine, J. Savulescu. "Withdrawal aversion and the equivalence test" *American Journal of Bioethics* 19:3 (2019) p21–28.

418 N. Daniels, J. Sabin, *Setting limits fairly: Learning to share resources for health*, 2nd ed. (New York: Oxford University Press, 2008)

419 R. W. M. Law, "Resource-intense Treatments in a Resource-finite Environment" In: Medical Futility in Paediatrics: Interdisciplinary and International Perspectives, ed. K. A. Choong (Budapest: Trivent, 2019); V. R. Droog, J. van Exel,

Where end-of-life care is concerned, such decisions may not only be a matter of life and death, but also shapes what it means by a dignified end to life. Perhaps, medical resources strategically dedicated to end-of-life care and early palliative interventions might potentially offer a means to effective resource allocation.[420]

C. End of Life Decision-making from the Perspective of Resource Allocation

Inappropriate access to resource-intensive medical interventions may place financial burdens on the NHS. From a resource allocation perspective, devoting resources into life-sustaining treatments to save critically impaired patients with poor prognoses may not necessarily produce benefit to society or be conducive to the maximal utility of available resources.[421] Some commentators observe that this might be an injustice to those (who are not at the end of life) being deprived of medical treatment.[422] Therefore, resources invested to treat one patient may in effect preclude another to the same treatment.[423]

Whilst professional codes of practice affirm that physicians are not obliged to provide treatments on patient demand or to keep their patients healthy,[424] any rights of the patient to specific treatment are likely to be limited.[425] The GMC advises that physicians may offer to their patients

---

W. Brouwer, "Who Should Receive Treatment? An Empirical Enquiry into the Relationship between Societal Views and Preferences Concerning Healthcare Priority Setting" *PLoS ONE* 13:6 (2018) e0198761

420 E. French, M. De Nardi, E. Kelly, "End-of-life medical spending in last twelve months of life is lower than previously reported" *Health Affairs* 36:7 (2017) p 1211–1217

421 N. A. Al-Saad, C. Skedgel, J. Nortje, "Principles of Resource Allocation in Critical Care" *BJA Education* 17:12 (2017) p 390–395.

422 A. Puyol., "The Uncomfortable Truths of Healthcare Prioritisation," in *Prioritising Health Services or Muddling Through*, ed. J. E. del Llano-Señarís and S. Peiró-Moreno (Madrid: Springer Healthcare, 2018), p 125–143

423 J. Glover, "The Role of Physicians in the Allocation of Health Care: Is Some Justice Better than None?" *Kennedy Institute of Ethics Journal* 29:1 (2019) p 1–31

424 GMC (2008) *Withholding and withdrawing life-prolonging treatments: Good practice in decision making*, General Medical Council, London

425 L. McCrossan, R. Siegmeth, "Demands and Requests for 'Inappropriate' or 'Inadvisable' Treatments at the End of Life: What Do You Do at 2 o'clock in the Morning When …?," *British Journal of Anaesthesia* 119:S1 (2017) p i90-i98.

"*treatment that are clinically appropriate and of greatest benefit to which the patient can either accept or decline*."[426] Moreover, the GMC in its publication 'Treatment and care towards the end of life' advises physicians that: "*you should not withdraw or decide not to start treatment if doing so would involve significant risk for the patient and the only justification is resource constraints*."[427] Though the publication provides a practical approach for the physician on end-of-life care, it recognises that "*Decisions about what treatment options can be offered may be complicated by resource constraints – such as funding restrictions on certain treatments in the NHS*".[428] The regulator appreciates that "*In such circumstances, you must provide as good a standard of care as you can for the patient, whilst balancing sometimes competing duties towards the wider population, funding bodies, and employers*".[429]

The relationship between an individual's quantity and quality of life and the values attributed to it, is difficult to characterise.[430] Understandably, this relationship is likely to encompass the complex combination of social, economic, clinical, and ethical issues pertinent to the individual. Therefore, to simply analyse end-of-life care through the lens of resource allocation without due regard to these factors may undervalue what palliative care can contribute to the patient and to the wider society. Hence, it is unsurprising that the wider public would expect that should they themselves require future end-of-life care, the option of high quality palliative care ought to be available irrespective of the likely costs involved.[431]

Decision-making relating to end-of-life care is a difficult process for the healthcare professional and is often wrought with ethical dilemmas.[432]

---

426 General Medical Council. *Consent: Patients and Doctors Making Decisions Together* (Manchester: General Medical Council, 2008) https://www.gmc-uk.org/ethical-guidance/ethical-guidance-for-doctors/consent/part-2-making-decisions-about-investigations-and-treatment (accessed June 4, 2020).

427 General Medical Council. *Treatment and Care Towards the End of Life: Good Practice in Decision-making*. Manchester: General Medical Council, 2010: para 39. https://www.gmc-uk.org/-/media/documents/Treatment_and_care_towards_the_end_of_life___English_1015.pdf_48902105.pdf (accessed June 4, 2020).

428 Ibidem, para 37

429 General Medical Council. *Good medical practice* (Manchester, General Medical Council, 2013), para 56.

430 A. Gawande, "Quantity and Quality of Life – Duties of Care in Life-Limiting Illness" *JAMA* 315:3 (2016) p267–269

431 S. Mitchell, A. Tan, S. Moine, J. Dale, A. Murray Scott, "Primary palliative care needs urgent attention" *BMJ* 365 (2019) I1827

432 E. J. Draper, M. A. Hillen, M. Moors, J. C.F. Ket, H. W.M. van Laarhoven. I. Henselmans, "Relationship between physicians' death anxiety and medical

Clinicians may be reluctant to diagnose a patient as dying and hence may continue to recommend treatments irrespective of whether it would change the overall prognosis of the clinical condition. Perceivably, apprehension among healthcare professionals with holding end-of-life discussions with their patients may reflect their professional failures. In such circumstances, patients may have a medical history of having previously undergone resource-intensive treatments. Therefore, altered expectations, heightened emotions and a sense of defeat may affect end of life decision-making.

The supply of and the demand for end-of-life care is dependent on the age demographics, social deprivation, and the ethnicity mix of the local population. The priorities in palliative care of the dying individual are similar irrespective of the underlying medical condition.[433] The shift of focus from disease-based cures to symptom-based care can be facilitated by specialist teams in palliative medicine. The identification of relevant best interests, priorities, and preferences often begins with an understanding between the clinician and the patient that the medical condition suffered is incurable, terminal, and that nothing more can be done to alter the likely clinical course of the condition. Subsequent individualised end-of-life care plans are formulated based on those clinical priorities and patient preferences. Resources and support afforded end-of-life care planning thus heavily influences patient access to a responsive palliative care service.[434]

D. The Impact of Resource Allocation on End-of-Life Care

Optimising and achieving a high-quality end-of-life care service may materially be cost-saving in the long term.[435] Patients receiving appropriate end-of-life care may experience fewer unanticipated clinical "crises"; as a consequence, they contribute to an improved quality of life with fewer

---

communication and decision-making: A systematic review" *Patient Education and Counseling* 102:2 (2019) p 266–274

433 K. A. Lorenz, J. Lynn, S. M. Dy, L. R. Shugarman, A. Wilkinson, R. A. Mularski, *et al.* "Evidence for Improving Palliative Care at the End of Life: A Systematic Review" *Annals of Internal Medicine* 148:2 (2008) p147–159

434 A. Haycox, "Optimizing Decision Making and Resource Allocation in Palliative Care" *Journal of Pain and Symptom Management* 38:1 (2009) p45–53

435 Ibidem, at p 48

hospitalisations.[436] Ensuring effective resource allocation to palliative care is dependent on two factors: enabling that resources allocated to end-of-life care achieve maximal patient benefit *and* that the effect of the total allocated resources leads to optimal palliative healthcare delivery.

The value an individual would place on the quality of life over quantity (*or vice versa*) is often difficult to determine from a resource allocation perspective. Though patient objectives in end-of-life care delivery are individualised and specific, the concept of what a "dignified death" means is near-universal.[437] Palliative care provisions often require continual reassessments to ensure appropriate responses to each patient's dynamic physical and psychological care needs nearing end of life.[438] Responding to change in care needs requires effective mobilisation of medical resources. Those resources may simply extend beyond money, for example: adequately trained healthcare professionals, administrators to coordinate care delivery or availability of hospice care beds.[439]

Palliative care in the NHS present unique challenges to resource allocation.[440] The NHS deploys a high degree of control on how the healthcare system conducts its clinical activities across all specialties. In relation to palliative medicine, the NHS is a minority stakeholder. The voluntary sector currently provide approximately 80 % of all adult inpatient palliative care at community hospices; whereas the NHS hold only a minority of inpatient beds dedicated to end-of-life care.[441] These peculiar arrangements make cost-effectiveness analyses on end-of-life care rather challenging and open to regional variations. Therefore, the optimal model of end-of-life care cannot be entirely determined nationally. Indeed, overarching bench-

---

436 M. Chapman, N. Johnston, C. Lovell, L. Forbat, W. M. Liu, "Avoiding costly hospitalisation at end of life: findings from a specialist palliative care pilot in residential care for older adults" *BMJ Supportive & Palliative Care* 8 (2018) p102–109.

437 C. J. Evans, L. Ison, C. Ellis-Smith, C. Nicholson, A. Costa, A. O. Oluyase, *et al.* "Service Delivery Models to Maximize Quality of Life for Older People at the End of Life: A Rapid Review" *The Milbank Quarterly* 97 (2019) p113–175.

438 J. Russell, "Conversational planning about end-of-life care: health care provider reported resources, prioritization, and knowledge" *Journal of Communication in Healthcare* 11:1 (2018) p 48–55

439 S. Pearce, D. Kelly, W. Stevens, "'More than just money'– widening the understanding of the costs involved in cancer care" *Journal of Advanced Nursing* 33 (2001) p371–379.

440 J. Abel, A. Kellehear, "Palliative care reimagined: a needed shift" *BMJ Supportive & Palliative Care* 6 (2016) p21–26.

441 P. Edmonds, "Organization of palliative care services" *Medicine* 32:4 (2004) p2–3

marking end-of-life care principles promulgated nationally could guide palliative care at the local level.[442]

Any evaluative assessment of the impact that resource allocation exerts on palliative care requires a beginning and an end. Insofar as patient-centred care is concerned, the process begins with the patient requiring end-of-life care having exhausted active therapies in the effort to treat the terminal illness; and ends with the patient's death.[443] A major barrier to the evaluation of end-of-life healthcare is that it is often not standardised across the NHS.[444] Therefore, clear definitions of end-of-life care and consistent parameters by which to assess the quality and appropriateness of the care offered are essential. With better healthcare planning in palliative and end-of-life care, finer cost-effective analyses, and improved standardisation of service delivery, it follows that these can contribute to productive resource allocation.[445]

Whilst early patient access to end-of-life care interventions may be a strategy to conserve finite resources by minimising life-sustaining treatments that may be deemed inappropriate, futile, or not cost-effective, decision-making of this nature is rather complicated.[446] Conceivably, clinical situations may arise where patients and their families dispute clinical recommendations of palliative care. The reasons that motivate patients to demand life-sustaining treatment that are contrary to medical opinion are complex.[447] These are likely to be highly personal and are of specific importance to the individual and to their families. As such, reasons un-

---

442 J. L. Phillips, E. J. Halcomb, P. M. Davidson, "End-of-Life Care Pathways in Acute and Hospice Care: An Integrative Review" *Journal of Pain and Symptom Management* 41:5 (2011) p 940–955

443 N. R. O'Connor, D. J. Casarett, "Which Patients Need Palliative Care Most? Challenges of Rationing in Medicine's Newest Specialty" *Journal of Palliative Medicine* 19:7 (2016) p696–7

444 N. Ahmed, J. E. Bestall, S. H. Ahmedzai, S. A. Payne, D. Clark, B. Noble, "Systematic review of the problems and issues of accessing specialist palliative care by patients, carers and health and social care professionals" *Palliative Medicine* 18:6 (2004) p 525–542.

445 L. M. Fleck, "Controlling Healthcare Costs – Just Cost Effectiveness or 'Just' Cost Effectiveness?" *Cambridge Quarterly of Healthcare Ethics* 27 (2018) p271–283

446 R. Müller, S. Kaiser, "Perceptions of medical futility in clinical practice – A qualitative systematic review" *Journal of Critical Care* 48 (2018) p78–84.

447 D. Wilkinson, R. Truog, J. Savulescu, "In favour of Medical Dissensus: Why we Should Agree to Disagree about End-of-Life Decisions" *Bioethics* 30:2 (2016) p109–118

derlying patient demand for clinically inappropriate or medically futile treatments should be handled sensitively.

Decisions to delay end-of-life care and continuing with life-sustaining treatment whilst the court formulates its judgement are not unusual. Whether these decision are made at the bedside or in a courtroom, it remains the case that they are likely to be challenging. Likely precipitants for such legal disputes may include disagreements between the healthcare professionals and the patient (and the family) concerning appropriate treatment and the decision-making processes deployed that led to the recommendation of end-of-life care. Where a legal dispute occurs concerning withdrawal of life sustaining treatment in favour for palliative care, the court would seek to determine whether a common ground exist between the clinicians and patient (*and* family) involved. This will be explored in the next section.

E. Legal issues arising from withdrawal of treatment at end-of-life

In English case law, doctors are not legally bound to provide treatments that are considered clinically inappropriate or medically futile *irrespective of demand*.[448] Some commentators have stated that doctors are acting ethically if: (i) *they do not provide treatment judged inappropriate, futile, or contrary to the best interests of the patient*;[449] and (ii) *they do not provide treatment where resources are not available for this*.[450] Whilst most disagreements on life-sustaining treatment may eventually be settled through dialogue between clinicians and patients, breakdown of trust between the parties may lead to a protracted dispute. Judicial review may be brought if patients (or their family) believe that medical resource allocative decisions affecting them were illegal, irrational, or on grounds of procedural impropriety.[451]

448 *Re J (A Minor) (Wardship: Medical Treatment)* [1990] 3 All ER 930.

449 T. M. Pope, "Legal Duties of Clinicians When Terminally Ill Patients with Cancer or Their Surrogates Insist on 'Futile' Treatment," *ASCO Post* (March 2018).

450 D. Wilkinson, S. Petrou, J. Savulescu, "Expensive Care? Resource-Based Thresholds for Potentially Inappropriate Treatment in Intensive Care," *Monash Bioethics Review* 35 (2018) p 2–23.

451 *Re B* [1981] 1 WLR 421; *Re C (A Minor)* [1989] 2 All ER 782; *Re J (A Minor) (Wardship: Medical Treatment)* [1990] 3 All ER 930; *Re R (Adult: Medical Treatment)* [1996] 2 FLR 99.

Based on existing case law, the court may support refusal to provide a particular medical treatment if it can be demonstrated that the treatment is medically contraindicated.[452] Courts recognise that doctors cannot be compelled to pursue a particular course of treatment for a patient, but it can determine whether the treatment would be in the patient's best medical interests. In the widely publicised case of *R v Cambridge Health Authority ex parte B*, which concerned a 10-year-old child with acute leukaemia, the child's father sought to overturn the decision of refusal from the health authority to fund further chemotherapy and a bone marrow transplant over palliative care.[453] The health authority believed that any *benefits* of further chemotherapy and transplant were unproven and that the *costs* had greatly outweighed all perceived benefits. In the ruling, Laws J opined that decision-makers must "*do more than to toll the bell of tight resources*" and that the health authority must clarify their decision-making processes that had led them to refuse treatment. This judgement was subsequently overturned at the Court of Appeal and that "*courts should concentrate on the lawfulness of the decision rather than on its merits.*" Sir Thomas Bingham MR developed this further:

I have no doubt that in a perfect world any treatment which a patient or a patient's family sought would be provided if doctors were willing to give it, no matter how much it cost, particularly when a life was potentially at stake. It would however, in my view, be shutting one's eyes to the real world if the court were to proceed on the basis that we do live in such a world. It is common knowledge that health authorities of all kinds are constantly pressed to make ends meet. They [health authorities] cannot pay their nurses as much as they would like; they cannot provide all the treatments they would like; they cannot purchase all the extremely expensive medical equipment they would like; they cannot carry out all the research they would like; they cannot build all the hospitals and specialist units they would like. Difficult and agonising judgments have to be made as to how a limited budget is best allocated to the maximum advantage of the maximum number of patients. This is not a judgment which the court can make. In my judgment, it is not something that a health authority such as this authority can be fairly criticised for not advancing before the court.[454]

452 *Re J (A Minor) (Child in Care: Medical Treatment)* [1992] 2 All ER 614; *Burke v GMC* [2005] EWCA Civ 1003.

453 *R v Cambridge Health Authority ex parte B* [1995] 1 WLR 898.

454 *R v Cambridge Health Authority* [1995] EWCA Civ 43.

The Court of Appeal judgment had in effect determined that the remit of the court was neither to investigate actual decisions nor to consider matters about how finite resources are spent. The court held that its role was to provide scrutiny on whether the processes that led to a particular clinical decision was legal or rational. In that regard, courts may consider whether those making the decisions had the power to do so, whether appropriate procedures were adhered to, the relevant clinical circumstances, and whether those decisions were proportionate. Courts are likely to regard clinicians to be acting reasonably if their decisions were based on established clinical guidelines.[455]

Traditionally, courts have argued that they lacked the clinical expertise to adjudicate on disputes about allocative decisions.[456] Many judges have expressed that decisions regarding treatment should be well left to those who have the necessary competence.[457] This has led to commentators suggesting that the court's over-reliance on medical opinion may affect its impartiality when presiding over disputes between patients and medical professionals over matters involving limited resources.[458] Moreover, judges are likely to apply terms such as "futility, best interests, quality of life, and suffering" when in reality the treatment is unlikely to yield any substantial benefit.[459] In the case of *Re J (a minor) (wardship: medical treatment)*, Lord Donaldson made a cursory comment on finite resources, being mindful not to engage with resource allocation: "[I]t is outwith the scope of this judgment to give any guidance as to the considerations which should determine such an allocation…"[460]

Similarly, in the seminal case of *Airedale NHS Trust v Bland*, the court was likewise very reluctant to enter into any discourse on resource alloca-

---

455 In *Re C (A Baby)* [1996] 2 FCR 569, "[t]he courts do not instruct doctors how they should perform their clinical and professional duties."

456 K. Syrett, "Of Resources, Rationality and Rights: Emerging Trends in the Judicial Review of Allocative Decisions," *Web Journal of Current Legal Issues* (2000). http://www.bailii.org/uk/other/journals/ WebJCLI/2000/issue1/syrett1.html (accessed July 16, 2020).

457 In *R v Central Birmingham Health Authority, ex parte Collier* (1988): "It is not for this court, or indeed any court, to substitute its own judgment for the judgment of those who are responsible for the allocation of resources."

458 K. Syrett, "Courts, Expertise and Resource Allocation: Is There a Judicial 'Legitimacy Problem'?" *Public Health Ethics* 7:2 (2014): 112–122.

459 N. Bhatia, *Critically Impaired Infants and End of Life Decision-making* (Abingdon: Routledge, 2017) p198.

460 *Re J (a minor) (wardship: medical treatment)* [1991] 1 Fam. 33

tion.[461] In the attempt to avoid discussion on the matter, Hoffman LJ intimated that:

The resources of the National Health Service are not limitless and choices have to be made. This qualification on moral duty to provide care did not enter into the argument in this case at all. The Airedale NHS Trust invited us to decide the case on the assumption that its resources were unlimited and we have done so. But one is bound to observe that the cost of keeping a patient like Anthony Bland alive is very considerable and that in another case the health authority might conclude that its resources were better devoted to other patients. We do not have to consider such a case, but in principle the allocation of resources between patients is a matter for the health authority and not for the courts.

Careful not to guide healthcare professionals on how finite resources should be spent, Lord Browne-Wilkinson in *Bland* gave his perspective:

In addition to these ethical questions, the new technology raises practical problems. Given that there are limited resources available for medical care, is it right to devote money to sustaining the lives of those who are, and always will be, unaware of their own existence rather than to treating those who, in a real sense, can be benefited, e.g. those deprived of dialysis for want of resources.

Though it is correct to assume that the NHS has a statutory duty to provide medical treatment, courts appear to appreciate that with finite resources, there cannot be an expectation or duty to provide all conceivable treatments.[462] In *R (on the Application of Coughlan & Ors) v North & East Devon Health Authority*, the court recognised that the Secretary of State for Health though he had a duty to promote a comprehensive healthcare service, he is also entitled to consider the amount of resources available to him and the demands placed on those services under his charge.[463] Furthermore, in *R v Secretary of State for Social Services*, the Court of Appeal determined that there is no absolute duty to provide treatment irrespective of economic decisions taken at the national level.[464]

Legal challenges against healthcare rationing and resource allocation can only be successful on procedural grounds or if it judged to be unreasonable and individual circumstances overlooked. If health authorities cite

461 *Airedale NHS Trust v Bland* [1993] UKHL 17

462 National Health Service Act 2006 s.1 (1b).

463 *R (On the Application of Coughlan & Ors) v North & East Devon Health Authority* [1999] EWCA Civ 1871 para 26.

464 *R v. Secretary of State for Social Services, ex parte Hincks* [1980] 1 B.M.L.R. 93.

that the lack of funding for a particular treatments or indicate that funds are required for higher priority patients, then any legal challenge to clinical decision-making based on these consideration is unlikely to succeed.[465] As the case law demonstrate here, the nub of all legal thinking in relation to resource allocation is that there is no legally enforceable individual right to treatment. Hence, garnering legal support to facilitate patient access to NHS medical treatment is ineffectual.

F. Conclusion

In an ideal world where healthcare resources are infinite, rationing and prioritisation would simply be academic arguments. This is not the case with a healthcare system like the NHS. Notwithstanding the medical advances that enable healthcare professionals to prolong life, financial pressures on the resources affects all who engage with the NHS. As patients cannot receive every treatment conceivable, the imperative for healthcare planners to demonstrate maximal utility from finite resources is inexorable. Medical professionals are compelled to provide cost-effective treatment and to conduct themselves as being fair to all patients using the resources available.

Individuals approaching end of life may not necessarily benefit from continued life-sustaining treatment if such medical interventions interferes with quality of life. Discourses on end-of-life encapsulate the delicate balance between quality and quantity of life and are often wrought with ethical and legal issues. Clinical decision-making in such circumstances could be better facilitated with earlier involvement of dedicated specialists in palliative care, though end-of-life care delivery presents unique resource challenges to the NHS. Historically, little resources were invested into palliative care and the specialty looked towards the voluntary sector to address funding shortfalls. With better investment of NHS resources into a clinically effective end-of-life care service, this measure may on the whole be cost saving as inappropriate or futile treatment may be reduced. Access to resource-intensive treatments may then be available to those who would benefit quickly and maximally.

465 S. Bhattacharya, C. Ghosh, I. Khan, M. Shroti, "Legal support to gain access to medical treatment in the current healthcare system is unproductive" *Medico-Legal Journal* 87:2 (2019) p85–88

When clinicians and their patients do not agree on decisions recommending palliative care, legal action seeking support from the court as a means to demand a particular treatment is neither productive nor helpful. Money to fund treatment may suddenly appear, though this is likely to be due to diversion of existing resources in response to the threat of going to the courtroom. Whilst there have been publicised legal cases where treatments have been denied on grounds of limited resources, the courts have been rather reluctant to engage with the issue. As a consequence, there is no evidence in English case law that taking legal action against clinical decisions would necessarily secure desired treatment(s) demanded for by patients nearing end of life.

Tetsu Isobe, Professeur, Keio University (Tokyo), Haluna Kawashima, Project Associate Professor, Keio University (Tokyo), *Hard law, soft law or self-discipline, which regulation for the medicine at the final stage of life in Japan?*

A. Introduction: End of Life situation in Japan

If there is no End-of-life Act in Japan, it seems to be not only because of social and political debate on the matter but also due to the legal consistency in the regulation of medical practices.

On top of all, let us briefly overview the social background of end-of-life regulation. According to official demographic statistics, in 1960, nearly 70 % of people died at home, and about 20 % died at the hospital. Nowadays, 75 % of people die at the hospital, just under 10 % die in care house, and only 13 % die at home[466]. An overwhelming majority of people dies outside their homes, mostly in hospitals. Consequently, hospitals may be regarded as an environment where unnecessary life-prolonging treatments are performed to many patients who may rather need palliative care. The question of what to do to prevent the patient's pain cannot be avoided.

Faced with this situation, two major policy flows can be highlighted at the moment.

Firstly, home health care and attendance at death bed at home have been promoted. If the patient, his or her family decides so, it must also

466 Ministry of internal affairs, *e-stat*, https://www.e-stat.go.jp/dbview?sid=0003214716 (visited on the 31 August 2020).

be legally acceptable not to take the patient to the hospital even if his or her condition worsens[467]. To make this legally possible, it is necessary to prospect the appropriate legal interpretation or law making.

Secondly, it is desirable that palliative care and medicine such as pain management be enhanced. Even in recent years, the number of hospitals with the specialized department remains small, and eligible subjects to palliative cares are also limited to some patients suffering from cancer. As a consequence, the enhancement of the quality, as well as the quantity of palliative care, is further required.

Based on the above background, the present article looks back at Japan's discussion on euthanasia and death with dignity before pointing out the legal problems that the country is facing in search of better end-of-life medicine system.

B. Euthanasia and Death with dignity

I. Definition and legal framework

The discussion from a criminal law perspective was focused on *euthanasia* where the influence of German law is overwhelmingly strong: many oppose the legalization of euthanasia in fear of eugenic genocide practised in the name of euthanasia. However, there is also a growing debate that euthanasia may be legalized as one of the choices of how to die. The examples of euthanasia laws of the Netherlands and Belgium or the Death with dignity Act in Oregon are often and comprehensively studied in Japan.

Since homicide with consent and suicide assistance are punished in Japan by Article 202 of the Penal Code, any act resulting in shortening someone's life is illegal even though the consent of the person concerned

467 Recently, end-of-life care in the emergency service is discussed. The main questions are, for example, how to respond to the patient in terminal stage who wishes not to be transported to the hospital or not to receive any cardiopulmonary resuscitation (Tokyo Fire Department, Emergency Service Discussion Report, February 2019). Because law requires doctor's diagnosis of death for the patient dead at home without prior medical consultation in 24 hours, it remains to be questioned whether he or she should be transported to the hospital from home only to confirm his or her death, or how to link home, hospital and emergency services.

has been obtained. In order to legalize euthanasia, consistency with such legal disposition is required.

What about the constitutionality of thos dispositions of the Penal Code? While the right to self-determination is supposed to be guaranteed by Article 13 of the Constitution, there is still discussion about whether said right includes the "right to self-determination to death". Even in the affirmative, it is not considered that the Constitution assures individuals a possibility to "obtain" assistance to death. Therefore, according to formal constitutional law studies, Article 202 of the Penal Code cannot be unconstitutional.

Based on the above legal framework, various discussions have been made to enable euthanasia and cessation of treatment.

There are various definitions of euthanasia, but it is often understood as the act which hastens the patient's death by active action (so-called "active euthanasia"). This is the subject of punishment under homicide with consent and suicide assistance. Most of the doctrine considers that in principle, such an act must be regarded as unlawful even with the consent of the person concerned, and there is extremely little room for exceptional justification. Therefore, it must be asked in which situations illegality or liability may be prevented or denied. In the past, so-called mercy killing was ruled to be a justification[468], but the Yokohama district court set up more modern justification requirements centred on the right to self-determination of the patient, as we will see later.

On the other hand, death with dignity may be understood as a situation whereby a medical practitioner refrains from a therapeutic intervention that would have extended the life of a patient suffering from a disease (so-called "reluctant euthanasia"). Recently, it is preferred to refer to it merely as "cessation of treatment" which differs from the withholding of the treatment, which means not to start treatment from the beginning.

1. Courts findings

The Tokai University Hospital Case examined by the Yokohama district court established the legal criteria for euthanasia as well as the cessation of treatment[469]. At Tokai University Hospital, a doctor first took away the drip infusion, catheter and respirator from a 67-year-old man in the terminal stage of cancer and comatose after a request from the patient's

---

468 Nagoya Court of appeal, 22 December 1967, Kokeishu vol. 15, no. 9, p. 674.
469 Tribunal Yokohama, 28 March 1995, Hanji, no 1530, p. 28.

son. The doctor finally injected potassium into the patient, following a request to "please ease him" by the patient's son. The doctor was accused not of withdrawing the vital care but for the injection of potassium. However, the tribunal laid down criteria both for death with dignity and for euthanasia.

First, the criteria for the legally acceptable death with dignity is the following.

1. There is no hope of recovery, and the patient is in a situation where death is inevitable.
2. There is the patient's will to seek the cessation of treatment at the time

Second, the criteria for legally acceptable euthanasia is the following.

1. The patient is suffering from insupportable physical pain.
2. The patient is in a situation where death is inevitable and imminent.
3. All the measures were taken to remove the patient's pain and ease him or her, and there is no alternative way.
4. There is an expression of the patient's will to seek his or her life at the time.

In the case of cessation of treatment, the patient's intention is not limited to explicit and is sufficient to find the estimated will with the support of the so-called "living will", or his or her family. On the contrary, explicit expression of the patient is required for euthanasia.

Since this decision, some academics considered that there is the possibility to acknowledge "an act of euthanasia and cessation of treatment permitted by law". On the one hand, however, regarding euthanasia, it seemed to practitioners that the conditions laid down by the tribunal are impossible to correctly fulfil, not only because of their ambiguity but also due to the difficulty of confirming the sincere will of the patient. On the other hand, it is possible to proceed legally to the cessation of treatment without special law.

The medical professionals were misguided and considered that "no-starting the treatment is not punishable because it means an omission. However, the cessation of treatment is punishable because it means a positive action". In the medical field, even when neither the doctor nor the patient or his/her family thought the treatment was a good solution, the treatment could not be stopped. Under these circumstances, it was very significant that the Supreme Court recognised the possibility of justifying the positive act of cessation of therapy in Kawasaki Cooperative Hospital's case[470], hereinafter described.

The tribunal's judgement in the Tokai Hospital Case was never appealed and therefore final so that it was not clear what position the Supreme Court stood in this respect. The Kawasaki Cooperative Hospital Case was the first case where it has decided on the legality of the cessation of treatment.

In this case, the patient is a 58-year-old man in a vegetative state who lapsed after multiple attacks of asthma. The doctor, believing that leaving the patient to die naturally would be good for him and being asked his family to remove the tracheal tube. However, with his air way closed, the patient showed rough and painful movements and the patient's family asked the doctor to ease the patient. The doctor administered the fatal dose of Myobloc and let him die after trying several medications to suppress his suffering in vain. In this case, the acts of doctors were examined as regards to the cessation of treatment and not for euthanasia. The Supreme Court stated as follows

> According to the developments of the facts..., during the period from when the victim had a severe bronchial asthma attack and was hospitalized until the removal of the tube in question was performed, no electroencephalogram or other test was performed as needed for determining the expected length of the remaining life of the victim. In light of the fact, in addition to this, that the removal of the tube was performed only two weeks after the victim had developed the disease, <u>it can be found that at the time of the removal, it was impossible to make an accurate determination as to the possibility of the victim's recovery or the expected length of his remaining life (...). As it is found from the circumstances described above, the victim's family members did not make such request after being properly informed of the victim's conditions, etc.</u> Nor can it be said that the aforementioned act of removing the tube was performed based on the presumed will of the victim. Taking into consideration all of these factors, we should say that the aforementioned act of removing the tube cannot be regarded as cessation of treatment that is legally permitted (emphasis added).

Why was the physician found guilty? Firstly, because she had not taken all the measures to correctly evaluate the remaining life of the patient. Secondly, because the patient's will had not been confirmed without the

470 Supreme Court, ch. 3, 7 December 2009, penal, vol. 63, no. 10m p. 1899.

basis of a liable medical diagnosis, the patient – in this case, his family – could not have made his will properly and sincerely. We might say that the doctor's act would have been lawful if these appropriate procedures had been met by her. It is thus legally important to make sure the practitioners follow the due process before ceasing treatment.

C. Moving toward the enactment of "Euthanasia Act" or "Death with Dignity Act" in question

There has long been a movement in Japan to enact euthanasia and death with dignity laws, but so far, it has not resulted in an official draft law. The draft law is promoted by groups typically like "Japan Society for The Life and Death" announced in 1978, and recently in a movement among parliament group called "the Parliamentary federation for reflection on the legislation of death with dignity" (Chairman, Teruhiko Masuko, member of the Democratic Party of Japan). Those revendications aim to legalise euthanasia and "death with dignity" by law, in order to make the patients will carried out by the medical team in a better fashion, but in vain. Why is it so?

On top of the reasons, we should remind the medical law mechanisms in Japan.

Since the first medical system called Isei issued on the 18th August 1874, Japan's medical-related laws have mainly been established on the regulation of medical professionals and medical facilities regulation. The principle underlying this system was that the government refrained from intervention in the medical content. The suitability and opportunity of medical acts are contingent upon each patient's condition and their will, the skill and experience of individual doctors, and individual medical environment such as available equipment. Therefore, an *a priori* and uniformed regulation is not appropriate to the medical act, and it has been entrusted to an *a posteriori* regulation by the Civil and Penal Code for each individual case. In such a principle, the discretion of the doctor who performs the treatment must be respected as much as possible. The Physicians Act is a good example[471]. On the one hand, this law defines physicians' qualification and put in place necessary regulations to assure the fitness of doctors to

471 See. Haluna KAWASHIMA and Tetsu ISOBE, "Le monopole médical au Japon" *in.* LECA, Antoine(dir.) *Le monopole médical en question : France, Etats-Unis, Canada, Japon, Brésil, Vietnam.* LEH Edition, 2019, pp. 185–196.

the highest level. On the other hand, the law establishes a minimum level of regulation from the viewpoint of public health and let qualified doctors apply their skills as freely as possible. Coupling those aspects, the legislator thought that it would be possible to provide the appropriate medical care to the people. In general, medical practices, the high discretion of medical practitioners such as a doctor, is highly respected, and it must remain so. This is because practitioners are experts who place the patient's life and health first and act in their pursuit.

Those are the basic standpoints of the Japanese medical law system. The Japanese legislator is very cautious in prioritising medical care content directly by law or setting up a permit system. The exceptions are extremely limited to the field of organ transplantation and regenerative medicine, etc. The regulation of medical care content is expected to be settled *ex-post-facto* under the Civil Code and punishment under Penal Code when it is necessary for each individual case. This is one of many sound medical systems.

Whether this principle should be applied to end-of-life medicine or, on the contrary, whether end-of-life medicine is so particular that special rules should be sought[472].

According to the principle, if there is a possible treatment and the patient accepts it, the doctors should continue to take care of the patient and apply it to them. On the contrary, if there is neither possible treatment nor the prospect of further improvement, and the patient does not wish to receive any treatment, it might be one of the appropriate steps to stop the treatment. In such a case, to adopt the best legal interpretation to respect the patient's life, the distinctions between an act and an omission, or the non-starting or the withholding of treatment do not bear significance anymore. It can be said that the interpretation to be applied to end-of-life medicine is assimilated to that of the standard medicine, when we seek the interpretation for a better life until the end, while there are various end-of-life choices and self-determination of patients, different life prognosis, and recovery possibilities. In other words, death with dignity is only one aspect of medicine at the end of life. Medicine at the end-of-life does not differ in essence from ordinal medical care, so its evaluation criteria should not be different from that of the ordinal medical practices. If the requirements

472 See. Haluna KAWASHIMA. "La prise de décision dans la médecine au dernier stade de la vie au Japon", E. AUBIN, E. KASAGI, S. KOJIMA, L. LEVOYER et T. SAITO (dir.) *Comment maintenir la qualité de vie des personnes âgées en France et au Japon?*, 2020, pp. 69–73.

for ordinal medical care are not defined by law, the current absence of a provision on end-of-life medicine should follow and deem normal.

However, the cessation of treatment can be considered homicide in certain cases. It is necessary to discuss at least the due process for the legitimate cessation of treatment. The debate over end-of-life medicine in Japan is gradually emphasizing this decision-making process.

I. Guidelines on the decision-making process

In the Kawasaki Cooperative Hospital Case, the Supreme Court has clearly acknowledged the existence of a "legally acceptable cessation of treatment". Still, it specifies neither its requirements nor its ground. Law should not unilaterally fixe the legal requirements on the contents of medical care for the consistency in Japanese medical regulations, and the court insights are appreciated in this way. Stopping the treatment only at the doctor's discretion was a significant factor in the issue, facing the importance of the patient's will. The same type of issue continued to be posed in practice, such as in the so-called Imizu City Hospital case.

Based on the lessons learned from those cases, the Ministry of Health, Labor and Welfare (MHLW) and the medical associations have made increasingly active efforts to examine the appropriate process for determining treatment policies for end-of-life care, and several guidelines have been established. The MHLW has established the *Guidelines on the decision-making process in end-of-life medicine.* These guidelines were straightforward in terms of content and only recommended to "take the best treatment policy" "based on the patient's intention". Simultaneously, there are guidelines established by the medical associations by their initiative, such as the Japan Society of Emergency Medicine's "Proposals for End-of-Life Care in Emergency Medicine" (November 2007). These guidelines were adopted through the careful process with public consultation procedures and provide a definition of end-of-life in emergency medicine as well as a decision process, a way to confirm the will of the patient or his/her family, and a modality of cessation of treatment (including suspension of hydration). A number of other guidelines have been established, such as by the Japanese Academy of Pediatric or the Japanese Geriatrics Medical Association.

We cannot go into all of these guidelines, but we may depict the legal landscape as follows.

At the administrative level, the basic policies and targets are set up: so the technical due process is not taken into account. At the practical level, we may need practical and process guidelines for the end-of-life medicine which propose the appropriate way to confirm the will of the patient and precise the range of possible medical solutions which can vary based on the condition of the patient such as cancer or chronic disease, pediatric, elderly or emergency, etc. The scientific societies draft such practical guidelines according to their field of expertise and their own reasoning and through the reliable process to consider different opinions. It can be said that a "multi-layered structure" with the national guidelines and the practical guidelines is established. Such a normative structure seems to be meaningful as a method to make effective use of the medical profession's autonomy as an institutional foundation.

Suppose there has been no case of prosecution of homicide in the case of cessation of treatment after the Kawasaki Cooperative Hospital case. In that case, it can be considered that these guidelines have contributed to the improvement of the situation. The guidelines are not law, but they show the best process that medical professionals should follow properly to assess to the best the patient's condition and respect the patient's will. Such act performed in accordance with those best practices is conceived as what the Supreme Court has recognised "legally acceptable cessations of treatment".

II. Remaining challenges

The Japanese legal framework of end-of-life care may be seen as defective because there is no recognition by law concerning the status of "advanced directive" or "living will" and "trusted person", and of the rights of patients, especially those who are particularly vulnerable such as minors and legally incompetent persons. However, it seems that the Guidelines of the MHLW shows some hints on this matter.

Initially, these Guidelines were made in 2007 in response to the case of removing a ventilator in Imizu City Hospital, which happened in March 2006[473]. The original Guidelines only define what the appropriate medical care is. It proposed that the medical personnel provide their patients with appropriate information and explanation. The patient's decision made after discussion with them should be the basis of end-of-life treatment poli-

473 In this case, the doctor committed in the withdrawal of respirator from in total seven patients who have been unconscious and had no hope of recovery between 2000 and 2005. The case was sent to the prosecutor, but the doctor was not accused because of insufficient evidence to prove the causation.

cy. Besides, the end-of-life treatment policy must be carefully determined by the medical team rather than at the doctor's discretion.

Then, in March 2018, a significant revision was issued[474].

This revision's background is the ageing of the population and the necessity for the construction of comprehensive community care. It is also remarkable that the concept of ACP (Advanced Care Planning) has become popular, mainly in the UK and the United States, but also among Japanese academics. Especially, the following revisions were made.

In the form, the name of the guidelines was changed to "Guidelines on the decision-making process for medicine and care in the final stages of life" so that the guidelines can also be applied in the home health care and nursing care, and clarified that care workers were included in the medical and care team.

Concerning the respect of patient's will, the basic stand point was shown. The will of the patient can vary according to changes in his or her mental and physical condition, so that the guidelines emphasise the importance of having a discussion, on a daily basis and repeatedly, about the care policy and the life that he or she wants to live. This aims to enable the care team to confirm the patient's will properly in a direct, opportune and express manner. It is also mentioned that the discussion between the patient, family and the care team should be summarised in a document each time and shared between them.

At the same time, the concept of a trusted person was introduced. Before the patient comes to be in a state where he or she cannot communicate his or her will, the Guidelines highlight the importance of designating a person who can be trusted, such as a family member, but not only. In light of the recent social evolution whereby the number of single households is increasing, the conventional family was expanded to the "family and so on" which also includes close friends, etc.

All of this may help the vulnerable people be assured of their interests while the Guidelines do not mention them. There can be various sensitive questions: for example, how is the patient's interest evaluated when he or she has a conflict with some family members? It may be necessary for such a patient to be able to design a trusted person. The Guidelines also recommend that the care team decides the end-of-life care plan after constant discussion with the patient. If the patient cannot express his or her will, the discussion should be held with several members of the patient's

474 The Guidelines were renamed to "Guidelines for the Final Stage Decision Process of Life" in March 2015.

family and a trusted person. If the patient does not have any family or the family leaves the final decision to the care team, the patient's best interest should be sought. By doing so, the Guidelines cover a wide range of people (vulnerable or not vulnerable) and encourage the care team to make a case by case decision for the interest of the patient, which is, for health care workers, not very far from what they ordinarily do in any medical practice.

D. Conclusion

In countries with which Japan shares many social conditions, such as France or Germany, end-of-life medicine itself is a subject of law.

On the contrary, Japan chose, for the moment, to integrate end-of-life medicine into ordinal medicine. The medical professionals are always at the heart of the medical decision-making on the individual patient. If the legislator doesn't intervene in the personal medical practice, it is medical societies that propose appropriate medical treatment as a form of guidelines in order to support practitioners. The self-discipline of medical professional plays a significant role in practice.

On the other hand, it is true that these guidelines were brought by social, academic, technical and case law developments in Japan and overseas. With society changing, reasonable consideration or accommodation to patient's rights, especially to patients in particular vulnerability, will be required in end-of-life medicine. It can be said that practitioners should flexibly approach each patient and respond to the social requirements in the Japanese medical system. However, the limit of their initiative would be the start of the intervention of the public authority. In the case of end-of-life medicine, the patients' procedural protection comes to be emphasised through the Ministry Guidelines. As long as the Guidelines work effectively in practice, the law makers may not be urged to take up its pen.

Bibliographies

Katsunori KAI, "Euthanasia and death with dignity in Japanese law". *International Journal of bioethique* (1998) vol. 21, no. 4, p.135.

Saku MACHINO, "患者の自己決定権と医師の治療義務". Penal law journal, no. 8 (2007) p. 49.

Hitoshi SAEKI, "末期医療と患者の意思・家族の意思. "Juriste, no. 1251(2003)p.106.

Hitoshi SAEKI,"治療の不開始・中止に関する一考察". Lawyers Association journal, vol. 72, no. 6(2020)p.1 – 29.

Satoko TATSUI, "治療不開始/中止行為の刑法的評価--「治療行為」としての正当化の試み". Meiji Gakuin Law Journal, vol. 86(2009) p.57.

Koichi JIMBA, "Emerging Legal and Bioethical Issues Associated with End-of-Life Care for Elderly Prisoners in Japan". *Medicine and Law* (2019) vol. 38, p.597.

Anand N Raut, PhD, Assistant Professor, Maharshtra National Law University Mumbai, *Select Religious Practices and Death: An analysis from Indian legal Perspective*

Abstract

The Constitution of India guarantees the Right to life with dignity, Freedom of religion, conscience and the right to freely profess, practice, propagate religion subject to public order, morality and health. It has often happened that certain religious practices were per se violative of fundamental rights or fell within the reasonable restrictions laid down by the Constitution. Supreme Court laid such anomalies and disputes to rest by either at times disallowing such practices or allowing certain practices if they fell within the ambit of essential religious practices. Recognizing which religious practice is essential and which not has always been tricky and a matter of debate. After practising certain exercises like fasting un to death or taking Samadhi if the practitioner dies, it gives rise to inquiries like whether such practices are permissible under freedom of religion. The Constitution of India does not recognise the Right to die as a facet of the Right to life. Hon'ble Supreme Court of India has recognized only passive euthanasia as a mode of exercising the Right to die with dignity. So it may also be argued that following such religious practices is neither part of Freedom of religion nor the Right to life or die with dignity rather, it is suicide and the practitioner being mentally ill needs care and help.

The paper attempts to explore such select religious practices in India, death, freedom of religion, right to die with dignity, suicide as mental illness and honestly attempts to test them on the touchstone of Constitutional validity.

Keywords – Right to live, Right to die, Freedom of religion, Death

A. Introduction

Constitution of India unequivocally and expressly bestows the right to equality and equal protection of laws, non-discrimination by State on the grounds of religion, race, caste, sex, place of birth or any of them, to live with dignity, to freedom of speech and expression, assemble peaceably, form associations, movement, residence, profession, occupation, trade or business, free compulsory education, right against ex post facto law, double jeopardy and self-incrimination, freedom of religion etc. but is silent upon Right to die. Judiciary in India interpreted Constitution and, at times with an activist robe, included a number of rights within the ambit of fundamental right even though the same were not expressly mentioned in the Constitution. The most crucial is Article 21, which protects the right to life with dignity and can be taken away only with the due procedure established by law. Life meant not just survival of animal existence or adequate nutrition, clothing and shelter but also reading, writing and expressing one's self[475] suitable accommodation allowing to grow physically, mentally and intellectually, means of livelihood,[476] wrongful interference by phone tapping during telephonic communication.[477]It is because of such nature and scope Article 21 of the Constitution of India is helmed as a reservoir of rights. The Constitution of India also recognized Freedom of religion and the right to practice it with reasonable restrictions. After practising certain religious practices, the practitioner may die, so should it be called suicide? or may they be allowed as freedom of religion expressed by the person practising it if the same is not barred by reasonable restrictions? If following such practices are considered as suicide per se, and then law regulating suicide may be attracted, and the practitioner would be sent to rehabilitation.

B. Right to Life and Suicide

The journey of the Right to die to be recognized as a fundamental right was not so easy. Suicide was considered a criminal act under the law[478], and the right to die was not considered part and parcel of the right to life. Law Commission of India[479] advocated the abolition of a law penalising suicide. In State v. Sanjay Kumar Bhatia[480] Hon'ble court observed that

475 Francis Carolie v Delhi AIR 1981 SC 746

476 Olega Tellis v. Bombay Municipal Corporation AIR 1986 SC 180

477 R M Malkani v. State of Maharashtra AIR 1973, SC 157

478 Section 309 Indian Penal Code 1860

479 42nd Report of 1971

480 1986 (10) DRJ 31

"continuance of Section 309 Indian Penal Code is an anachronism unworthy of a humane society like ours." This view got some support in Maruti Shripati Dubal v. State of Maharashtra[481], wherein the Hon'ble Bombay High Court observed that the aforementioned law was violative of the right to equality and the right to live with dignity was to be struck down. The discussion centred around was that as freedom of speech and expression includes freedom not to speak, freedom of business and occupation includes freedom not to do business similarly right to life included right to die. Hon'ble Delhi High Court observed that starting prosecutions under Section 309[482] itself is a mindless mechanical procedure, especially against a person attempting to commit suicide and belonging to a poorer section of society, as it would add further insult to injury.[483] Finally in P Rathinam v. Union of India[484] held that an act of suicide could not be said to be against religion, morality or public policy, and an act of attempted suicide has no baneful effect on society. Further, suicide or attempt to commit it causes no harm to others, because of which State's interference with the personal liberty of the persons concerned is not called for and hence Section 309 of IPC was declared unconstitutional.

Unfortunately, Supreme Court reversed its stand in Gian Kaur v. Union of India[485] and stated that 'to give meaning and content to the word 'life' in Article 21, it has been construed as life with human dignity. Any aspect of life which makes it dignified may be read into it but not that which extinguishes it and is, therefore, inconsistent with the continued existence of life, resulting in effacing the right itself. If any, the right to die is inherently inconsistent with the right to life' as is death' with life'. And hence Section 309 was again held constitutional. Law Commission of India[486] recommended that a person attempting to commit suicide needs medical care and attention.[487] Then came Aruna Shaunbag's case[488], in which the fate of a terminally ill patient had to be decided, and discussion centred

---

481 1987 (1) Bom CR 499

482 Indian Penal Code 1860

483 Court on Own Motion v. Yogesh Sharma Civil Appeal No. 230 of 1985

484 1994 AIR 1844

485 1996 AIR 946

486 196th Report on Medical Treatment to Terminally Ill Patients (Protection Of Patients And Medical Practitioners) 2006

487 Law Commission of India, 196th Report on Medical Treatment to Terminally Ill Patients (Protection Of Patients And Medical Practitioners) 2006 https://lawcommissionofindia.nic.in/reports/rep196.pdf

488 WRIT PETITION (CRIMINAL) NO. 115 OF 2009

on euthanasia or physician-assisted suicide. The discussion eventually led to determine whether the right to life included the right to die. Here Apex Court was of the view that Section 309 was anachronistic and recommended parliament of India to consider the feasibility of deleting the same. It also laid down the procedure of recognizing the right to die of the patient in a permanent vegetative state by removal of life support system on application to and intervention of High Court by near relative or friend. However, interestingly in one of the earlier instances in Naresh Marotrao Sakhre v. Union of India,[489] Hon'ble Court has also observed that Suicide is an act of self-destruction or self-killing. At the same time, Euthanasia or mercy killing implies the intervention of other human agency to end the life, and hence both concepts are factually and legally different. Suicide has now been decriminalized, and attempting to commit suicide is considered to be the result of severe stress. Law imposes a duty upon the Government to provide care, treatment and rehabilitation to a person who has severe stress and has attempted to commit suicide to reduce the risk of recurrence of attempt to commit suicide.

The prominent questions that remain to be answered are i. Whether following of certain religious practice always means an attempt to commit suicide and hence be treated as mental illness ii. Whether such religious practice is religious freedom and hence protected by the Constitution of India

I. Freedom of Religion as a fundamental right in India

The preamble of the Indian Constitution recognizes India as a secular State and bestows freedom of religion. Article 25 to Article 28 recognizes freedom of conscience and the right freely to profess, practise and propagate religion, and religious denominations shall have the right to maintain an institution for religious affairs, manage matters of faith: Freedom as to payment of taxes for promotion of any particular religion, Freedom as to attendance at religious instruction or religious worship in certain educational institutions. These freedoms are not absolute and have reasonable restrictions upon them in the form of public order, morality and health. Fundamental right not allows for entertaining such religious beliefs as may be approved by one's judgment or conscience but also to exhibit one's beliefs and ideas by such overt acts and practices which are sanctioned by

489 1994 (2) MhLj 1850

religion. Practices that are protected by the Constitution are to be decided by the courts with reference to the doctrine of a particular religion and include practices regarded by the community as part of its religion.[490] In another landmark case, while discussing the scope of freedom of religion and carrying out religious practice Hon'ble Supreme Court of India held that 'if a practice is to be treated as a part of the religion then it must be regarded by the said religion as its essential and integral part; otherwise even purely secular practices which are not an essential or an integral part of religion would be clothed with a religious form and may make a claim for being treated as religious practices under Article 26 of Indian Constitution. Also, practices may be carefully scrutinized as they may have sprung from merely superstitious beliefs and are extraneous and unessential accretions to religion itself, and to provide protection under Article, such practices need to constitute an essential and integral part of a religion.'[491] So, 'activities associated with religion but do not really constitute an essential part of it can be regulated by State. What constitutes the essential part of a religion is primarily to be ascertained with reference to the doctrines of that religion itself if the tenets of any religious sect of the Hindus prescribe that offerings of food should be given to the idol at particular hours of the day etc. Would be regarded as parts of religion and the mere fact that they involve the expenditure of money or employment of priests and servants or the use of marketable commodities would not make them secular activities partaking of a commercial or economic character.'[492] Only obligatory overt act to exhibit religious belief was protected.[493] It has to be stressed that protection under Article 25 and 26 is given to only those religious practices which form an essential and integral part of religion for e.g. "A mosque is not an essential part of the practice of the religion of Islam and namaz (prayer) by Muslims can be offered anywhere, even in open."[494] Also the practice of capturing and worshipping live cobra snake was not considered essential to the religion.[495] 'The protection guaranteed under

490 Seshammal v. State of Tamil Nadu (1972) 2 S.C.C. 11

491 Durgah Committee, Ajmer v. Syed Hussain Ali, AIR 1961 SC

492 The Commissioner, Hindu Religious Endowments, Madras v. Sri Lakshmindra Thirtha Swamiar of Shirur Mutt 1954 AIR 282, See Generally Tilkayat Shri Govind Maharaj v. State of Rajasthan AIR 1963 SC 1638

493 Mohammad Hanif Quareshi v. State of Bihar, AIR 1958 SC

494 Dr. M. Ismail Faruqui Etc, Mohd v. Union Of India And Others AIR 1995 SC 605

495 Gramsabha of Village Battis Shirala v. Union of India and Ors' Writ Petition No 8645 of 2013

Article 25 and 26 is not confined to matters of doctrine or belief but extend to acts in pursuance of religion like, rituals, observance, ceremonies, and modes of worship which are essential to religion'. Essential means core beliefs over which religion is founded or cornerstone of practice over which the superstructure is religion built.[496]

The moot question is how to identify whether the practice is essential or not. Two tests laid down in determining whether practice essential or not is i. Whether the nature of religion would be changed in the absence of the practice and absence or alteration will change its fundamental character ii. core belief upon which religion is founded.[497]

Also, Freedom of religion is curtailed by the Constitution of India if it is against public health, morality, law and order.[498] Playing of loud microphones or loudspeakers,[499] sale of firecrackers,[500] refusal to get inoculated against contagious disease[501] is a threat to public health. Carrying lethal weapons like daggers,[502]communal violence[503], outraging religious sentiments[504] etc., is a threat to public order and dedicating girl to Devdasi,[505] exclusion of woman from religious practices[506] etc. is immoral.

II. Select religious practices, death and Mental illness

"Relation between religion and spirituality on one hand and religion and mental health is multi-faceted and complex"[507] so it has to be scrutinised

496 Commissioner of Police v. Acharya Jagdishwarananda Avadhuta 2004 12 SCC 770

497 Ibid

498 Article 25 of Constitution of India 1950

499 Church Of God (Full Gospel) In v K.K.R. Majestic Colony Welfare AIR 2000 SC 2773 See generally Masud Alam v. Commissioner of Police, A.I.R. 1956 Cal. 9.

500 Re: Noise Pollution (2005) 5 SCC 733

501 J. Choudhury v. The State, AIR 1963 Orissa 216.

502 Acharya Jagadiswaranda Avadhuta v. Commissioner of Police Calcutta, AIR 1984 SC 51

503 Shyamal Ranjan Mukherjee v Nirmal Ranjan Mukherjee [AIR 2008 (NOC) 568 (All.),

504 Public Prosecutor v. P. Ramaswamy ,AIR 1964 Mad 258'

505 See Immoral Traffic Prevention Act 1956

506 2018 SCC OnLine SC 1690

507 Bhugara Dinesh, "Commentary: Religion, religious attitudes and suicide", International Journal of Epidemiology' 2010; 39:1496–1498 doi:10.1093/ije/dyq232

carefully. Suicide[508] is forbidden in many religions. Christianity, Islam, Buddhism, Judaism and even in Hinduism, however, there are certain exceptions mentioned in 'holy scripts like smritis, epics, puranas.'[509] It mentioned only when an individual has achieved the highest aesthetic power were authorised to take such actions of ending one's life (Thakur 107).[510] Certain Upanishad speaks of achieving immortality and states that one who knows both not knowledge and knowledge overcomes death through not knowledge and obtains immortality through knowledge.[511] It has also been advised that after attaining a particular age (Seventy Five years) man has to lead a life of a hermit and to subsist on air and water walk towards north-easterly direction till body sinks down in response (F Max Muller 204).[512] In India, there are and were various practices that involve ending one's life like Johar, Sati, Samadhi, Prayopaveshan, Atmarpana, Santhara, Mahaprasthana etc.

1. Johar – Jauhar meant mass immolation by woman.[513]. 'It was done by Rajput women to avoid capture and rape and thereby maintain the boundary lines of the community'.[514] The same was also considered a manifestation of truthfulness, exemplified by a woman's self-sacrifice.[515]

---

508 Durkheim Emile, Suicide. A Study In Sociology Durkheim, Translated by Tr Spaulding and Simpson Routledge 1952 discusses that Suicide is all cases of death resulting directly or indirectly from a positive or negative act of the victim himself, which he knows will produce this result. Suicide is egoistic, altruistic, fatalistic.

509 See Kane P.V, 'History of Dharmashastra', Bhandarkar Oriental Research Insitute, Pune, 2006

510 Thakur Upendra, 'History of suicide,' Munshi Ram Manohar Lal, 1963, p 107

511 See Generally Various Oriental scholars, 'The Sacred Books of the East' Ed. F. Max Müller Vol. I, London, Oxford University, https://holybooks-lichtenbergpress.netdna-ssl.com/wp-content/uploads/01.SacredBooksEast.VarOrSch.v1v2v3comb.Muller.Buhler.Legge_.Oxf_.1879.1897..pdf

512 ("The hermit in the forest", Manu's Code (See : Laws of Manu, translated by George Buhler, Sacred Books of the East edited by F.Max Muller, (1967 Reprint) Vol.25, page 204,J Shlokas 31 ad 32)

513 Harlen Lindsay, 'Religion and Rajput Women The Ethic of Protection in Contemporary Narratives' University of California Press 1991 Chp 6, p 184, https://publishing.cdlib.org/ucpressebooks/view?docId=ft2g5004kg&chunk.id=d0e11569&toc.depth=100&toc.id=d0e11481&brand=ucpress;query=jauhar#1

514 Hardgrove, Anne. "Sati Worship and Marwari Public Identity in India." The Journal of Asian Studies, vol. 58, no. 3, 1999, pp. 723–752 Oct 15, 2019 JSTOR, www.jstor.org/stable/2659117.

515 Ibid

It's an age-old practice, and there has been no reported incidence of Johar over a century.

2. Sati – Sati is 'burning of a widow on the pyre of her husband's dead body'[516]. It was a glorified Hindu tradition and was commemorated by erecting a monument in the sacred memory of a woman who performed Sati.[517] Attempt to commit Sati,[518] abatement to Sati[519] and glorification[520] of practice and glorification of Sati[521] has been illegalized by law in India. Also, any temple of structure used for any form of worship or the performance of any ceremony carried on with a view to perpetuate the honour of or to preserve the memory of any person in respect of whom Sati is to be demolished.[522] Rajasthan Sati (Prevention) Act 1987 and Rajasthan Sati (Prevention) Ordinance, 1987 enacted to prohibit Sati has been held Constitutional and non-violative of Article 25 and 26 of the Indian Constitution.[523] Onkar Singh v. State of Rajasthan it has been held that religious freedom does not mean evil customs to be saddled on the society on the basis of religious freedom. While discussing Tej Singh v. State1958 RLW 19 Hon'ble Court, while relying upon Shastric texts, held that Sati is kind of blind faith and was never regarded as an integral part of religion also rarely it was practised. Also, bad customs like child marriage, Dev dasi, untouchability, animal sacrifice etc. were abandoned. Today's culture, society and societal needs have to be given thought to while discussing religion in modern times.' There have been no incidents of Sati in the recent past.

3. Prayopavesana – It is abstaining from food, mediate and approach death. It's considered as an act of expiation or for the acquisition of reli-

---

516 Singh, B. (2011). THE PRESENT STATUS OF "SATI" MEMORIALS OF MEDIEVAL RAJASTHAN. Proceedings of the Indian History Congress, 72, 1263–1272. Oct 15, 2020, from http://www.jstor.org/stable/44145738

517 SHUKLA, G. British Attitude Towards the Practice of Sati in Gujarat in the 19th Century. Proceedings of the Indian History Congress, 48, 480–482. Retrieved Oct 18, 2020, from http://www.jstor.org/stable/44141743

518 Section 3 of The Commission Of Sati (Prevention) Act, 1987

519 Section 4 of The Commission Of Sati (Prevention) Act, 1987

520 Section 5 of The Commission Of Sati (Prevention) Act, 1987

521 Section 2 (c) of The Commission Of Sati (Prevention) Act, 1987 Sati means the burning or burying alive of (i) any widow along with the body of her deceased husband or any other relative or with any article, object or thing associated with the husband or such relative; or (ii) any woman along with the body of any of her relatives, irrespective of whether such burning or burying is claimed to be voluntary on the part of the widow or the women or other-wise;

522 Section 7 The Commission Of Sati (Prevention) Act, 1987

523 State of Rajasthan v Hat Singh & Ors Appeal (crl.) 671–678 of 1987

gious merit.[524] Samadhi is a state of awareness that may be eternal. In Jeeva samadhi, it's said that the energy remains in and around the body as if it were still alive, and the body will not decay over time either (or extremely slowly as in some cases).[525] Mahasamadhi is consciously leaving the body while in a deep meditative state.[526] It may be noted that there have been no reported instances of Prayopavesana or Jeeva Samadhi, Mahasamadhi in the recent past.

4. Santhara – Janis believes in achieving liberation of the soul from samsara through right faith, right, right knowledge and right conduct. In the Jain community, ritual death is identified with distinctive characteristics likewise (proficient), less wise (partially proficient), foolish.[527] a. Savicara Bhaktapratayakhyana means an encounter with death by healthy, thoughtful, and pious aspirant in normal spiritual circumstance by fast unto death, b. Ingini means death after identifying nature of the soul and one's desire to terminate existence[528] c. Prayopagamana is death by denying self-help d. Samadhi yoga, Samadhi means concentration, and yoga means the operation of the mind, speech and body conducive to it[529] i.e. meditation unto death, e. Sanyasa death by renouncing external and internal bondage f. Sallekhana is a praiseworthy process of emasculating the body or scratching out the body to serve the soul.[530] It is also facing death voluntarily by ascetic or householder when normal life as per the religion is not possible due to famine, old age incurable disease, etc. after subjugations of all passions abandonment of worldly attachments by the observance of austerities gradually abstaining food and water and simultaneous mediation on the real self until soul departs from the body.[531] The underlying principle is that man is the master of his own destiny and should face death in such a way that prevent the influx of new karmas even at the last moment of his life and liberate from the bondage of karma.[532]The

---

524 https://www.wisdomlib.org/definition/prayopaveshana

525 https://soonyata.home.xs4all.nl/jeevasamadhi.htm

526 See Blackman, Sushila Graceful Exits: How Great Beings Die: Death Stories Of Tibetan, Hindu & Zen Masters. New York: Weatherhill. (1997). ISBN 0-8348-0391-7.

527 Settar.S, Pursuing Death : philosophy and practice of voluntary termination of life, Institute of Indian Art History, Karnatak University, Dharwad Chp 1 p3

528 Chp IV, pg87

529 Utta su IX, 4, p 34

530 Chp VIII, p 176

531 J. Tukol T.K, 'Sallekhanā is not Suicide,' LD Institute of Indology, Ahemadabad, Section 2 p 7,

532 Ibid

vow of Sanlekhana find its mention in Ratnakaranda Shravakacara, Tatwarthadigamasutra, etc. Recently in India Rajasthan High Court held that Santhara (a religious practice of fasting un to death practised in the Jain Community) is not an essential religious practice and hence cannot be allowed.[533] This decision caused a hue and cried, especially amongst the Jain community. The case was then appealed to Supreme Court, which stayed the order of Rajasthan High Court.

But can it be said that the person who practices the aforesaid suffers from mental illness[534]? Whether aforesaid practices amount to suicide? Are these practices unlawful or are they protected by the Constitution of India? The answer to this question would be another question i.e. Do these practices stand the test of essential religious practice? i.e. is it integral to religion? Are they prescribed by doctrines of religion? Is it an obligatory overt act to exhibit religious belief? Is it not confined to matters of doctrine or belief but extend to acts in pursuance of religion like rituals, observance, ceremonies, and modes of worship which are essential to religion? And most importantly, whether i. nature of religion would be changed in the absence of the practice and absence or alteration will change its fundamental character ii. Such practices are core belief upon which religion is founded.[535] The Constitution of India also mandates that freedom of religious practice shall not be available if it is against public order, morality and health, and if it is so, then the State may enact a law curtailing such religious freedom. After close scrutiny of practices mentioned aforesaid, it may be concluded that religious practices like Johar, Sati do not pass the test of essential religious practice laid down by the Hon'ble Supreme Court of India. However, Santhara in Jainism or Jeeva Samadhi stand at a different pedestal. Such religious practices are not per se a threat to public order, morality and health. One of the core values of the Jain religion is Ahimsa, and it may be very well argued that Santhara comes within the ambit of Ahimsa. The rest of all it may be

533 Nikhil Soni v. Union of India DB Civil Writ Petition 7414 of 2016

534 Section 2 (s) of Mental Healthcare Act 2017 defines mental illness" means a substantial disorder of thinking, mood, perception, orientation or memory that grossly impairs judgment, behaviour, capacity to recognise reality or ability to meet the ordinary demands of life, mental conditions associated with the abuse of alcohol and drugs, but does not include mental retardation which is a condition of arrested or incomplete development of mind of a person, specially characterised by subnormality of intelligence

535 'Commissioner of Police v. Acharya Jagdishwarananda Avadhuta 2004 12 SCC 770'

definitely said that Santhara is fasting unto death but not suicide. Suicide is generally committed by persons suffering from a mental disorder like depression or alcohol use disorder, impulsive decisions in a moment of crisis due to failure to handle life crisis like financial problems etc., chronic pain and illness etc.[536] Jainism does not allow a person with aforesaid conditions to follow Santhara, and that's why those who undergo Santhara strictly as prescribed by Jainism cannot be said to have been committed suicide or said to have been suffering from mental illness. The Law of mental healthcare categorically mentions that mental illness shall not be determined on the basis that a person belongs to a particular cultural or religious group or in conformity with religious beliefs prevailing in-person community.[537] Similarly, those to achieve moksha or abandon worldly attachments liberate themselves from the attachment of the body to attain union with God or achieve immortality by realising the true nature of the soul or letting the body go to attain spiritual goals[538] cannot be said to commit suicide. The array of literature in India suggests that death is viewed as a part of human life, just as birth is, and it marks the end of the embodied nature of the self in this world and the passage to the next form of existence of the 'self', the soul.[539] Freedom of religion is curtailed by the Constitution of India if it is against public health, morality, law and order. So such instances which do not pose a threat to public health, morality, law and order,[540] are not practised by minors or unsound minded, nor the person practising is overpowered by passions to end the life out of stress or mental dereliction or is forced or unduly influenced by other to take up such practice then it may not be brought under the ambit of Mental Health Care law as its not suicide nor mental illness and falls within the ambit of freedom of religion.

C. Conclusion

It may be concluded that certain religious practices may not always mean an attempt to commit suicide. Deciding to near the end of one's life

536 Suicide, Sept 15 2019 https://www.who.int/news-room/fact-sheets/detail/suicide

537 Section 3(3) (a), (b) Mental Healthcare Act 2017

538 See Solayan, M., & Barvin, A. M. (2007). The concept of death in Cankam and English metaphysical poetry. Journal of Tamil Studies (71), 88–92

539 See Hamilton Inbadas (2018) Indian philosophical foundations of spirituality at the end of life, Mortality, 23:4, 320–333, DOI: 10.1080/13576275.2017.1351936

540 'Article 25 of Constitution of India 1950'

through a systematic process for spiritual and religious reasons is different from committing suicide due to mental disorder or stress. Former is an exercise of freedom of religion which may be an essential religious practice and is Constitutionally protected, while later needs care and help.

Prasannanshu Prasannanshu, Professor National Law University Delhi,
The Legal and Linguo-Cultural Aspects of End of Life in India

Abstract: *Law, in a nutshell, is a set of norms established by various means to protect and enhance human life. Therefore, it is not unreasonable to believe that law is majorly concerned with circumstances that can be influenced by human action leading to termination of life. Birth is an accident, but death is a certainty, this means that we all have to enter a stage where death is imminent, and as a corollary, as certain as the death is the period preceding it. This stage of life may be called the end-of-life situation (ELS), it may last a few seconds or less or may be protracted over years or decades depending upon the circumstances, perceptions, and definitions. Several human interventions are possible in this stage, including of the person whose death is imminent and the people around such a person. The consequences of these actions may accelerate or retard death. This possibility of manipulation and modification of life span and quality of life immediately attracts the attention of law towards end-of-life situations. Law has a cultural context, and at the same time, language and culture are inseparables, hence this paper sets out to look at the Legal and Linguo-Cultural aspects of End of Life, especially in the Indian context.*
Keywords: *Law, Linguo-Cultural, End of Life, India.*

Introduction:

End of life: End-of-life situation/stage (ELS) may be described as a period immediately preceding death. Logically, since death is an inevitable reality of human life, so is ELS as it is inseparably associated with it. ELS may be very brief or protracted over decades. Further, ELS may be manipulated by the action of the individuals themselves or someone else. Figure 1 illustrates this. This leads to a situation where law has a say, as any human action affecting the society or any of its members directly or indirectly invites the attention of law.

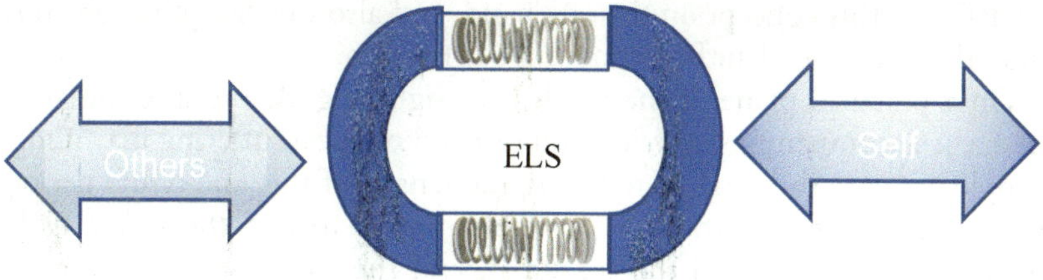

Figure 1 Stretchability of End of Life Stage

This gives an insight into why the issue of end of life and the presence of interventions of the nature of modifying its quality and length become so important. If we look at it from a different angle, human action leading to the termination of life is actually an action to decrease the end-of-life period. We may, by going to an extreme, consider whole of the life in some mathematical way as the 'end-of-life period'. To prevent this unpleasant description, perhaps we will need a firmer definition of end-of-life that even delimits the period of end of life. As per the 'normal' or 'intuitive' thinking, end-of-life may be defined as the period when a person's death becomes imminent or foreseeable. However, we may still say that every newborn baby's death is also both imminent and foreseeable! Possibly we may resolve this problem of definition at least to a certain degree by calling end-of-life as the period during which death of a person becomes psychologically visible. This definition rests upon the premise that we, the human beings, ordinarily know the inevitability of death but are somehow, during the normal course of life, under the illusion that it is far, unreal, or just a hypothesis. It is also interesting to note that 'end of life' is frequently not defined or described in research articles dealing with end-of-life issues, this was found to be the case in several of the papers on the issue of end of life, surveyed by the author, e.g. Given & Reinhard (2017), De Vries & Gutman (2016), Page (2014), Neil, Coady, Thompson, & Kuhse (2007), and Ideis (2008).[541] This show the difficulty in capturing

---

541 Given, B., & Reinhard, S. (2017). Caregiving at the End of Life: The Challenges for Family Caregivers. Generations: Journal of the American Society on Aging, 41(1), 50–57. doi:10.2307/26556266
De Vries, B., & Gutman, G. (2016). End-of-Life Preparations: Among LGBT Older Adults. Generations: Journal of the American Society on Aging, 40(2), 46–48. doi:10.2307/26556200

or defining this concept on the one hand, and also the deceptive 'obviousness' that lets several authors ignore the definition.

On a practical plane, if the death is in sight, e.g. due to a terminal illness, the accompanying physical and/or psychological suffering may nudge people towards thinking of reducing the length of this end-of-life period. In fact, there are two options available, one is to end the suffering by medicines and care, and the second is, end the suffering by ending the life itself. In end-of-life situations where suffering is inescapable, the first option that comes to mind is palliative care. However, palliative care may not be able to provide all or some of the following: i) increase in the life span ii) reduction or elimination of suffering iii) kindling again the absence of the desire or will to live. In view of this, the care givers, or the individuals themselves, at times, develop a desire to end life. This will necessitate certain actions to reduce the end or life period and to hasten the onset of death. The presence of these actions during the end-of-life period overwhelms even the legal thinking, provisions, and interpretations, at times.

Whenever a law is made, several possibilities must be kept in mind; especially the possibilities of abuse and misuse. End-of-life interventions are literally a matter of life and death, and hence the cautions of law cannot be underestimated or undermined. There again are two possibilities for end of life: one is that the person whose death is approaching loses the wish to live and decides to die with the least possible suffering. However, this decision may be taken under a spell of great pain or depression. This decision can also be influenced by religious and spiritual factors like in the case of ancient Indian practices of *samadhi maran, sallekhana, santhara, ichcha mrutyu etc*., and the European Cathar Endura. Essentially, this action is very similar to what is traditionally known as 'suicide'. Prasannanshu (2019)[542] has recommended the use of a 'more descriptive and inclusive

---

Page, L. (2014). The end of life. BMJ: British Medical Journal, 348. Retrieved November 24, 2020, from https://www.jstor.org/stable/26513627

Ideis, M. (2008). End-of-Life Care. The American Journal of Nursing, 108(11), 14–14. Retrieved November 24, 2020, from http://www.jstor.org/stable/4038504 6

Neil, D., Coady, C., Thompson, J., & Kuhse, H. (2007). End-of-Life Decisions in Medical Practice: A Survey of Doctors in Victoria (Australia). Journal of Medical Ethics, 33(12), 721–725. Retrieved November 24, 2020, from http://www.jstor.o rg/stable/27719996

542 Prasannanshu. (2019). Wilful Self–Termination of Life: Evolution across Jurisprudences, and Linguistic Exploration of Hyponyms. In Interactions between

coined expression like Wilful Self–Termination of Life' (WISTOL)', in place of 'suicide' as 'it is value-neutral, and it helps in putting together, and classification of the actions of taking one's life'.

There is no absolute answer to resolve this situation, it is a choice between the devil and the deep sea: on the one side is an individual's suffering and the freedom to make very important decisions about their life and death, and on the other side is a possibility of a most horrendous misuse. This is such a deep psychological, philosophical, religious, cultural, and legal matter that we can forget about any universal approach, and even fixing national or regional solutions is hardly in the realm of the possible.

If euthanasia is allowed, then many individuals may become a victim of the greed or vengeance of people who they are dependent upon in a potentially helpless stage. They may also fall prey to their treatable psychological states that may be transient in nature. Human life is too precious for the society to be allowed to dissipate in the face of the slightest of doubts or possibilities of misuse. This is the dilemma faced by the courts and lawmakers across the world. Finding a perfect solution is like any possibility of approaching infinity. However, several experiments have been made and are being made in the legal systems by introducing as many practical safeguards as possible. This task becomes manifold challenging when the person whose life is at stake is not conscious or capable of taking a decision by virtue of lack of communication or cognition.

Again, the solution is safeguarded, but in this case, the safeguards are for checking the authenticity of the motives of the person who is supposed to be the representative of the will of the individual in ELS. This is another matter that perhaps in such a matter of extreme implications, even the self cannot be trusted to be reliable. This is exactly why suicide is not a legal option in many jurisprudences, and even if it is decriminalized, it is not legalized.

It is a matter of sociological, psychological, philosophical, cultural, and jurisprudential dimensions dealing with the nature of 'reality', the rights of an individual and the society in matters that may appear to be very

Culture and Law in India and Europe (Influence réciproque entre culture et droit en Inde et Europe; Wechselwirkungen zwischen Kultur und Recht in Indien und Europa). Edited by Jörg Luther, Prasannanshu, and Stephanie Rohlfing–Dijoux. (ISBN 978–88–255–2474–1). DOI 10.4399/978882552474113. pp 169–213, Italy: Aracne editrice. Publisher link: http://www.aracneeditrice.it/aracneweb/index.php/pubblicazione.html?item=9788825524741)

individual-centric or personal. The debate rages between i) an individual's right over their life, ii) whether the right over life includes the right to choose between life and death? iii) the role of the society (or its agencies, like the court) in protecting an individual against harm iv) the limits of the protective role of the society v) the supremacy or equality of the role of a society and an individual's rights, vi) the wisdom of an individual against the collective wisdom of the society is also a matter of debate. Then there are issues, like what is more important, to live, or to escape suffering? In other words, is life supreme and sacrosanct beyond everything else and in all circumstances?

A recent development in this field has been the concept of the living will where an individual during their life span and during the period when their cognitive and communicative abilities are reasonably normal are able to leave instructions for actions to be undertaken, on their behalf, concerning their life and death, treatment and care, in a situation when they are not in a position to take such decisions on their own.

A whole range of experiments and possibilities have been explored in different legal systems of different places and times. Still, there is no unanimity or common understanding on this complex issue. It can safely be predicted that such certainty is not even foreseeable. The causes lie in the discussion laid before the reader above. The conceptual, experiential, and perceptual parameters that lead to such decisions are too numerous, complex, abstract, intertwined, and of high stakes that arriving at an unequivocal solution for all times and places is extremely difficult. This may become clearer if we consider that deciding a matter of traffic violation or petty theft may be relatively simpler due to its usually lower stakes and fewer issues involved.

In India, several cases have been very impactful where the courts have grappled with the problems of ELS or concerning WISTOL, palliative care, e.g., decriminalization of suicide, and matters concerning euthanasia and *santhara.* These deliberations and approaches may be seen as attempts to arrive at a state of equilibrium between individual liberty, or right over one's life, and the society's responsibility towards an individual for their protection and wellbeing. This is also a tug-of-war between the society's 'right' over an individual's life, body, and freedom of will and that of individuals themselves.

All these matters in the realm of jurisprudence and culture are based upon the concepts of right and wrong, and obviously, they are not a fixed commodity. These ideas keep changing over time and across space and form an invisible superstructure or a cybersphere. The effect of these ideas is not limited to a particular matter or case. Instead, they represent the collective consciousness and the concept of right and wrong in a society. It is a jelly-like structure of concepts that is fluid and dynamic. This jelly or pudding is based upon a multitude of cultural ingredients, including religion, language, law, history, geographical conditions, etc. therefore, it is not fixed for all human societies. It is interesting to note what Kassim and Alias (2016) say: 'With the influential development of patient autonomy and the right to self-determination, a patient's religious affiliation constitutes a key component in medical decision making. This is particularly pertinent in issues involving end-of-life decisions such as withdrawing and withholding treatment, medical futility, nutritional feeding and do-not-resuscitate orders. These issues affect not only the patient's values and beliefs but also the family unit and members of the medical profession. The law also plays an intervening role in resolving conflicts between the sanctity of life and quality of life that are very much pronounced in this aspect of healthcare.[543]

Positive laws in most modern countries are ideally secular, and it is seldom, with not very frequent exceptions, that laws are designed and deployed with an explicit religious consideration. However, via the route of culture, religion, and all other beliefs somehow make a difference. This is a difficult to observe, measure, and capture phenomenon, as a lot of it must be going on subconsciously, invisibly, and possibly in the form of 'judicial activism'. We see that even within Europe, some countries allow abortion while others do not. Likewise, the laws of these countries differ in matters of WISTOL, e.g. suicide and euthanasia.

Indian approaches:

We have to remember that any culture is strongly influenced by a multitude of factors including history, wars, victories and defeats, business, other cultural exchanges, historical thoughts, religious beliefs, technological advances, present challenges, e.g. pressure of diseases, pollution, population explosion, economic and political conditions. In the light of this we can see how Indian courts of late have been taking approaches that may be

543 Kassim, P., & Alias, F. (2016). Religious, Ethical and Legal Considerations in End-of-Life Issues: Fundamental Requisites for Medical Decision Making. Journal of Religion and Health, 55(1), 119–134. Retrieved November 25, 2020, from http://www.jstor.org/stable/26749231

seen as experiments or attempts to reconcile the current Indian cultural realities in consonance with the needs of the hour. This may be construed in the context of the recent judgements on homosexuality, divorce, animal issues (e.g. jallikattu, and religious sacrifice), suicide, euthanasia, adultery, live-in relations, age of consent, the concept of adulthood, etc.

Some people may find the changing stance of the Indian courts on the issue of suicide perplexing, but the foregoing discussion would help us understand that the dynamic nature of our social and mental constructs is likely the underlying cause. This can also be seen along with the individual variations of perceptions, cultural backgrounds, and beliefs of the same or different judges deciding the same matter at different times. Seng's (1996) following statement hints at this, 'In fact, the court came to the conclusion that the question of whether suicide is against public policy has to depend on the system of jurisprudence and criminal justice in place in the country in question. It cannot be, therefore, the case that every act which is considered by English law to be a crime is necessarily so regarded in India or some other country.' Seng has also said, 'In fact, the Indian Court in Scottish Union and National Insurance Co v NR Jahan Begum opined that public policy with regards to suicide must be determined by the sense in which the law and public opinion of the country in which it takes place understand it.'

Seng (1996)[544] also opines that '...it appears to be trite law in India that suicide itself is not an offence.' and goes on to elaborate that the Indian Penal Code has made an attempt to suicide an offence, but not the suicide itself, as the offender, in that case, would not obviously be available for punishment.

This is somewhat different from the medieval European situation when the family members of the person who committed suicide had to suffer the fury of the church and the law. In this regard, Healy (2006) has noted, '...it had been normal in classical times to punish suicides by confiscating the goods of the deceased and denying their bodies the usual burial rites, and that only with St Augustine, and later Thomas Aquinas, had Christian attitudes become more uniformly hostile and punishments more severe. The Reformation and expansion of the state had led to the harsh treatment

544 Seng, L. (1996). SUICIDE AND LIFE POLICIES – A FRESH PERSPECTIVE. Singapore Journal of Legal Studies, 79–110. Retrieved November 16, 2020, from http://www.jstor.org/stable/24866843

of suicides under the Tudors and early Stuarts, ...[545]'. It may be argued that this change has arisen with the growing understanding that an individual's crimes cannot make anyone else, including the family members, liable for punishments. This understanding, in turn, may be seen to have developed from the growing respect of the individuality of every human being, including that of the offender and the people around them. Further, there is a recognition of the fact that suicide is a step taken in extreme duress, and people who attempt killing themselves need help and sympathy rather than bitterness and harsh treatment.

Article 21of the Indian Constitution

Law is there to protect human life and to make it liveable, or meaningful, as far as possible. Umpteen number of additions, interpretations, and enlargements of the scope of Article 21[546] of the Indian constitution has been done, as noted by Khosla & Semwal (2011)[547] in the following words:

> 'Equality before law and equal protection of law formed the bedrock of several human rights decisions delivered by the Courts[27548]. In doing so, the right to life under Article 21 was expanded so as to include in it: the right to travel, right to privacy, right to a speedy trial, right to a fair trial, right against torture and custodial violence, right to free legal aid, right to education, right to health and medical care, right to pollution-free environment, safe drinking water, right to quality life and right against sexual harassment of the working women etc.'

This is perhaps the most potent field with unending possibilities for legal reforms and 'Judicial Activism'. Arguably, in a simplistic manner, it may

545 Healy, R. (2006). Suicide in Early Modern and Modern Europe. The Historical Journal, 49(3), 903–919. Retrieved November 25, 2020, from http://www.jstor.org/stable/4091587

546 Art. 21 of the Constitution of India: No person shall be deprived of his life or personal liberty except according to procedure established by law.

547 Khosla, S., & Semwal, M. (2011). HUMAN RIGHTS JURISPRUDENCE IN INDIAN CONSTITUTION RIGHT TO EQUALITY AND LIFE: CONCEPT AND SUBSTANCE. The Indian Journal of Political Science, 72(4), 927–936. Retrieved November 15, 2020, from http://www.jstor.org/stable/41856528

548 N. Trivedi (Ed.), World of All Human Rights, Universal Law Publishing Co., New Delhi, 2010, p. 69.

be claimed that Article 21 represents the Constitution of India in a nutshell or its spirit.

There have been suggestions that the right to life incorporates the right to death also. For example, Chetwynd (2004) has mentioned: 'In 2002 Diane Pretty went to the European Court of Human Rights to gain a ruling about assisted suicide. In the course of this, she argued that the right to life implied a right to die.[549]' However, this is a vexed linguistic and philosophical question, somewhat paradoxical in nature and in no way resolvable in language or law. Its solution, if any, lies in the philosophy behind law or the philosophy of law.

Singh (2012) has quoted two judgements of the Indian courts to show how the law is struggling with arriving at an answer, as follows: 'In 1994, the Supreme Court in P. Kathinam v. Union of India held that the right to life includes the right to die also. However, in Gian Kaur v. State of Punjab, it was held by the five-judge bench of the Supreme Court that the "right to life" guaranteed by article 21 of the Constitution does not include the "right to die".[550]' Bedau (1968) also came face to face with this problem and has noted that '*...it is natural to see the right to life classically as having reference mainly to questions affecting the termination of life* (*e.g., suicide, homicide, euthanasia, the death penalty, warfare*)[551].'

Obsession and obstruction:

From another perspective Law is obsessed with 'life'. Life is, of course, very important and the central preoccupation of our individual and collective consciousness, but at the same time, when an important thing becomes an obsession, it starts hindering our normal existence. This is true of this 'obsession with life' also.

It is well known that life is an accident, but death is a surety: and hence a lopsided emphasis on life may hinder or distort the cycle of life

549 Chetwynd, S. (2004). Right to Life, Right to Die and Assisted Suicide. Journal of Applied Philosophy, 21(2), 173–182. Retrieved November 25, 2020, from http://www.jstor.org/stable/24355193

550 Singh, S. (2012). EUTHANASIA AND ASSISTED SUICIDE: REVISITING THE SANCTITY OF LIFE PRINCIPLE. Journal of the Indian Law Institute, 54(2), 196–231. Retrieved November 23, 2020, from http://www.jstor.org/stable/43953537

551 Bedau, H. (1968). THE RIGHT TO LIFE. The Monist, 52(4), 550–572. Retrieved November 23, 2020, from http://www.jstor.org/stable/27902102

and death. When we think of life, there should be some thought for death also. It appears natural to us that we seldom think of death as it is considered the most negative of things, unpleasant, and an avoidable topic in conversations. However, we must know that this is not an avoidable thing so we should think and plan about death, or rather the end-of-life situation for ourselves and our dear ones. Indian courts are also accepting and advocating 'living will', as in several other jurisdictions, is accepted by similar or other names, e.g. 'advance health care directive'.

India has a predominance of Hindu populations and a large number of Muslims and Christians. She also boasts of having Buddhists, Jews, Parsees, and Jains in significant numbers. This will provide us with an important axis of cultural considerations here.

> 'At the census 2001, out of 1028 million population, little over 827 million (80.5 %) have returned themselves as followers of Hindu religion, 138 million (13.4 %) as Muslims or the followers of Islam, 24 million (2.3 %) as Christians, 19 million (1.9 %) as Sikh, 8 million (0.80 %) as Buddhists and 4 million (0.4 %) are Jain. In addition, over 6 million have reported professing other religions and faiths including tribal religions, different from six main religions.'[552]

This distribution indicates plurality on the one hand and the distinct possibility of the greatest influence of Hinduism on the lingo-cultural context on the other. India is recognized as a linguistic area[553], and analogically, she may be considered a cultural area, or rather a lingo-cultural area. Buckham (1892), more than a century ago, realized the complexity and difficulty of defining culture and said, 'Culture is a concept which is well-nigh indefinable.'[554] Still, culture is an all-encompassing reality of human coexistence with others, and it may be described as a way of life that includes the outlooks, perspectives, philosophies and attitudes towards different elements of nature and society that a person faces individually and collectively, in living together with others. Culture helps us in coexistence as it gives thinking patterns and norms to us that allow us to accept certain behaviours and mutual rights and duties. It tells us what to do in the

---

552 Source: https://censusindia.gov.in/Census_And_You/religion.aspx

553 Emeneau, M. (1956). India as a Linguistic Area. Language, 32(1), 3–16. doi:10.2307/410649

554 BUCKHAM, J. (1892). WHAT IS CULTURE? The Journal of Education, 36(24 (899)), 395–395. Retrieved November 23, 2020, from http://www.jstor.org/stable/44037407

face of a problem or a situation posing a challenge. Death is one such matter that may be called the biggest challenge that a person, a family or a society may face. It is inevitable that different cultures have developed different perspectives towards death. These perspectives form a part of the collective subconscious and consciousness of the cultural units or communities. When we talk of the norms, we somehow can draw a connection with the positive laws. This is not very explicitly acknowledged, but when we talk of the customary law in the Indian context, we see a rarely visible connection between the two. In fact, customary law and positive laws are, more often than not, in conflict with each other. We may get a glimpse in the following examples: African customary law of South Africa as touched upon by Vincent (2009)[555] and Sierra's (1995) work 'on the relationship between customary law and state law in the context of the administration of justice by and toward Indians', i.e. the natives of Mexico[556].

However, by saying the following about Justice Krishna Iyer: 'He not only delivered justice as per traditional norms but always tried to achieve social justice in a welfare state[557].' Ahmad (2015) has given a glimpse of the value associated with Law's traditions or culture in popular modern Indian thinking.

Cultures somehow tend to have some absolute wrongs and some lesser ones. In most cultures, death is the most negative thing. However, in the Indian Hindu, Jain, etc., contexts, death is not an absolutely negative thing. Death in these cultures, anyway, is not the final reality since there is a belief in life after death in an infinite cycle of rebirths. Life is rather seen as purposeful, and the purpose is more or less seen in terms of '*purusharths*' or ends of life. There are four purusharthas, viz. *dharm, arth, kama*, and *moksha*, corresponding roughly with duties, wealth, desires, and ultimate liberation from the cycle of rebirths. If we look at it from a different perspective, the real termination of life is *moksha* and not a simple death. With *moksha,* there is an absoluteness of cessation of the

555 Vincent, L. (2009). Polygamy in the Recognition of Customary Marriages Act. Agenda: Empowering Women for Gender Equity, (82), 58–65. Retrieved November 23, 2020, from http://www.jstor.org/stable/41321368

556 Sierra, M. (1995). Indian Rights and Customary Law in Mexico: A Study of the Nahuas in the Sierra de Puebla. Law & Society Review, 29(2), 227–254. doi:10.2307/3054011

557 Ahmad, F. (2015). UNDERSTANDING ISLAMIC LAW IN INDIA: AN ASSESSMENT OF THE CONTRIBUTION OF JUSTICE V.R. KRISHNA IYER: A TRIBUTE. Journal of the Indian Law Institute, 57(3), 307–332. Retrieved November 23, 2020, from http://www.jstor.org/stable/44782785

possibility of biological life. An outcome of this cultural reality can be witnessed when an older person who has great-great-grandchildren dies, their funeral procession is taken out with music and celebration, rather than crying and lamentations. It is an acknowledgement of the fact that the deceased completed their life (present birth) successfully.

Notes on contributors

Florence Bellivier is a professor of private law at the University of Paris Nanterre, where she co-directs the Centre for Criminal Law and Criminology. A specialist in the links between law and scientific developments, she is interested in the upheavals in criminal and civil law brought about by biotechnologies. Her publications include *Contrats et vivant*, (with C. Noiville, LGDJ, 2006), *Les biobanques* (with C. Noiville, PUF, 2009), *Droit des personnes* (LGDJ, 2015), and *Droit des crimes internationaux* (with M. Eudes and I. Fouchard, PUF, 2018). She is an alternate member of the National Advisory Commission on Human Rights. She co-edits, with Christine Noiville, the *Cahiers Droit, Sciences &Technologies*.

Kartina A. Choong is a Reader in Medical Law and Ethics at the University of Central Lancashire, UK, having previously held academic appointments at the Universities of Durham, Reading and Leeds Metropolitan. She obtained her Law degree from the University of Cardiff before qualifying as a Barrister (Honourable Society of Lincoln's Inn, London). She holds Master degrees in Healthcare Ethics and Applied Social Research from the University of Manchester, and in Islamic Studies from the University of Leeds. Her PhD in Medical Law was awarded by the University of Manchester. Her main areas of research interests, on which she has published widely, include medical futility, religiously- and culturally-sensitive end-of-life care, medical mediation, professional liability, access to health records, consent and confidentiality. She is an Accredited Mediator and a Fellow of the UK Higher Education Academy.

Birgit Daiber is an Associate Professor at the Seoul National University School of Law. She completed her First and Second Legal State Exam in Munich and holds a Master Degree in European Law (LL.M.Eur.) from Saarland University and a Doctorate in Law from Ludwig-Maximilians University Munich. Her main areas of research interest are German Constitutional Law, EU Law, the European Convention on Human Rights and Constitutional History. In her research she profits from the practical insight she could gain at the German Federal Constitutional Court, the Court of Justice of the European Union, the German Federal Parliament, the Parliament of Bavaria and the European Department of the German

Federal Ministry of Economics and Technology. Additionally, she benefits from research stays at the European Court of Human Rights, the Institute for the History of Modern Times and Contemporary History of the Austrian Academy of Sciences and the University Paris Nanterre. Currently she is a guest researcher at the University of Vienna.

Géraldine Demme is an associate Professor of Law at Paris Nanterre University since 2010. She holds a PhD in Antitrust Law from the University Paris II Panthéon-Assas. Her publication on vertical restraints was awarded the Vogel Prize for Economic Law and the Prize of the Swiss Institute of Comparative Law. She is Of-Counsel and Head of German Desk in a Paris law firm. At Nanterre University she teaches within the integrated French-German Law Curriculum, mainly Economic and Criminal Law. She is member of the Multidisciplinary and Multi-Language Research Centre (CRPM) at Paris Nanterre University.

Michael Eichberger, Professor, Dr., Judge in the German administrative jurisdiction since 1984, finally at the Federal Administrative Court in Leipzig from 1998 to 2006. From 2006 to 2018 Justice at the Federal Constitutional Court of Germany. From 1998 to 2017 teaching environmental law at the Eberhard Karls University Tübingen. President of the German Section of the International Commission of Jurists; since November 2018 Vicepresident.

Sophie Garcelon is a professional coach, dedicated to the health sector. She accompanies managers and medical teams through individual, team and organization coaching programs developed by her firm, Wingsanté, created in 2016. She also provides courses relating to medical liability and medical risk management. Sophie started her career as a lawyer at the Paris Bar, before holding various positions with French insurance companies specializing in medical liability. She holds Master's degrees in International Commercial Law (University Paris Nanterre) and in Insurance Law (University Lyon III). Sophie is certified in medical risk management (CNAM), was trained as a Crew resource management expert with the Haute Autorité de Santé (HAS) and is in the process of certification in Professional Coaching (Vincent Lenhardt – JBS-Lyon school). She has organized or personally carried out missions in more than 150 hospitals of health institutions.

Uwe Hellmann received his doctorate (Dr. iur.) in 1986 and his habilitation (Dr. iur. habil.) in 1992 at the University of Osnabrück. From 1994 until his retirement in 2021, he was head of the Department of Criminal Law and Economic Criminal Law at the University of Potsdam. He continues to head the Research Centre for Russian Law there and is chairman of the German branch of the "Association of Criminologists and Criminalists" founded in Russia. His research focuses on property offences, economic and fiscal criminal law as well as criminal procedural law. He is involved in numerous cooperation with foreign universities. He is co-editor of two publication series and member of the scientific advisory boards of several journals published in Russia. He is a visiting professor at the University of Paris Nanterre and the University of Szeged (Hungary).

Tetsu Isobe is a Professor at Keio University Law School, Tokyo. His main research areas are Administrative Law and Health Law. While conducting overseas research as a visited scholar at Jean Moulin University Lyon III between 2015–2017, he is designated as a Corresponding Member of Pontifical Academy for life. He serves as an expert in various public organs such as an examiner in Administrative Law for the National Bar Examination, a chairman of the Committee on Oversight of Pharmaceuticals and Medical Devices Safety Regulation, a member of the Expert Panel on Bioethics of the Cabinet Office's Council for Science, Technology and Innovation, and also an ad-hoc member of the Subcommittee for COVID-19 in the Council for Pandemic Influenza Countermesures. His major work is Rethinking Administrative Law through Cases (Coauthored, 2016, in Japanese) and "La santé publique face à la crise sanitaire au Japon" (Coauthored with Haluna KAWASHIMA, Revue Droit & Santé vol. 96, 2020). He holds a Ph.D. in Law from Hitotsubashi University, Tokyo.

Haluna Kawashima is a Project Associate Professor at Keio University Global Research Institute (KGRI), Tokyo, where she is a subchief of an international research project on digital society and e-health. Before joining Keio University, she taught Health law, Communication law and Constitutional law in Teikyo University, Tokyo. Her major works are "La prise de décision dans la médecine au dernier stade de la vie" (ISS Research Series vol.69, 2020) and "Legal and philosophical reflection on traditional medicine and patient's right to personal liberty" (colloquium proceedings, VIII French Japanese International Bioethics Conference 2018, to be published). Her main areas of research interest are Health law, Bodily integrity and Fundamental rights law. She holds Master in Public Law from Aix-Marseille University and prepares thesis on bodily integrity in Constitutional law.

Richard Wai Ming Law is an Associate Specialist in Acute Internal Medicine at the University Hospitals Morecambe Bay NHS Foundation Trust and works at the Royal Lancaster Infirmary. He studies Medicine at the University of Leeds before qualifying as a General Medical Council registered medical practitioner. He is a currently practising physician in acute internal medicine. He holds a Master (LLM) degree in Law from the University of Central Lancashire. His main research interests in relation to clinical practice are medical futility,decision-making in the context of withdrawal of life-sustaining treatment, and resource allocation in relation to critical care.

Tobias Lettl holds the Chair of Civil Law, Commercial and Business Law at the Faculty of Law of the University of Potsdam since 1 April 2004. In addition to civil law, his teaching focuses on commercial and corporate law, unfair competition law, antitrust law and copyright law (especially media business law). These areas are also his main areas of research. A particular focus is on antitrust law. Furthermore, he has been a member of the editorial board of the journal WERTPAPIER-MITTEILUNGEN IV (WM) since 2005. From 2013 to 2015, Prof. Lettl was Dean of the Faculty of Law at the University of Potsdam.

Volker Lipp holds the Chair of Civil Law, Civil Procedure, Medical Law and Comparative Law at the Faculty of Law, University of Göttingen, Germany. He studied law in Mannheim, Heidelberg and Göttingen, became Dr. iur. in 1994 and Dr. iur. habil. in 1999. In 2000 he became full professor at the University of Göttingen. In 2011 he declined to join the University of Regensburg. Volker Lipp has been Visiting Professor at the University of Bergen, Norway, and at Chuo-University, Tokyo, Japan. He has been a member of the Central Ethics Commission at the German Medical Association since 2010, and of the German Ethics Council since 2016. He became Doctor et Professor honoris causa of Eötvös Lorand University, Budapest, Hungary, in 2016. His research focuses on general principles of private law and civil procedure, the law of persons and family law, and medical law, with a special focus on international and European civil procedure and private international law.

Jeanne Mesmin d'Estienne holds a PhD in Public Law from the University of Paris. She is Associate Professor of Law at the University of Lyon (FRANCE) and Abu Dhabi University (United Arab Emirates). Her main areas of research interest are medical law, public law, and relations between human sciences and legal concepts. She is associate lawyer at the JMDE AVOCATS (Lyon Bar) specializing in business public law and defense of victims in front of criminal jurisdictions.

Kerstin Peglow is a Professor of Law at the University Paris Nanterre since 2018 and Member of the German Bar Association Schleswig-Holstein since 1992. She holds a PhD in Corporate Law from the University Paris II Panthéon-Assas. At Nanterre University she teaches within the integrated French-German Law Curriculum for Bachelor, Master and PhD Levels. She is a member of the Pluridisciplinary and Multilingual Research Center (CRPM) at University Paris Nanterre since 2009. Her main areas of research are Language and Law and French-German Comparative Law.

Prasannanshu, Prasannanshu, LL.B., M.A. (Lingu., D.U.), M.A. (Gen. Lingu., Univ. of Groningen, The Netherlands), M.A. (Eng.), M.Sc. (Univ. of Potsdam, Germany), M.Phil. (D.U.), Ph.D. (D.U.). he is a Professor at the National Law University, Delhi; Director, Centre for Linguistic Justice and Endangered Languages, NLUD. Project Coordinator of 'Study and Research towards Preservation and Promotion of Indigenous and Endangered Languages'. He has been a Member of the Publication Committee of the Linguistic Society of India (2018–20); Visiting Professor, Université Paris Nanterre, France; Visiting Professor, Università Del Piemonte Orientale (UPO), Italy; Fellow of the Institute for Advanced Studies in the Humanities, Edinburgh, UK; and a British Academy Visiting Scholar. His areas of interest include Endangered Languages, Law and Culture, Law and Language, Law and Literature, Law and Poetry, Communication Skills, Linguistics, Neurolinguistics, Psycholinguistics, Clinical Linguistics, and Anthropological Linguistics. Website: prasannanshu.com; or https://sites.google.com/view/prasannanshu/home;

Anand N. Raut is Assistant Professor (Law) and presently serving as Head of Post Graduate Department at Maharashtra National Law University Mumbai. He is Deputy Director of Centre for Information Communication and Technology Law is also Member of Academic Council. He is holder of Doctorate Degree and advanced Diploma Programme in Cyber laws. He has cleared UGC NET and is a merit holder in graduation and post graduation. He has undertaken various research projects and has written research papers, reading material. He has been invited as a speaker at national and international conferences, seminars, workshops, panel consultations etc. His areas of interests are Information Technology law, Data Protection, Health Law, Contract and Property Law.

Stephanie Rohlfing-Dijoux is a Professor of Law at the University Paris Nanterre since 2008 and Lawyer at the Paris (France) and Munich (Germany) Bar since 1994. She holds a PhD in German Law from the University Frankfurt/Main and in Civil Law from the University Paris Sorbonne. At Nanterre University, she is in charge of the German-French integrated curriculum Law programs of the French-German University for Bachelor, Master and PhD Levels. She is a member of the French-German University's scientific commission since 2016 and a member of the multidisciplinary and multi-language research laboratory (CRPM) at Nanterre university. Her main areas of research interest are Culture and Law, Comparative Law and Medical Law. She is a guest professor at the Gandhinagar National Law University/India and the University of Mauritius.

Louis-Charles Viossat is Inspector General of Social Affairs (IGAS) at the French Ministries of Health and Social affairs and Labor. He is the author of several policy and evaluation reports on end of life and palliative care, among other areas of expertise. Louis-Charles has a 30-year public/private experience in France and abroad. He has been chief of staff to the minister of Health and Social Security (Prof. Mattei), deputy chief of staff to the Prime Minister (Mr. De Villepin) as well as Ambassador for Global Health. He has also been worked as a senior executive with various health firms (Eli Lilly, Abbott and AbbVie). He has recently supported the Ministry of Overseas territories and the Ministry of Health for Covid-19 crisis management. Chair of the Board of Centre-Inffo, a leading voice in vocational training in France, and Treasurer of the Friends of the Global Fund Europe, an international advocacy NGO focused on development issues, Louis-Charles teaches global social policies at Sciences Po Paris.